Floreana

A Woman's Pilgrimage
to the Galapagos

The
GALAPAGOS
ISLANDS

PACIFIC

Panama Canal

EQUATOR

Galapagos Is.

REPUBLIC
OF
ECUADOR

OCEAN

PINTA
(Abingdon)

MARCHENA
(Bindloe)

GENOVESA
(Tower)

EQUATOR

SANTIAGO
(James)

SEYMOUR

FERNANDINA
(Narborough)

SANTA CRUZ
(Indefatigable)

SANTA FÉ
(Barrington)

SAN CRISTOBAL
(Chatham)

Villamil

ISABELA
(Albemarle)

FLOREANA
(Charles)

ESPAÑOLA
(Hood)

Floreana

A Woman's Pilgrimage
to the Galapagos

Margret Wittmer

Translated from the German by
Oliver Coburn

Moyer Bell Limited
Mount Kisco, New York

To my sister
HANNAH WALBROEL
to
LADY DUKE-ELDER

and to all our English and American friends, who have helped so much through the years to make our life on Floreana more comfortable and contented.

Published by Moyer Bell Limited
Copyright © 1989 Margret Wittmer
First American Edition 1990

Published 1989 by Anthony Nelson Ltd., PO Box 9, Oswestry, Shropshire SY11 1BY. First published in German by Verlag Heinrich Scheffler in 1959 under the title *Postlagernd Floreana*. This translation first published by Michael Joseph Ltd., London, 1961.

**LIBRARY OF CONGRESS
CATALOGING-IN-PUBLICATION DATA**

Wittmer, Margret
  [Postlagernd Floreana. English]
  [Floreana / Margret Wittmer. —1st ed.

  p. cm.
1. Santa Maria Island (Galapagos Islands)—
Description and travel. 2. Natural history—
Galapagos Islands—Santa Maria Island.
3. Wittmer, Margret—Homes and haunts—Galapagos Islands—Santa Maria Island. I. Title

F3741.G2W512   1990
986.6'5—dc20   90–17747
ISBN 1–55921–001–X   CIP

Distributed by Rizzoli International

BOMC offers recordings and compact discs, cassettes and records. For information and catalog write to BOMR, Camp Hill, PA 17012.

Foreword

Anyone who wishes to visit the Galapagos Islands today must be a bit of an adventurer, for the journey to this remote archipelago is not easy. First you must fly to Ecuador, and spend at least one night in Guayaquil or Quito. A TAME flight then takes you to the island of Baltra, followed by a somewhat hazardous bus and ferry trip to Puerto Ayora on Santa Cruz Island. If you prefer, you can make a trip round the islands on a small chartered yacht. To do the journey in real comfort one must book a berth on one of the large cruising ships which make regular voyages round the islands, going ashore in a small dinghy or rubber boat with all the excitement of landing on an uninhabited island, while knowing that civilisation is anchored just off shore.

Imagine if you can, what this group of islands was like over half a century ago. There was no regular communication with the mainland, no roads, no electricity and no fresh water except for rainwater and a few isolated springs. There were no shops or services and certainly no hospitals or doctors. Even the climate was not easy, for it could change from a humid daytime heat to a very chilly night in the 'garua season'. Cockroaches, rats, mosquitoes and wild pigs abounded, doing their best to make life a misery, and to undo the hard work of the previous day. Yes, Galapagos was a hard place fifty years ago, and yet it was to this remote and inhospitable archipelago that Margret Wittmer, a young German hausfrau, came in 1932 with her husband, stepson, and two dogs.

Many people have tried to live in Galapagos and have gone home defeated, but Margret Wittmer was made of sterner stuff. She did not give in. Not only has she been there since 1932, but she has brought up a family, helped to make a farm out of virgin bush, built a hotel and run it as a business, and has also been postmistress of her island for as long as I can remember. Besides all this, she found time to write a book in order to share her remarkable experiences with others. I first met Margret Wittmer in 1963 soon after

I had arrived in the Galapagos after a five month voyage from Britain on the Charles Darwin Foundation's support vessel, Beagle. This was shortly after the death of her husband Heinz, but even then she was the matriarch not only of Floreana but of the whole island group. I was impressed by her personality, and every time that I visit her home in Black Beach I leave feeling what a remarkable character she is.

Having come from Britain at the beginning of the Beatles era, the swinging sixties, I soon learned to love the simplicity of life in these still primitive islands. Some of the comforts of modern living had arrived there by 1963, and it was difficult to imagine what life must have been like for those early settlers. Only those with character and determination were able to survive.

Galapagos has changed much since Margret Wittmer arrived, though Floreana, the island on which she has lived for the past 56 years has changed less than Santa Cruz and San Cristobal which have benefited from the development of farming and the growth of tourism. Both these islands have airports close by, so having easy access to mainland Ecuador, but Floreana, although it now boasts a concrete dock, a proper road, electricity and street lighting, still retains much of the charm and beauty which first attracted those early settlers.

What the future holds in store for Floreana and the Galapagos Islands is hard to foretell. The islands are now a National Park, fully protected by the Government of Ecuador. There is an excellent National Park Service which though always short of money has done a marvellous job in maintaining the balance between farming, tourism and conservation, but it is people like Margret Wittmer and her family who are in the first line of defence against the many threats to their island home. They appreciate the need to conserve and preserve their own islands more than any expert from outside ever can.

No-one who has visited the Galapagos will ever forget these mystical and magical islands, of which the most remarkable aspect is neither the tortoises, the marine iguanas, the woodpecker finch, the flightless cormorant nor even the beauty and the amazing solitude. It is the people who have adapted themselves to this once inhospitable place and who have made it their home. The fact that they are there makes it possible for us to visit the islands, and to wonder if these people have not made the best choice in leaving our so called civilisation.

Margret Wittmer's story is a truly remarkable one, a story of survival and determination, of ingenuity and skill, of desperation and of love. As the world we know becomes more and more accessible, this is a story which cannot be repeated. The experiences described in this book will not occur again, for no matter how remote an island may be today, it cannot be as remote as Floreana was in 1932 when Margret Wittmer first arrived there.

JULIAN FITTER

Chapter 1

The grey outlines of the little fishing-boat slowly faded in the mist lying over the sea, till at last they disappeared altogether.

She was the boat which had brought us here, and half an hour before we had been still aboard with her skipper and crew. Now we were on our own, 'stranded' on Floreana, this lonely island. Behind us lay the sea and the shifting mist, above us the sky, infinite as the sea and a dismal grey. Ahead lay the future we had ourselves chosen, our new life.

At the edge of the little bay where we had landed, the ground was a greyish white, studded with heavy black lava boulders, but with no trees or bushes, scarcely even a blade of grass: a forbidding scene. There were a few trees and bushes here and there a little further inland, but the trees had no leaves, and their dark grey, lifeless branches stood out against the wild and desolate landscape.

We turned round in silence, our eyes searching desperately for the little boat. There was no sign of her, the mist over the sea had long swallowed her up. We still did not speak, we felt too down-hearted. This was where we were going to live, this was to be our 'other Eden.'

Heinz and I were alone, for Harry had gone up the coast a bit with the two dogs. Harry was Heinz's twelve-year-old son and my stepson. We looked at each other, my husband and I, knowing without a word spoken that we were both thinking the same thing: there's no going back. We had 'burnt our boats' in the old phrase, or anyhow 'our boat' had gone; and it might be months before another ship put in here. I had twenty marks on me in German money, and a handful of sucres, the Ecuadorian currency. Even if a ship came, we couldn't get home on that.

The nearest mainland, part of Ecuador, was six hundred miles away. Surely no more lonely, forlorn and 'dead' place could be imagined than this island with the lovely name like a flower in bloom. But we had come to Floreana now, and there was no going back.

We walked a little way over the grey sand, past the black blocks of lava, knowing that many before us had tried to settle on this island, that all of those former settlers had failed, given up, gone away. We walked on into the silence. The sea lapped softly on the beach. Birds flew by, birds we had never seen before, with red crops and long black wings: probably frigate-birds. Then all was quiet again.

We stopped thinking of the few sucres we had on us, of the vast expanses of water cutting us off from the world. We would close our eyes to the dismal scene at our feet, we had not come here for that. Suddenly Hertha and Lump, our two Alsatians, began barking. They were mother and son, Lump being only a six-weeks-old puppy when we left Germany. We heard them chasing off, and Harry whistling them back excitedly.

Ahead of us a wild donkey galloped across the grey scrub. Its hide was a silvery grey, it had a black stripe going from the head right down and past the neck and also branching off down both shoulders—the shape looked like a cross. The dogs were still racing after it, we could hear their whining and the thud of its hooves. So after all there was something alive on the island.

Heinz and I watched the donkey and the dogs, and were revived ourselves by this sign of life. Instinctively we clasped hands: no looking back now—we walked on into our island. After a hundred yards we raised our eyes from the dreary grey shore with its lava rocks, to see a wall of pale green behind it. The ground was steaming from the heavy rain which had been falling. Behind the bare thorny scrub we discovered the first green trees: acacia-like algerobo, *palo santo*, and the dwarf mayuyu trees which were only to be found here on Floreana. More and more of them came out of the slight mist, varying in height and with various shades of green: they looked like theatre props arranged one behind the other.

'I think I'll just explore inland a bit,' said Heinz. 'You coming?'

'No, I'll stay here,' I answered, and watched him going off with Harry and the dogs through the gently rising bush.

Completely alone, I sat on one of the shelves of lava, dabbling my feet in the water of the Pacific Ocean, which stretched away in all its monotonous vastness. The sun had triumphed over the mist, and was shining almost straight down on to the island. It was not too hot, though, but pleasantly warming and comforting, since for the last six days and nights we had not a dry stitch of clothing on our bodies.

In the little bay where I sat, there were thousands of small silvery sardines playing. Further out I could see bigger fish leaping out of the water here and there. Flights of finches whirred in the air, and from the bush rising above the shore I could still hear the cry of the wild donkey; otherwise an uncanny silence reigned over Floreana. But I no longer felt so terribly alone as I had done in the first minutes. The sun was there, the donkeys were almost familiar to me, the birds flew very low over my head, having no fear. It was only birds of passage which would flee from us, if they came on to the island, because they had experience of man. 'The fear felt by birds and other creatures is an instinct directed exclusively against Man'—so Charles Darwin had written when he visited this group of volcanic islands, the Galapagos, almost a hundred years before me on the famous *Voyage of the Beagle*. It was the variation of individual species from one island to another, especially the tortoises and the finches, which crystallized Darwin's ideas for the *Origin of Species*.

I knew that the islands had animal and plant life which was unique. The giant tortoises, *galapagos* in Spanish, which gave the islands their name, were no longer extant on Floreana, but right in front of me were two iguanas, strange dragonesque creatures about three feet long, looking like some prehistoric reptile that ought to have become extinct ages ago. Apparently these marine iguanas were the world's only sea-going lizards.

I thought back to all I had read in books about the islands and about our new home, of which we were rather timidly taking possession. For a few moments I imagined myself sitting in my house in Cologne with a book open in front of me. But then I looked round, and saw that this was reality: the sea, the shore with its dark boulders, the two iguanas which waddled past me with only a brief curious glance at the strange creature above them.

Meanwhile Heinz had returned, and some fifty yards behind me had quickly put up our main tent—in case the rain started again—with a tarpaulin next to it covering our kitchen and stores: crates, boxes, hampers, sacks and cases, plants we had brought with us—bananas, sugar-cane, coffee, yucca, camotes, otoi—all in a jumble together. I decided that the big crate of books should be our table, and put a table cloth on it; some of the other crates would serve as chairs. It was beginning to look more comfortable, quite different anyhow from those first minutes when the boat sailed away, leaving us alone and disconsolate.

I let my thoughts stray back. Two months ago, July 1932, we had left Amsterdam. In Guayaquil, the chief port of Ecuador, we had seen the mainland for the last time. Then we were a week on the seas to reach Chatham, the main island of the Galapagos group, where the Ecuadorian governor lived. We had paid to go as far as Floreana, but the captain of our primitive little ship declared he could go no further. I didn't know why, but I did know—they had told me in Guayaquil—that it was hopeless trying to argue with an Ecuadorian on such a matter: if he wouldn't do a thing, he wouldn't. In this part of the world lots of things were different from the way they were back in Europe, and that was something you had to get used to. Right from the start of our new life I resolved to respect the customs and attitudes of these people, and on the whole I have managed it fairly well, although the excitable Rhinelander in me has often rebelled.

We were stuck at Chatham for three weeks, till the governor put at our disposal a fishing-boat which was to take us to Floreana. 'Tomorrow we'll be there,' the skipper promised proudly, a dark-skinned cheerful man with a chubby good-natured face. His craft, twenty-five feet long and six feet wide, was so tightly crammed with her three-man crew, us three, our two dogs and all the luggage, that it was almost impossible to move: you just 'sat tight' where you were. It was the end of August, when it is painfully cold in these waters, and to make matters still worse, I was seasick. But in twelve hours, we comforted ourselves, it would all be over.

The water came splashing into the boat, and in a few minutes we were all drenched to the skin. Besides which, it was raining. We were miserably cold, even the sugar-cane brandy the

12

governor had thoughtfully provided failed to warm us up. Our teeth chattered in chorus.

The night was pitch black, with no moon or stars. It was depressing and frightening to have only the endless expanses of sea around me. I had never before been in an open boat on a grim black night like this. Heinz tried to cheer me up, saying things like: 'It's really not so bad, it seems worse than it is because of the darkness. But that'll soon be over, and by dawn we'll be in sight of journey's end, *our* island.'

At dawn, sure enough, our skipper suddenly became excited, pointing towards the horizon. We saw a strip of grey land, and a small bay. 'Post Office Bay,' he told us. We even saw what looked like two or three derelict houses, the remains of a previous attempt at settlement by a party of Norwegians: they too, like the others before them, had failed to build a new life on Floreana. These reminders of their fate were not calculated to cheer us.

When it grew lighter, we could pick out details: first the volcanic mountains of varying sizes. The picture was still anything but inviting, everything grey on grey.

The Spaniards had sometimes called the Galapagos 'the enchanted islands,' because they seemed endowed with magical power to attract or repel ships; and we were now exposed to some of this magic. After two hours' sailing we approached Blackbeach Bay, south-west of Post Office Bay, where we were to land; but then the wind dropped completely. We were so near the 'promised land,' but could not move a yard closer all day. Thick clouds came down between us and our island. Hunger and thirst joined forces with cold and wet in oppressing us as the second night broke over the boat. The current was terribly strong, and must have driven us away from Floreana, further and further, at about three miles an hour.

Next morning the crew made desperate efforts to put in to the small harbour, but once more in vain. We were getting dangerously short of water. Coffee was brewed on the 'ship's oven,' a large empty food tin: one cup for each of us, that was all the water ration would allow. But this one cup of hot coffee was wonderfully reviving, with our bodies chilled to the bone as they were. Strange really: we were only a few miles from the Equator, and it had been cold enough to make our teeth chatter.

The third night on the dark sea began. It rained still harder than it had the two previous nights. Even the skipper lost some of his confidence, and tried vainly to hide what he must have been thinking: that we were right out of water, and might die of thirst.

By dawn next morning we had been driven so far by the current that we were nearer Isabela, largest island in the group, than we were to Floreana. But that was not too bad, for on Isabela we could get food and above all water.

We landed there that afternoon, glad to be on *terra firma* again. But I found it hard to walk now, I was landsick and couldn't eat a thing. After a few hours we returned to our boat. Praise be, we had water again, also a giant tortoise—one of the galapagos with its tasty meat, ten sacks of salt, a few sacks of coffee and a hundredweight of dried fish. The fish began to smell, and I was none too sure whether the sharks swarming greedily round the boat were after that or us.

That night, however, things were very cheerful on board. The crew began to roast bananas, and cook camotes (sweet potatoes): and without feeling guilty of extravagance we could brew a good strong coffee again. When the morning sun came through the mist, we felt a pleasant warmth for the first time. I could even sleep a bit, dog-tired as I was after all the hardships and fears of the last sleepless nights. When I woke, Floreana lay ahead of us, and an hour later the crew threw a big stone into the water to serve as anchor. A thick rope made us fast, and Floreana could not escape from us again. We were 'home' at last on 28th August, 1932.

It was too late to begin unloading, so we had to spend another night on board. But the boat was tossing no longer, and the rain had stopped. Again we could sleep, though still sitting up, of course; there was no room to lie down in that cockleshell. Against my secret expectations, especially that first night in the boat, I had somehow survived, and things really did not look quite so bad any more. Even so I was very glad when we finally began the disembarking operation beneath the rays of the morning sun. In the little landing boat, which cleared the water only by four or five inches, we got everything safely ashore: our luggage, our two Alsatians, and finally ourselves. Hertha and Lump were beside themselves with joy at having dry land under their paws again. I think they must have suffered just as much as we did during the dreadful crossing. They jumped on to the sandy beach and frisked around like wild things: dogs, I had reflected, are lucky to have shorter memories and fewer apprehensions about the future—they know how to enjoy the present.

I came back to the present myself, still sitting on my ledge of black lava. The ground near me was dry as a bone: stones, stones and more stones. It looked as if the Almighty had made it rain stones here for forty days and forty nights.

In my complete solitude I felt as if I were no longer on this earth but had landed on some distant and deserted planet. I have never before or since felt so small as I did in those minutes. I closed my eyes, and half in dream could see one of the lumps of stone growing bigger and bigger, till it was bigger than the island and the sea . . .

Then I heard the dogs bark, the grim picture was wiped away at once. I opened my eyes, and saw the stones again in their right proportion, also Heinz and Harry, who were looking at me with a smile. 'How about getting us something to eat?' Heinz said. 'After that we'll pay our social call.'

'Social call?' I started slightly. 'Oh yes, Dr Ritter.'

It was certainly our duty to visit the two people, Germans like ourselves, who had been living on our island for three years now, its only human inhabitants besides ourselves: Dr Karl Friedrich Ritter and his friend Frau Dore Strauch. For I suppose it was their example which had given us the idea of coming here in the first place: if they could do it, so could we.

Dr Ritter was a dentist who suddenly left Berlin in 1929, to live out a new 'nature philosophy' on Floreana away from the world—which he hated and despised. He was a vegetarian, practised nudism, and intended to prove that you could attain the age of a hundred and forty if you lived according to nature as interpreted by his philosophy. He was forty-three then, a year older than Heinz when we left Germany, and was accompanied to the site for his experiments in natural living, not by his wife, but by Dore Strauch, a qualified teacher (though she had never actually taught) and Ritter's most enthusiastic 'disciple.' For months after their sensational arrival on the island they were a topic of absorbing interest to the papers and illustrated magazines.

Heinz had evidently been deeply stirred by these reports, which he followed up by reading William Beebe's fascinating book, *Galapagos, End of the World*. I remember my astonishment in Christmas 1931, only a few weeks after we were married, when we were standing in front of a men's shop, I told him he ought to buy a new suit—and he replied: 'Yes, or a rifle, I can't decide which.'

'A rifle?' I asked blankly. 'What on earth do you want a rifle for?'

'In case we go to the Galapagos Islands,' was the answer. 'Just for two or three years, you know. It might do as Harry's sanatorium!'

Harry had had very bad eyesight from birth, had always been extremely delicate, and at this time we were more anxious than ever about his health. A doctor recommended two years in a sanatorium, but how could we afford that? Besides we knew that Harry would have been miserable if parted from us for two years. So Heinz thought of this solution, to leave the unhealthy conditions of city life, the social and economic insecurity then prevailing in Germany, and give Harry the peace of an 'enchanted island.' Heinz was secretary to Dr Adenauer, then *Oberbürgermeister* of Cologne, and it meant throwing up a good job. His colleagues would have been startled and shocked, and in fact he took his annual fortnight's holiday without saying anything to them about it: we meant to leave at the end of that fortnight.

We had made arrangements to sell the flat, and had invested all our savings on equipment and supplies, notably a good set of tools both for agriculture and household use, and plenty of food stores. We took two hundredweights each of rice and beans, a hundredweight of flour, twenty-five pounds each of coffee and Quaker oats, five pounds of cocoa; plus three bottles of brandy, washing soap, matches, oil, tinned milk, and potatoes and onions for planting; a bale of yellow material for extra clothing needs; and a typewriter, in case any of our experiences should be worth putting down on paper.

While we were at Chatham, we bought many more seeds and plants: sugar-cane, yucca (a sort of tapioca), banana shoots, coffee beans, otois and camotes (two sorts of sweet potato), pineapple, pumpkins, mangoes, papaws and avocados, also a cock and two hens.

We knew everyone would try to dissuade us from the crazy

16

course we were taking, so we felt it was better to keep our plans a complete secret even from friends and relatives; my father and sister were as much in the dark as any. The eve of our departure, the second Saturday of Heinz's leave, when my sister said 'Good night, see you tomorrow as usual'—we always met on Sunday afternoons—it was all I could do to answer a slightly strained 'good night,' without hinting in any way that I might not be seeing her again for two or three years at least. The next morning a messenger dropped in to her the keys of our flat, with letters of explanation for her and my father—Heinz had also written one to Dr Adenauer—and by that time we had set off on our long journey to emulate Dr Ritter.

We had been told a few more details about him in Guayaquil. We knew that he had had all his teeth pulled out while he was still in Berlin; as a vegetarian he considered them superfluous, and as a dentist he no doubt dreaded having any kind of dental trouble on a lonely island, with all the complications that might ensue. He kept a set of steel dentures for special occasions, we learnt, but did not use them for chewing. Altogether he seemed a most peculiar character, this Ritter, and we had also been well warned of the fact that he did not like being disturbed in his 'island retreat.' Still, we were only calling on the two of them out of politeness, we had no intention of intruding on their lives. We had our own lives to build, for ourselves, for Harry, and for the other children we might be blessed with. We wanted to be settlers in a more ordinary sense than Ritter, to build a farm out of this wilderness by the labour of our hands. But he need not be afraid: we meant to 'live and let live' in its most literal sense.

The first meal I made for the three of us was a huge rice pudding. We ate it avidly, and it tasted marvellous. Then we had our first swim: the water was icy, but some sort of immersion was urgently necessary! Feeling clean and refreshed, we set out for Ritter's house which was about five hundred feet above sea level. It was called Frido (derived from Friedrich-Dore). We took half an hour to get there, and as we slowly climbed, my limbs still felt weak and tired from the ordeal of the last days and nights.

Frido turned out to be a sort of bungalow, four stakes with a corrugated iron roof over them. As we found out later, there was a cage of wire mesh inside, enclosing another four stakes. The cage was about ten feet in diameter, and had two beds in it.

Dr Ritter had probably seen us coming. He stood in his garden, waiting for us. Heinz nudged me, and murmured: 'There he is.'

Despite all I had heard, I had a slight shock when I first saw the former Berlin dentist. Admittedly I couldn't have expected an elegant figure in a white coat, and it was a relief to find that he was apparently no longer a nudist, for he was wearing trousers and a shirt. He was short and thick-set, with a mop of untidy black hair above a deeply wrinkled brow, a broad flat nose in a triangular face, with a black moustache. Altogether he looked rather frightening, and if I had been on my own, I might almost have fled. His eyes shifted uneasily as he inspected me, and had a gleam in them which suggested the fanatic. A boor, I thought, but sincere enough; and I liked him better, anyhow, than the woman standing with him, also short and rather untidy looking. He greeted me politely enough, but when Dore Strauch shook hands with me, she made a face as if she had burnt her fingers. 'Aren't you a bit too well dressed for the Galapagos, Frau Wittmer?' she remarked with an acid smile.

I checked my first impulse to answer just as rudely, for after all we were going to be neighbours and would have to get on together somehow.

'Oh well,' I said, forcing a smile myself, 'I like to put on something decent when I go visiting, even here! But I promise you for work I'll wear an overall.' After this she made no further attempts at conversation for the moment.

'This is my garden,' I heard Ritter telling Heinz. I went over and joined them on a tour of his domain. It was only a small plot of land, about half an acre. This was the strip of ground he had cleared, sown and planted; his 'farm' looked pretty well cultivated —more so than he did himself.

For the first time we saw all the things that grew here: bananas, coconut and date palms, tamarinds, ciruela plums, mangoes, figs, papaws. There was a hen-house with about twenty chickens squawking away in it. We found all this wonderful.

In our eyes Dr Ritter was by now real landed gentry, whereas we at the moment had nothing—except good-will, our hands, and a certain amount of native intelligence: and down at the coast, of course, our picks and *machetes* and carefully packed young plants.

Dr Ritter had escaped from 'civilisation,' because he hated it, hated the unnatural life people lived in their over-bred civilisation. This was the sort of thing I had read about him in the papers. He lived only on what he grew himself, and I heard him say proudly: 'One can live on nothing but figs.' He was a misanthropist who had cut himself off from the world for three years and didn't want to know anything about it; yet suddenly he asked Heinz: 'How do things look? In Germany, for instance. Ever been in Berlin?'

I sensed a slight note of homesickness in his voice, a longing, however deeply repressed, for the world he had once lived in. I felt certain somehow that he was not so set on his solitude that he meant to live in it for ever. Heinz told him about Germany, and he listened intently.

Meanwhile Dore had limped up to join us—she had one leg that was almost paralysed. As I found out later, it troubled her most when she was in a state of anxiety or nervous excitement. She began giving me proofs of her erudition, quoting Nietzsche and Lao-tse. Oh dear!—at that moment I couldn't have 'cared less' about either; I was thinking of all the work we had ahead of us to clear even the smallest strip and plant it, so that we should at least have something to eat! When we were on our way to Floreana, I had pictured a romantic south sea island, a paradise of peace and plenty, where work had little place. The books and press reports we had read in Germany had not warned us adequately that it would be a herculean task to make a living in our new self-chosen home.

Chapter 2

The first day on Floreana was ending. Days here, I knew, were not so long as at home, for we were almost on the Equator; twelve hours day and twelve hours night, all through the year.

I was sitting on a shelf of lava again, thinking about the past day—and the morrow. Nothing would fall into our laps here, that I realised already. Should we be strong enough to defy all the difficulties put in our way by nature? Was the island friendly to us or hostile? Should we have enough to eat when our meagre reserves had been used up? Idle questions, of course; only the next weeks and months would answer them.

I felt like dozing off a bit, but a housewife had duties even, or more especially, on a lonely island. I slid carefully down from the sharp ledge and went over to the fire. It could not be allowed to go out, for we had to economise even on things like matches.

Heinz and Harry were exploring. Perhaps they had gone off to the pirates' cave which was to be our home till we had built a house. Wherever they had gone, I knew they would come back ravenous, so I must get down to making supper.

Beans were on the menu this evening. There was still a little water in the water-bag, but I had to go very carefully with it, for the spring was a good way off. I diluted our precious water with a third of sea-water. A big onion and some otoi tubers—which were supposed to have more starch in them than ordinary potatoes did—also went into the stew. I imagined for the moment that I had some pork to add; the very thought made my mouth water.

In the distance, in the thick bush which began above the coast, I could hear the lowing of wild cattle. I too had company now : two donkeys stood near me, shaking their heads as they watched this strange creature cooking bean stew without pork. One of them even followed me when I walked a little way up the shore to collect some dry wood; he let me carry the wood myself, though. Whenever I came near him, he went bounding away.

Donkeys were the island's road-builders. In the course of many years, that is, they had tramped out regular tracks, the only roads there were. On one of these I walked through the bush, grey and dried up, with none of the lush green we had found only five hundred feet higher at Dr Ritter's 'Frido.' From here I could see Blackbeach Bay, which was not very big but much bigger than the little bay near by where we had landed. This bay had once been built by men, because the sea at Blackbeach was too rough. Those men had long abandoned the island, they were just beaten by it.

The tide was out, and the sea had gone back a long way. I could see black lava rocks sticking out of the shallow water, as on the beach. On our forced visit to Isabela I had watched the natives jumping barefoot from one slippery lava stone to the next; I thought I would emulate them. I was somewhat downcast, literally, by my lack of success: I kept on slipping, and preferred to wade back through the shallows. Then I lost quite a lot of my thin blouse on the arid thorn-bushes with which the donkeys' track was seamed. With their thick hides, of course, they did not have to worry; we should need to get more like the donkeys, I decided.

'You must have a look at it all yourself,' said Heinz that evening when he came back from his reconnaissance trip. 'I've found a wonderful spring, and three caves near it will do splendidly for our temporary residence, better anyhow than this windy tent. When I think of that rain starting . . .'

So we were to move in the morning, up where the spring was and the caves. This would solve the water problem, the all-important one just then, for there was only a tiny drop left in the water-bag.

We slept magnificently in the house tent our first night on Floreana. The tent had a rubber ground-sheet and air-beds—though in fact we didn't really need mattresses at all. The sand on the shore was as soft as any couch.

The next morning we had coffee warmed up from the evening's brew. Then we 'washed up' the cups in the sea, packed them, and were ready to start loading for the move. We took only the bare essentials, bedclothes, some crockery and cutlery, rations and tools. Everything else we left behind: our ten crates, that is, containing all our possessions, carefully packed in waterproof paper to protect them against damp. We had brought hundreds of things, but no furniture; that was something we should have to make ourselves.

Our rucksacks weighed pretty heavy when we moved off. Heinz had loaded on our cock and two hens, saying that you couldn't leave the poor creatures to their own devices on the beach. But we were not unduly worried, for on his reconnaissance the day before he had only taken two hours to get to the caves. Slowly, step by step, we went up a narrow donkey-path. On both sides there were prickly cacti. Bone-dry clay and ashes crumbled beneath our feet.

The track began to climb more steeply, and we were soon groaning under our load. But six hundred feet up, an hour away from the coast, we were out of the dried-up belt, and the scene was less bleak. The lemon trees had green leaves, and in between them there were scattered clusters of orange trees, with ripe fruit which gleamed at us invitingly. The soil was no longer dry, dusty clay; it was now dark, almost black, and very moist. We had left behind, too, the braying of the donkeys which lived near the coast; instead we were welcomed up here by the dull lowing of the wild cattle.

'I must have a rest,' I said, exhausted. What ages this journey was taking. In the shade of an orange grove by the track we stopped, took off our packs and had a breather. Heinz looked first at his watch, then at me with a funny expression on his face.

'What's the matter?' I asked apprehensively.

'We've been going three hours already.'

'Oh dear, I thought we must be almost there.'

'So did I,' Heinz admitted a little sheepishly.

The air was heavy and misty. The clouds above were descending lower and lower, lying right over the trees; the rain was bound to come soon. Already at this altitude the climate was quite different from that in the dry belt on the coast. This was a phenomenon perhaps unique to Floreana: differences of altitude of three hundred feet corresponded to more than three times as much on the mainland, so that you got the most varied climatic conditions within a very confined area. That is why tropical plants grew here almost next to European ones: potatoes and bananas in close proximity.

'Isn't it curious!' said Heinz. 'But we ought to postpone our discussions of the climate for another time, don't you think?'

'We ought indeed,' I said. The bush was steaming, the hill ahead of us where the caves were, or were supposed to be, was already wrapped in a thick cloud. Visibility was down to a few yards.

When we left our tent on the shore, I had taken along a reel of white thread against all eventualities. In this strange solitude I had half unconsciously been thinking of fairy-tales about people losing their way in the woods, like Hansel and Gretel. I was in the rear of our procession, and without Heinz or Harry noticing, I left a long bit of thread on a branch every hundred yards or so.

It began to rain. The ground became slippery. We slid about on our rubber soles. And we had gone wrong somewhere, that was now clear. Harry and I stayed behind with Lump under an orange tree, while Heinz took Hertha and set out to regain his bearings. Of course he discovered the white thread on the branches, and realised who had put them there; he also realised very soon that we had been going round in a circle. But after that he quickly found the right way to the caves, and in six hours we had made it at last: six hours for a journey you could do comfortably in two hours.

Anyhow, there were the caves, three of them together, one bigger than the others, under the slope of a hill. 'Our house,' said Heinz tersely.

Three big dark openings gaped at us. 'You forgot to close the doors yesterday,' I remarked, taking refuge in facetiousness to hide my feelings. For really these dark holes didn't look inviting, and the switch from Cologne and Amsterdam to caveman life on Floreana was a little disconcerting.

The caves had been hollowed out of soft lava stone, which was brownish with some patches of white basalt added. They were pirates' hide-outs, and the island had others like them. 'Did the pirates build the caves?' asked Harry.

'They're supposed to have been made by men,' I told him, 'but I don't believe it. I've read that they were washed out by the sea from the soft stone. Floreana must once have been much

23

lower lying. Sand and sea-shells have been found under the lava, and it's hardly likely anyone bothered to take the shells five hundred feet up.'

I giggled, realising that in my learned discourse I had forgotten about the heavy rucksack still on my back, the weariness of my legs. Now I remembered them. We put down our luggage in front of the big cave. The hens squawked pitifully, as if it were they who had been marching up here for six hours.

We took a closer look at our new residence. The living-cave was the size of a pretty large room, and looked like a vault. The walls must have been finished by hand, and one wall even had a fireplace hewn out of it, with a chimney going through the 'ceiling'— for there was only a thin layer of lava above the cave. In front of the cave were papaw and melon trees; this was something else that was different on Floreana—melons grew on trees, not on the ground as at home.

The cave had two benches hewn out of one wall. Not exactly comfortable, of course, but at least something to sit on; and in fact, I was so tired when I sat down that I didn't notice at all how extremely hard they were. I saw, however, that the earlier occupants of one cave had also left some remnants of furniture : a table carpentered out of old crates, and two warped stools. We had not expected even that much comfort.

Right in front of the entrance there was a papaw tree heavy with ripe fruit, and near it bushes with yellow lemons. The lemons were not important at the moment, though; the thing that mattered most was water—the spring. Without that, life here would not be possible at all.

Footsore as we were, we had to go up to look at the spring. In contrast to our first grim view of the sandy lifeless shore with its black rocks, the scene was now enchanting: we were in a fairy ring of green trees. It was wonderfully cool and pleasantly dark in the shade of their thick foliage, after the glare of the sun which had beat down on us for the last part of our march.

The spring-water gushed and gurgled out, sparkling like quicksilver, and cool. We put our hands in it and held them against our burning faces; then we drank from our cupped hands the first gulps of water the island offered us. In that moment we forgot all the trials of the last days. Now at last we felt secure.

The water came from a bare slope about a hundred and fifty

feet high. It did not flow in one jet, but trickled out of the porous rock to join up below in a strong stream. 'Best water I've ever drunk,' was the unanimous opinion. It was icy cold.

In the course of the centuries the continual flow of the water had formed a big natural basin in the stony ground, and in this lush green ferns were growing. As we walked slowly back from the cool shade of the spring to our caves, bright-coloured canaries fluttered over us, settling on our head and hands. 'This really is like Paradise,' I murmured, but then at once thought of the interior of our 'house.' First of all it had to be cleaned up, we couldn't live in it as it was. I must start sweeping out at once— only we hadn't brought a broom. Still, brooms were no problem on Floreana. Heinz cut off a few twigs and tied them together— there was my broom.

Harry, meanwhile, was finding some dry leaves in the other caves so that we could make a fire. It smoked terribly, and the smoke made our eyes smart; the wood I had put on was wet. Up here, where it rained more than enough, it was going to be pretty hard to find dry wood.

'Didn't Dr Ritter tell us there were boars up here?' I asked Heinz.

'Say no more,' he answered, picking up his gun. 'Let's see if I can get a little joint to celebrate our house-warming.'

Perhaps the housekeeping was not going to be too difficult after all: no shops in Paradise, but you found what you wanted for daily life, right outside the cave in some cases. Harry pulled down a few papaws, and plucked ripe oranges and lemons from the trees growing almost into our 'front door.' Water was boiling in the saucepan, and we were only waiting for Heinz to bring the promised meat. A crazy idea really, I thought: we had only just got here, and already we expected 'civilised meals.'

When Heinz returned from his first boar-hunt on Floreana, we both had a pleasant surprise. I had made a clean and fairly cosy living-room out of the filthy cave, and he had really got meat. He held up joyfully the steaming heart of a boar he had shot and at once carved up.

Then he went back into the bush with Harry, and each carried half a boar over his shoulder when they returned just in time for our first cave meal. It was dark by now, so I lit a candle and put it on the rickety table with its spotless white tablecloth—one of the delicacies of civilisation I was glad to keep. The candle's gleam sent a warm light through our cave. 'Happy?' asked Heinz, half gay, half anxious.

'Yes,' I said, 'very happy.' I think we all were. We had got through the first and hardest part, we had a roof over our heads once more, if it was only the stone roof of a former pirates' cave.

'Did pirates really live here once?' asked Harry.

'Yes,' said Heinz, 'but a long time ago. You needn't be afraid one of them will suddenly pop up.'

'Of course I'm not afraid,' said Harry with a laugh, looking happier than I had seen him look for a long time.

'It's over three hundred years,' Heinz went on, 'since the first pirates, or rather buccaneers, came to Floreana. That was when the ships of the Spaniards from Peru used to sail along the west coast with their rich cargoes. It was those ships the buccaneers were after, and they caught a whole lot of them too, precious cargoes and all.'

For half an hour we forgot about the present, and listened to Heinz talking about the past of Floreana, which had once belonged to the pirates and buccaneers.

William Dampier, a well-known English buccaneer, who died early in the eighteenth century, was also an excellent writer, and described some of his voyages in these waters. On one of these the buccaneers were sailing near the west coast of South America with three Spanish ships they had captured. When they heard that the Spaniards were pursuing them with warships, they sailed westwards, and found a hiding place on these islands, where they discovered all the necessities of life: meat, poultry, fish, fruits, and above all water.

Most of the buccaneers were English (though there were also some French), and they called the islands after English dukes and kings: York, Norfolk, Albemarle (which is Isabela), James and also Charles—which is our Floreana. The buccaneers were certainly good patriots.

Charles Island or Floreana, about eight miles long and five miles wide, was a favourite hiding place for the buccaneers, who at one time had up to a thousand men as crew for their ships. They had no unexpected attacks to fear from the Spaniards, because it was a long way from the shipping lanes, and because in those days it took some luck to find the island at all. After the conquest of Guayaquil, which brought them in a mass of booty and a big ransom, they could quietly withdraw again to their hideout and recuperate a little from their arduous labours.

'And they probably did so living in these caves,' Heinz concluded.

The candle had burnt down a good deal. We were still sitting round the decrepit table, letting the tale of those earlier 'cavemen' sink into our minds. Suddenly I remembered that I hadn't told Heinz and Harry about my strange discovery. While they were fetching the boar, I had found a yellowish bit of paper quite near the cave. 'There are even newspapers here,' I said, and enjoyed watching their incredulous faces.

'Well, at least I've found a bit of paper,' I went on, 'and in German too. What's more, it's from Cologne, and it's got an obituary of one of my parents' friends.' I showed them the crumbling piece of newspaper, and Heinz told us it must have come from a journalist he knew of, who had been sent out from Cologne to the Galapagos two years before, to write about the islands and Dr Ritter. But the thing was something more for me, a piece of home, a talisman. When I first found it, I felt as if I had discovered a meadow of four-leafed clover on the Equator.

It took us all of a week to bring the contents of our ten big crates up to the caves—and it rained all the time, to add to our troubles. Before we started, Heinz had gone up to Frido Farm to ask Ritter for the loan of a donkey as a carrier. But he was met by Dore, who told him they were always needing the donkey, it would be very inconvenient for them to lend it. Our 'removal' had therefore to be done by hand, a long and laborious business. We were hurt by the woman's unfriendly attitude, which confirmed my hunch that we were not going to find this couple easy neighbours.

However, Ritter came down a day or two later, and having heard that Heinz had shot a boar, asked if he might have the head and one of the hams, in exchange for some vegetables from his garden. He was most amiable, and we agreed to the exchange, although extremely surprised at a vegetarian wanting meat. We began to suspect that during his three years on the island he must have lapsed not only from his nudist principles, but from his vegetarian ones as well.

The other ham we meant to keep for ourselves, of course. I

27

put it on the fire late at night so that we could have boiled ham for breakfast. We went to sleep dead tired as usual, and when the cock crowed—he had been housed in one of the smaller caves with his two hens—Lump came waddling up wagging his tail. I could see the evidence of a crime in his fat tummy: while the water was still cold, he had hooked out the ham and made a very good meal of it. The boiled ham for breakfast was 'off,' but no matter, we had plenty of other meat.

Heinz and Harry went up to Frido and delivered the head and the other ham, luckily intact. Dore was not there. But when they went down to the shore, they caught her making a thorough examination of the remainder of our luggage. She made some very lame excuse, and once more Heinz let it go. I was furious when I heard, but he calmed me down: 'Live and let live, as you said at first. After all she won't do us much harm if we keep out of her way—and that's what we're going to do, aren't we?'

'All right,' I said, 'but it seems a pity when we happen to be five Germans, the only inhabitants of Floreana, that they should be so unpleasant.'

'Never mind,' said Heinz, 'remember there'll soon be a sixth; and he or she will keep you quite busy, I dare say, not worrying about those two.'

Yes, if all went well, the first native of Floreana would soon be born. When we left Europe in June, I was already expecting a child, though it was not certain till we were on the high seas. My sister, whom I had left so abruptly in Cologne, impulsively rushed over to Amsterdam to see me off, and I was pretty sick most of the time until we sailed. She was horrified at the idea that I was probably pregnant and would have to have my first baby on an uninhabited Pacific island with no doctor or midwife or drugs, not even a telephone. I had shared her apprehension at the time, though I tried not to show it. But now I was looking forward to the day: the new arrival was due somewhere round the end of December.

Meanwhile we had to clear the bush and plant. I thought anxiously of the future. If we didn't soon have a crop we had planted and sown ourselves, we should be obliged in the coming months to live on a basic diet of oranges and wild boars; and even the oranges wouldn't last indefinitely.

As well as bush Floreana had wide stretches where no tree or shrub grew; it was only in the rainy season that the bare ground was covered with a shimmer of green. But you couldn't grow anything on these flats. Wait a minute, why couldn't you, though? Why go through the terrible labour of clearing the bush?

'Because nothing does grow where there aren't any bushes and trees standing,' Heinz enlightened me. I had been born and brought up in a town, had worked in a bank till I was married; I realised anew my ignorance of farming and 'settling.' But he went on to explain, and it sounded simple enough: where nothing grew, it meant no humus had formed; and without humus not even weeds or bush could get a footing.

Floreana was a very young isle, only a few hundred years old, which came into being through volcanic eruptions. It had been known for three hundred years. But there were no trees here which were three hundred years old, nor was there any virgin forest: how were trees to grow three hundred years ago on the bare lava? Even today there were no trees with trunks more than about a foot in diameter. In the area most suitable for settling the trees were chiefly lemon, which grew to about twenty-five feet; in between them were lemon bushes which could not grow so high, because the trees took away their light.

Before we had even got all our belongings up to the caves, Heinz had started on the clearing operations. Trees and bushes had to be cut down with axe or *machete*. He cut the branches off the trunks, which we saved up towards the building of our house. The branches and boughs were thrown into big heaps and burnt when they were dry. Their ashes gave us fertiliser.

The roots of trees and bushes could mostly be left standing, thank heavens. Where bananas, coffee or sugar-cane were planted, they did no harm, because these plants were placed fairly far away from each other. In the vegetable garden, however, there was no help for it, the root-stocks had to be dug out.

When the trees and bushes were down, the ground was worked with the pick, turned over and hoed. Then we had the soil which one day was to feed the family: the humus. It was not very deep, about four inches at most, and underneath were clay and stone. But the humus was fertile—though it would still be months before we could harvest our own produce.

29

It was weeks, in fact, before the first piece was cleared, enough anyhow to enable us in due course to live more or less from our own produce: weeks of laborious work which filled the whole day. And the days were so short, and there were such thousands of other things to be done besides.

Sometimes Heinz gave up a day to hunting. We needed meat, he especially for his labours. One time he would shoot a small boar, another time a bull. We had so much meat soon that we couldn't eat it all at once, and we had to learn how to preserve it by smoking it, so that it would keep for a while despite the damp.

For it had gone on raining incessantly. Four or five hours of sunshine a week were more than average, and we were grateful for every bit: on the whole, the climate up here was rather depressing, I felt, for an expectant mother!

Chapter 3

For once the sun was shining and I sat outside the 'living-cave,' sewing the first baby things. I was having trouble with the needles, and had to discard quite a lot in the end because they had rusted. I wished I had brought my sewing machine! That was one of the hundreds of necessities I had left at home as so much useless ballast, all of them things I could sorely do with now. What about dashing off a letter, though? They could be sent by return of post, even if it took some time to reach me. I said something like this to Dr Ritter, who burst out laughing. 'Return of post is wonderful,' he said. 'It's now the end of September, eh? You can't count on getting any post for six months or so.'

'But I've read about Post Office Bay. Surely mail arrives there pretty regularly?'

Ritter shook his head, still chuckling. 'My dear Frau Wittmer, it's not as regular as that. You ask your husband.'

'He's right, of course,' said Heinz, when Ritter had gone. 'I suppose mail isn't quite such a long-term business as it was in the days of the whalers, but even these days ships don't come here all that often in the winter, I imagine. Come to that, why should they? I don't suppose Ritter has many correspondents, now the hullaballoo about him has died down.'

'Did the whalers always stop here for mail?' Harry asked his father.

'Yes,' said Heinz, 'ever since their time it has been a sort of unwritten law for any ship that passed to heave-to outside Post Office Bay to pick up and deliver mail. One of the most fascinating things in Floreana's history, don't you think?'

We began to talk about the history of the islands. They were

31

known apparently to one of the Inca Kings, Tupa Yuquanqui, who came here with nearly a hundred men on big rafts, from the region where Ecuador's port of Esmeralda lies today. He returned months later with tales of great volcanic islands he had seen on his voyage, evidently the Galapagos; he had presumably witnessed an eruption on one of them, perhaps even Floreana. The traces of those long-past eruptions can still be seen on our island, the craters, small crateral lakes and lava rocks with which the island is strewn.

After that came the Spaniards, the real discoverers of the islands. In 1535 the King of Spain sent out the Bishop of Panama, Tomás de Berlanga, to report on conqueror Pizarro's progress. He set sail for Peru, but his becalmed vessels drifted out into the Pacific from the South American coast with stores coming to an end and only water enough for a few more days. Then they sighted land—where fresh water could be found; and the Spaniards had come to the Galapagos Islands.

They did not stay there long, but when they sailed away, they left behind something which has survived till this day, domestic animals. These were cattle and goats, probably not very many; perhaps they had run away from the Spaniards and hidden in the bush. In the course of time they multiplied exceedingly, and went wild again; in our first years, in fact, the cattle were often to be a real plague for us. Whether the dogs and cats now living wild on our island came over originally with the Spaniards, it is impossible to say; the donkeys swarming over Floreana today were probably brought over from neighbouring Chatham (or San Cristóbal, to give its Spanish name). Floreana never had any indigenous mammals, those on the island now were all brought from outside.

The Spaniards gave Spanish names to the islands, most of which have three names: Spanish, English (from the buccaneers), and the present official names given them by the Republic of Ecuador. After the Spaniards the Galapagos Islands became a *cache* for the buccaneers, and later on, in the early nineteenth century, a base for the whalers. The whalers built a supply depot for fresh meat on Floreana, and also established something else which is still functioning: the 'post office.'

This is perhaps rather a high-sounding name—mail-box would be more appropriate—for what is no more than a barrel fixed on a stake, in the bay which the whalers accordingly christened Post Office Bay. Each ship would drop mail on the outboard run, and pick it up on the voyage home: during the Anglo-American war of 1812, an American naval captain heard that British ships were cruising near the Galapagos, and headed for Post Office Bay. There in the barrel, waiting to be picked up by home-bound British whalers, he found a virtual roster of English ships and their whereabouts. Merely by lurking in Galapagan waters, and planting false notes of his own, he soon captured twelve vessels, and eventually destroyed a million tons of enemy shipping. This mail-box was to be our only means of communication with the outside world, and even if it took six months or more, as Dr Ritter and Heinz warned me, we were to find out that the mail never went astray.

For the scurvy-threatened whaling crews the Galapagos were a larder of plenty. The huge land tortoises provided fresh succulent meat, while the oil from their bodies was as pure as butter. Best of all, the giants would hibernate in a ship's damp hold for a year or more. They required neither food nor water, and their meat remained in prime condition. Whaling skippers were almost lyrical in their praise of tortoise meat, terming it far more delicious than chicken, pork or beef; they were so fond of it they stowed an estimated hundred thousand tortoises from the Galapagos in their holds. Often the crews lost track of exactly how many they had taken aboard, and back in New England at clean-up time many a landlubber must have bolted in terror when he stumbled across a five-foot reptile in the bilges. The whalers' depredations decimated the defenceless *galapagos*, however, and entire islands were stripped of their last tortoise; this included Floreana, though you could still find their immense shells on our island. We had been told that they might even now be abundant on the large island of Santiago which remained undeveloped and unexplored.

For three hundred years the Galapagos were a political no-man's-land, belonging to nobody; then in 1832 Ecuador declared them part of her territory. General Villamil landed from Ecuador, hoping to colonise them, and started on our island with eighty convicts whose sentences had been commuted from death to penal servitude. It was the General who gave the island its present name, in honour of Flores, the first President of Ecuador.

The site of the convicts' settlement was where we had settled now. The General called it 'Asilo de la Paz,' Asylum of Peace, but life up here was anything but peaceful, for his successor had to flee from the convicts. Those of them who survived were taken to other islands of the group. We liked the name, however, and hoped it would really prove an asylum of peace, where we could lead our own lives in peace and quiet. That was why we had come.

Unfortunately Floreana seemed to have been hostile to men ever since it was discovered; unless it was the fault of the men, not the island, that these and later attempts to settle here were all unsuccessful. Convicts were brought from Ecuador again in 1870, and again were settled near our caves. They grew chiefly coffee and tobacco, also lemons and oranges. The branches of the lemon trees twined over the ground, throwing out further roots into the earth, so that they soon formed thick, thorny lemon-hedges. Later on the pigs and cattle—domestic pigs and cattle gone wild again—ate the fruits and carried the seeds over half the island. They were the real planters! Tobacco was especially thriving here, extending further and further of its own accord. There would never be any shortage of tobacco, and that was a very comforting thought for Heinz, who liked to have his pipe going all day. (When he went into the bush for any length of time, he took a little tin with a wire handle containing glowing embers, so that he could always relight his pipe if it went out. Matches were too precious to be spared.)

A long time ago there had been another German on the island, a geologist called Wolf, who had been asked to survey it for the government of Ecuador; the first serviceable maps originated from him. But all his fine survey was wasted, for shortly after his visit there was a convicts' rising. The settlers divided, that is, into two hostile camps, there was a terrible battle, and at the end of it hardly any of either faction were left alive. The survivors were again taken elsewhere, and Floreana relapsed once more into oblivion.

The next attempt at settlement was in 1927, when Norwegians hoped to start a farm and a canned fish factory, but they too gave up. 'They've all failed,' said Heinz, filling himself a fresh pipe; but I wouldn't have it, I hated the word 'failure.' We hadn't left everything and travelled several thousand miles to be put off by defeatist precedents. At any rate we were here now, preceded by Ritter and Dore, and with the population soon to be increased by twenty per cent. I had already finished six vests for the baby. It is not so easy to shake off the habits of civilisation; even on a desert island you keep on doing crochet-work round a baby's vest. I'd also got a pillow for the baby, but not the stuffing. 'Have to feather our own nest,' remarked Heinz, and promised to shoot one of the sea-birds for pillow-stuffing.

Despite all these preparations, however, I was beginning to get rather apprehensive: partly about the house, of course. Heinz and Harry had so much else to do, and there were only three short months for building our house. But the cave wouldn't do for the nursery; the lava stone was so soft that the rain water kept seeping through. Apart from all this, having your first baby was a bit alarming in itself. 'We've at least got a qualified doctor on the island,' said Heinz comfortingly, 'so nothing much can go wrong.'

That was true, and the next time Ritter dropped in to see us for a few minutes, I asked him: 'You will help me, won't you, Dr Ritter, when the time comes?'

'I'm afraid not,' he said categorically, to my surprise and dismay. 'I didn't come to Floreana to practise as a doctor. I can't sit round here all the time, can I?—I've got too much to do. But you can let me know if you need me.'

How could any doctor be so heartless, I thought. How was I going to let him know when my labours began? Heinz wouldn't want to leave me on my own, and poor Harry's sight was so terribly bad he would never find the way to Frido.

Ritter evidently realised my disappointment, and did his best to soften the blow. 'You mustn't take it all so seriously, children are born every minute of the day—it's nothing to be frightened of. As you work hard and keep moving all the time, you'll find everything will go off smoothly.'

I can't say I found this much comfort; but I hoped he was right. It was now the middle of October: two months and a bit to go.

Still, there was plenty of hard work all right to keep me on the move, to stop me thinking too much about my natural childbirth. We all began to feel how tough nature made it for people who wanted to live on Floreana, and I sometimes understood only too well how some of our predecessors had left the island, in sheer desperation at nature, both animate and inanimate, which could so easily destroy all they had laboriously created.

On the other hand, there were some things about it which were indeed as I had imagined paradise. The fruit grew and ripened without our help, and wherever oranges and lemons were in bloom, the air was scented as if with eau-de-cologne. The birds were completely fearless. Doves, those symbols of peace, came flying up and hopped around in front of our feet. Then there were the fly-catchers, some coloured like our canaries, others black with a red head and breast. When I was working in the garden, they would dance right in front of my hoe quite unconcerned and pick up every worm they could find in the loose earth. Now and then a frigate-bird would fly past, with the metallic gloss of its feathers and its scarlet pouch, looking like some exotic flower. And there were always yellow and purple butterflies frisking about through the warm damp air. Yes, it was in many ways quite idyllic.

We were thrilled to see the first tender leaves in our vegetable garden, and revelled by anticipation in the delights of eating home produce. But we had not reckoned with the bulls, the wild cattle, that is. Day and night we could hear them bellowing in the bush; at times it sounded so menacing I would find myself holding my breath in apprehension.

One day I was 'at home' by myself. In the first days we had said: 'Now we're here, but we're not yet at home.' I wasn't quite sure when we *could* consider ourselves as being at home; perhaps after our first crop, it feels so good eating something you've grown yourself. That was why we were so pleased about the vegetables.

I went into my 'kitchen garden,' thinking I must do some weeding, for the weeds shot up like anything. To my horror I found that the radishes, lettuce and parsley had been trampled down, and by the tracks I could see that a bull must have broken in during the night. The little plantation was fenced in with a proper hedge, laboriously built with stakes and thorn-bush. The bull had simply shoved it aside with his horns, and laid waste everything we had spent so much trouble on. We had cleared the land, cut down trees and bushes, hacked out the roots, tilled the soil, covered it with the mud which had collected under the spring, and cherished lovingly the little green plants that came up. Now this was all in vain.

We worked on our fence day after day, mending it and re-inforcing it. Night after night the bulls came, tore through it again, trampled on our young plants, picked off the young banana leaves, the camotes, the maize. It seemed as if we were working to feed the bulls, and in the end might not have any-thing left to feed ourselves with! We were near despairing, like the others before us.

'The bulls were here first,' I said. 'In a way all this really belongs to them. We're the intruders.'

'Only the old bulls,' Heinz answered. 'The next generation was born in a different part of the island. They haven't any rights here, and they won't trouble us either; they'll stay where they were born, and where they feel at home. But there's no room for us *and* the old bulls to live here, so I'm afraid we must go by the law of nature: survival of the fittest.'

One night, therefore, when our particular enemy had come into the garden, enticed by the sweet banana leaves, Heinz shot him. We were rid of this disturber of the peace, we had meat again for a long time, and also fat—the kidneys were deeply embedded in fat, which we could melt down to make grease for candles. We also had the bull's hide, perhaps we could make shoes out of it. We needed them badly, for our own shoes had long perished from the thorns in the bush and the sharp lava stones. We had had to get used to going barefoot.

The hide needed stretching to dry it out, but up here it now rained almost all the time; on the coast it was fine and dry. We often needed a jersey here, while five hundred feet below a tropical heat reigned. So Heinz packed the heavy bull's hide in a rucksack and set off for the fine-weather belt, where he spread it out to dry in the blazing heat of the sun. After that we should somehow make leather of it.

I was quite often alone all day, and in between digging and planting and sewing and weeding and cooking, I kept a diary, despite some chaff from Heinz. 'How's the book going?' he would say in the evening. 'Hope you've not been at it so long you've forgotten our dinner. Harry and I are hungry as wolves.'

Wolves—that reminded me. While working on our garden in the afternoon, I had suddenly remembered something I wanted to enter in my diary. As I went into the half dark cave, a great wild dog dashed up, barking furiously. I think he got almost as much of a shock as I did. I screamed, he shot past me and away out of the cave again. He was a big yellow beast with a huge head. I had long had a secret suspicion that strange beasts were creeping into the cave when I was not there, for I had sometimes found bits of meat in it when I came back, but of course it might have been our own dogs. Now I knew they were innocent, and who the offenders were, the strange wild predators, like the one I had just met. These dogs were scarcely the same species any more as our Alsatians; they had grown up in the wilds and were more like wolves than dogs. I felt uneasy at the thought of living cheek by jowl with such creatures. How would they behave towards men when they were really hungry?

I went to our workshop cave and found one of the traps we had brought with us. I set it that evening, baiting it with a piece of dried meat. The next morning we found a big white dog, caught by its forepaw. Heinz gave it a bullet, cleaned the trap and set it again. The next two days we again caught a dog in it each morning.

Hertha, our Alsatian bitch, slept in front of our house-tent near the cave. Lump, the puppy, slept with Harry in the cave near the closed door (which we had meanwhile made). In the middle of that third night we were awoken by wild barking. Heinz got up, took his gun and went outside. In the faint moonlight he saw the dim outline of a dog on a rocky ledge. He knew it couldn't be one of our dogs, for Hertha was tied up outside the tent.

He fired. When he came back to the tent, he saw to his horror that Hertha was no longer on the chain. She had torn free, run ahead of Heinz, and waited for him on the rock. The next morning we found our loyal friend's body there, shot by her master in mistake. After the loss of his beloved Hertha, Heinz made even more of a favourite of young Lump, much to the detriment of Lump's training . . .

Soon we had been on Floreana three months. We lived simply, worked hard and were content. We were making good progress with our new home—our log cabin, twenty-two feet by twelve, to be built with our own hands. The wood of the lechoso tree, the only wood suitable for building, took over half an hour to drag up, log by log—for we were not yet the possessors of a donkey. So it was slow work, but we were past the first primitive stage, and we could see the house going up: that was a splendid feeling. All three of us were in good health. Harry had grown a lot, and was much sturdier too, a good strong boy he looked at thirteen. If only his eyesight would improve, as we hoped it might in this quiet green solitude.

Solitude? We did not feel lonely. Our day, the short tropical day, was so full we had no time for brooding. Theatres, films, entertainment?—we did not miss them. From our cave we had a wonderful view over the sea. In the evening we could watch glorious sunsets, we saw bright birds wheeling round and the flowers shining in their brilliant colours. All that more than made up for the life of civilisation which we had left behind.

On occasions we even had our excitements. One evening after work we were sitting outside the cave just after the sun had set. Dusk was coming down quickly, when suddenly the sky went a fiery red. Huge flames shot up, from the direction of Isabela. We held our breath, and began to guess what was happening: a volcano had erupted. It was a magnificent spectacle to enjoy from a distance, but there were volcanoes on Floreana too; suppose one should open its maw and scatter fire and ashes over the island? What should we do? Flee? But where?

The next day we felt a slight earth tremor but there were no other repercussions!

Chapter 4

In the middle of October we had a day of great excitement: the day our first visitors came.

I was busy with housework, quite unprepared for 'receiving,' when I heard Lump barking. There was a sound of rustling in the bush, which gradually grew nearer, and I could hear talking, with odd words blown across by the wind. Then, through the green of trees and bushes, I could see people approaching. I came out to meet them, and joyfully greeted an Austrian called Hagen whom we had met on Chatham. We did not know him well, of course, but he seemed like an old friend, and here he was coming to see us. Now I saw a small slim woman of about forty riding up on a donkey. Walking by the side of the donkey was a young man with flaxen hair, perhaps in his late twenties. Hagen introduced the woman as Baroness Wagner, and her escort as Herr Lorenz. Behind them came the captain of the ship which had brought them here.

The baroness dismounted. 'Where's the spring?' she demanded imperiously, foregoing any of the normal courtesies.

Rather taken aback, I pointed towards the spring. 'Just over there.'

She went over to it, followed by Lorenz, who took off her shoes like a devoted servant and proceeded to wash her feet thoroughly—in our drinking water.

After the ceremony had been completed, as she complained of being very tired, I said: 'If our tent will do, perhaps you would care to rest for a bit.'

With a vague murmur of thanks she accepted the offer. Lorenz, who also looked in need of rest, followed her into the tent. What an extraordinary couple, I thought.

Directly after this Heinz came in from his work, and wanted to know all about it. He too was delighted to see Hagen and the captain, but the little they could tell us about the baroness and her party was somewhat worrying. There were two men with her besides Lorenz, one German like Lorenz, the other an Ecuadorian; she had apparently brought them all with her from Paris. 'There's something not quite right about her,' Hagen told us. 'I noticed some funny things on the boat. I'd be a bit careful if I were you.'

'Oh dear,' I said to Heinz, 'that doesn't sound too good.'

'Well, I don't suppose they're staying long,' he answered philosophically.

'I'm afraid they may be,' said Hagen. 'They've brought a whole heap of stuff with them, not to mention cows and calves and two donkeys.'

We went on chatting for a while, and Hagen asked how we were getting on. He looked at the progress of our house, then came out with the depressing information that we were thatching the roof (with sugar-cane) the wrong way. We had been starting from the top, so that the gap between the top layer and the next one opened upwards instead of downwards, which would thus let the rain in. What we must do, he said, was to start from the bottom and continue to the top. A lot of hard work had been wasted, and it would all have to be redone. The baroness reappeared after her siesta. 'You won't mind, will you,' she asked, 'if we live quite near you just to start with?'

Heinz and I looked at each other. We didn't want to be unfriendly, but still! 'All right,' he said a little doubtfully, 'for the time being you can live in our orange grove. Near the little spring.'

The captain had brought us rice, and we bought a hundredweight off him for eleven sucres. The sack was down in Post Office Bay. Heinz said he hadn't got time to go and collect it at once, but the baroness offered to keep it for us—'in return for your kind hospitality,' she said—'and you can fetch it on Sunday.' We were overjoyed about the rice, it was wonderful to have it in reserve for the coming months.

There was something even more precious: our first mail: the baroness had brought a packet for us and a packet for the household at Frido Farm. 'You'll take Dr Ritter his, won't you?' she asked. 'I must be getting back to Post Office Bay, my party are waiting for me in the little wooden hut.' The wooden hut had been built by the Norwegian would-be settlers; it was right on the beach, and we had seen it on our first view of the island.

Hagen and the captain went off with the baroness and Lorenz, and when we were on our own again, Heinz shook his head. 'So now we've got neighbours,' he sighed. 'Three men and a woman.'

'Yes,' I said, 'and right outside our front door at that. But let's forget about them for a moment, I'm dying to see what the postman's brought!'

His eyes lit up. 'Hooray for mail!' he cried, with an excitement he rarely showed. 'This is the moment we've been waiting for.'

We dived into the packet, falling greedily on newspapers and magazines my family were sending out, and a splendid pile of personal letters with the little everyday details of life as we had known it such a short time, such an age, ago. They made Germany seem very near for the moment, though nobody, of course, had heard from us since we reached Floreana, and most of the letters struck the note of 'How are you getting on? . . . Let us know if you need anything . . . Longing to hear from you . . .' It would take weeks to answer them all.

And how *were* we getting on? Well, besides our new neighbours and the need to redo our thatching, we had other worries, especially a new bull. The previous night, despite the barbed-wire fence, he had again broken into our field of maize, which must have been particularly to his liking—because there was enough greenery for his consumption outside the fence. Heinz finished mending the fence, then went up to Frido with their packet of mail.

When he began talking about the new arrivals on the island, Ritter put up a hand to stop him. 'I know that lot already, they were up here yesterday, in fact they spent the night with me—some of it anyhow.' He gave a slight chuckle. 'The lady had to make do with a hammock, and she got pretty cold, so she told Lorenz, this gentleman-in-waiting of hers, to light a fire in our stove. As you can imagine, we weren't too pleased to have her giving orders like that in our house, and Dore told her so in no uncertain terms. In the end she went off to Post Office Bay, highly offended, breathing fire and slaughter against us.'

'Well anyhow,' said Heinz, 'here's a packet of mail she asked us to bring you.'

'That's funny,' Ritter said. 'Why didn't she bring it herself when she came here?' He took the letters. 'Damn it all, they've been opened.' His face was black as thunder.

'Not by me,' Heinz assured him hastily. Ritter shook his head in disgust. 'No, of course it wasn't you.' He began opening the letters and glancing through them. 'She's even taken photos out of some of them, the dirty bitch.'

'I see,' said Heinz, 'that's why she left your mail with us, so that you should think we'd opened it. Perhaps she wants to have us at loggerheads for her own good reasons. As far as I'm concerned, the less we have to do with them the better.'

'Goes for me too,' grunted Ritter. 'I'm not very fond of my fellow men and women, as I think you know.'

Two days later Lorenz came to us and introduced the Ecuadorian, a man called Valdivieso. The two of them had brought the cows up, and they put up a small tent where they were going to sleep. Valdivieso spoke only Spanish and French, while we spoke no French and little Spanish; we had to talk to him mainly through Lorenz as interpreter. Lorenz also gave us some of Valdivieso's background: 'About five years ago he was still a peon—just a common labourer, you know—on the island of Isabela. One day he smuggled himself on to a merchant ship that had put in there, and got to Europe as a stowaway. He worked on the railways in France, then he met the baroness, and she thought he'd be useful out here.' As I was to find out later, Lorenz was quite ready to gossip with strangers about the rest of his party.

On the Sunday Heinz and Harry went down to Post Office Bay to fetch the rice we had bought from the captain. Meeting them on the beach, the baroness took them to the little hut where she apparently spent the days. She received her guests in sporting attire: shirt blouse, riding breeches and high riding boots, a whip in her hand and for some reason a revolver in her belt; she was heavily made up. After offering Heinz a chair, she took up a graceful position reclining on a couch, there to grant him an audience; Harry she ignored throughout. Waving an elegant hand in the direction of another man in the room, she

43

introduced him as Monsieur Robert Philipson, 'my husband.' Although Philipson was a German and the baroness an Austrian, we discovered later that French was indeed the party's *lingua franca*.

Should she really be called Baroness Wagner-Philipson, Heinz wondered, studying the husband for a moment. Philipson, he told me afterwards, seemed a good deal younger than the baroness, about Lorenz's age, good-looking, with dark curly hair and at first meeting anyhow a rather off-hand manner. Monsieur Philipson regretted he had hardly a minute to spare for his visitors. 'So sorry,' he drawled. 'I'm just in the middle of an article I'm writing, and I simply must get it finished so that I can send it off at once.'

Heinz made no comment, but only just restrained a grin as this enthusiastic feature-writer left, determined to catch the evening post with his copy—on an island where ships only called every few weeks or months.

'You know my plans, don't you?' said the baroness.

Heinz shook his head.

'Oh, but haven't I told you about them?' she smiled, and looking very important handed him a Guayaquil newspaper. From this he managed to make out that she was intending to build a hotel on Floreana for American millionaires (to be called Hacienda Paradiso), assisted by her 'partners,' Philipson and Lorenz, as architect and engineer respectively. Before Heinz could ask any questions about this rather alarming prospect, the baroness had abruptly switched to another subject, Dr Ritter. Her lips curled as she spoke of him: 'Dentist and doctor indeed! Dental mechanic at most, more likely a male nurse . . .'

Heinz felt more and more embarrassed as she went on in this vein, and as soon as he could, he asked for the rice.

The baroness smiled sweetly. 'Oh yes, of course, the rice. That will be twenty-eight sucres.'

'What!' gasped Heinz. 'Twenty-eight sucres? But I bought it from the captain. For eleven sucres.'

'It costs twenty-eight sucres,' the baroness repeated, playing with her whip. 'If you want it, that is.'

Heinz stood up. 'I should be obliged, baroness,' he said coldly, 'if you would look for somewhere else to stay. You will *not* be welcome in our orange grove.'

44

Her features hardened. 'I wouldn't dream of looking for anywhere else, there's no other suitable place here. Not till my hotel
is up. I shall be staying in the orange grove as long as I like—or
were you thinking of throwing me out, by any chance?' She
laughed. 'We have three men, you know, and I can count as a
fourth man in some respects.' She touched her revolver significantly, and gave Heinz a baleful look.

We renounced our rice. We weren't going to starve without
it, and from now on we intended to give the baroness as wide a
berth as possible. But a few days later Heinz met her 'gentleman-
in-waiting' in the bush.

'Psst!' hissed Lorenz melodramatically, disappearing into thick
undergrowth. Heinz followed him. 'Nobody can hear us?' he
asked, looking apprehensively all round him.

'I don't think so, not just here,' said Heinz. 'What on earth is
it?'

'The baroness says I'm not to speak to you or your wife,'
Lorenz explained in a scared whisper. It was obvious that he was
only too eager to talk, particularly in German (as he was always
obliged to speak French with the others). In the strictest confidence he began to tell Heinz about the baroness and Philipson.

'They aren't really married, you know, that business about "my
husband" is just for show. Her husband's a Frenchman called
Bousquet, and she signs herself Baroness Wagner de Bousquet.
He was an airman in the war, then he became a business man,
and met her in Constantinople—she was a dancer there. Before
that, during the war, I mean, she was a spy, so I've heard. Don't
know if it's true, but when you know her you wouldn't put it
past her. She's not divorced from Bousquet either, but I think
he's glad to be rid of her.'

'Really?' said Heinz in response to all this information, then
came to the point which was interesting him as much as anything. 'Tell me, Herr Lorenz, did anyone open Dr Ritter's
letters?'

Lorenz hesitated, but his garrulity overcame his nervousness.
'Yes,' he admitted, 'the baroness did, she wanted to know the sort
of people he was in touch with. I think she opened some of yours
too.'

We had been too excited on opening our mail to have noticed, but now we had been warned: there was a spy living very near us, perhaps a former professional spy. It was a disturbing thought, but most of the time we managed to forget it in the advance of our own schemes. The house-building was coming along nicely, and I began to build a hen-coop from the waste wood. At present we had only two hens, sitting on ten eggs, but the raising of poultry was one of my big plans and Dr Ritter had promised to let me have three more. These and the coop were a modest beginning towards my fine chicken farm of the future.

On 15th November, about four weeks later, we had more visitors. Estampa, a Norwegian who lived on Santa Cruz, had brought a globe-trotting German called Franke in a little fishing boat he owned. Franke wanted to write an account of his travels in the solitude of Floreana.

They dropped anchor outside Post Office Bay, and landed on a small raft. The first person they met on the island was the baroness. Franke told her his plans, and asked her politely: 'Could you possibly give me a roof, just for a little . . .?'

'I couldn't,' she said. This curt refusal might have seemed strange for a woman intending to set up as hotelier, but the fact was that her hotel guests must be millionaires at least, as she had told us at the outset, and Franke plainly did not come into this class.

He went inland and up to Frido Farm. Dr Ritter also refused, though less bluntly than the baroness, saying: 'I'm afraid I need absolute peace and quiet for my scientific work, and anyhow there really isn't room, as you can see.'

'Go and see if the Wittmers can help,' he advised, so Franke came on to us, about an hour's walk. But alas, we could not possibly put them up either. We ourselves were still only cave-dwellers, with barely enough room for ourselves; and in six weeks I was expecting my child. My condition was beginning to cause me discomfort, so I really could not have 'anyone to stay.' Franke was very disappointed. 'I suppose there's nothing for it,' he said, 'but to get Estampa to sail me back to Santa Cruz.'

On their way down to Post Office Bay, he and Estampa shot a calf, which they hoped to take back to Santa Cruz. The baroness must have heard the shot, and when she saw the two

46

men coming along with the calf, she charged out of the hut: 'That was my calf!' she shouted, drawing the revolver from her belt. 'Stay just where you are . . . Philipson! Valdivieso!' she called.

They came out of the chalet and took up their stand near her. 'Destroy that raft!' she ordered.

Her henchmen obeyed, and she kept the revolver pointed straight at her two captives: she looked quite capable of shooting them like dogs if they made any move, so they had to stand there helplessly, watching their landing-raft being smashed up. When this operation was completed, she glared at them, turned on her heel, and went back to the chalet without a word. Philipson and Valdivieso followed her.

Finding themselves apparently stranded on Floreana, Estampa and Franke retired to Frido for a council of war. Ritter asked Estampa to stay with him to make a detailed report of what had happened, which could be sent to the governor at Chatham with a strong letter of complaint about the baroness's fantastic behaviour. Ritter knew that Heinz kept a collapsible dinghy hidden in the bushes near Blackbeach Bay (it had to be hidden lest the baroness should simply requisition it, like the rice), so he sent Franke off to us, asking if the dinghy could be used in this emergency. The plan was that Heinz should take Franke round in it to the fishing boat anchored outside Post Office Bay, which Franke would sail back to Blackbeach (with the dinghy on board) to pick up Estampa.

The first part of the plan worked all right. Heinz and Harry got Franke safely out to the boat. Unfortunately he had no idea how to handle her—a fact of which he had strangely not informed us—and began drifting further and further off course. There was nothing for it but for Heinz and Harry to return to Blackbeach in the dinghy, collect Estampa, and sail back to the boat somewhere off Post Office Bay.

From Blackbeach to Post Office Bay it was normally about two hours' distance in the dinghy. The weather was stormy, with a high sea, much too high a sea for so small a craft, so that Heinz and Harry were literally risking their lives to help the two castaways: it seemed a pity, in retrospect, that Estampa had not been the one taken in the dinghy, and Franke left writing a report with Ritter. Besides the danger, the whole business took

47

about twice as long as originally planned—and I could not imagine why my menfolk didn't come back.

I was up by the caves, alone except for the faithful Lump. As long as it was light, I worked in the garden. Then I collected wood and dry sugar-cane to go on building my hen-coop. Then I got supper ready. It was quite dark by now, the chickens had long gone to sleep. The silence all round me was eerie, seldom have I found the island's silence so oppressive and sinister as I did that evening. First of all, there was the feeling that something might jump out of the darkness and attack me; then came a mounting fear of what had happened to Heinz and Harry.

I crouched on a stool in front of the flickering fire. Lump lay in front of me with his head on my lap. Sometimes he looked up at me, his eyes questioning. We both listened for the slightest noise from outside. Now and then there were rustling sounds, and from the bush a cow's deep lowing percolated to the cave. The minutes went by like an age, I felt unable to get up to light the hurricane lamp. I was in the grip of a vast fear, stronger than I had ever felt in my life.

Suppose something *had* happened to them, suppose the little boat had capsized? I could hear the terrific waves breaking on the shore, that endless monotonous roar. The dinghy was so thin, and I knew there were swarms of sharks round the coast, sharks with waiting teeth . . . I put a hand over my eyes, but it could not blot out the grisly pictures which crowded in on my mind. I felt Lump's head pressing closer to me; he at least was alive and with me.

Suppose they didn't come back? What on earth should I do then—left alone on this island, with our child due in six weeks' time? The fire was almost out now, a faint glow was all the light left in the cave. I still couldn't nerve myself to get up and poke it, put on more wood. I could not move a single step.

Outside the cave the stars twinkled in the sky. The muffled roar of the breakers still rumbled in my ears. I felt there was nothing in the world but me and space, endless space.

Suddenly the wind seemed to blow a word over to me, a cry perhaps. Surely someone had called? Then there was silence again. No, I was deceiving myself, the darkness and the wind had tricked me.

Lump took his nose off my lap, raised his head and barked.

Not a bark really, more of a growl, low and restrained. I saw his ears sharply pricked, his tail slowly beginning to wag. Again a sound, a word shattered by the wind.

'Lumpi!' I called hoarsely.

At that he jumped up, ran out of the cave, and barked, louder and louder. Then he came running in again, nuzzled against me, and raced out again, his ears flying. Then despite the wind I heard it quite distinctly: 'Hullo!'

Heinz—it could only be Heinz, that was his call. My legs were shaking as I got up. I saw them, first as faint outlines, in the entrance to the cave. Heinz and Harry! Thank God! Thank God for bringing them back to me safe and sound.

'Heinz!' I cried, staggering forward. 'Harry!' Heinz caught me in his arms, and we stayed like that for minutes, not speaking. 'Well,' I said at last, 'I'm afraid supper may be spoiled, but I'm glad you're back.'

That was my first bad day on the island. I never wanted another like it.

The weather seemed to change. It was getting very hot except when there was rain; we were approaching the season of tropical heat. Most of the plants, if they were not near the stream, had their leaves drooping in the midday sun, only straightening up towards evening. If only we could have watered everything. But there wasn't enough water for that.

Apart from this our chief worry was the cattle, which were plaguing us unmercifully. Almost every night they broke into the garden, and one night we heard them munching away quite near the house. Lump barked furiously. Heinz got his gun and went after the dog's barking. There was only a faint moon, the outlines of a bull were all he could just see. He fired at the shadowy body, which caused immediate pandemonium. Several bulls raced out of the garden, bellowing.

The next morning we found a dead bull lying in the maize field. The others had torn up half the fence in their flight. We had another unexpected feast of freshly killed beef, but we did not enjoy it much—we were paying too dearly. We had to put an end to the cattle-plague, things simply could not go on like this. Here we were working and working, growing food, and all for the cattle. If they went on tearing everything up or trampling it down, we should have nothing left at all. There was only one thing for it: we must have a guard rota all night. Harry took the first shift from eight to midnight. I went till three in the morning, and the rest of the night Heinz was on duty.

I found it most eerie in the pitch-dark night. Wrapped in a warm coat, gun under my arm and torch in hand, I walked through the plantation. Lump escorted me, chasing every rat which scurried across the path. The second night I shot a cow which had broken in and was making a good meal of the runner beans.

The guard duties slowed up our other work, including progress on the house. It must be ready when the child came, but at the present rate it seemed very doubtful whether we should make that date. Yet there was something rather fascinating about these lonely watches in the still of the night. Above you was the sky, dark and overcast. The stars were seldom out, and the darkness all round seemed impenetrable. You sat there quite still so as not to betray your presence by a noise. But there were always sounds in the bush during the night. The pigs squeaked. Somewhere a donkey brayed. Cattle lowed and bellowed. A strange nocturnal concert, it took me a long time to get used to it. Many things were still strange. After all, we hadn't been here six months, and we had to allow ourselves longer than that to dig roots in our new environment.

It was strange too to have Christmas so near, in such different surroundings and climate. Five days before Christmas the temperature was 64 degrees by ten in the morning. Just after noon it was 82 in the shade.

Dr Ritter had asked us if we could give him beans and some other European vegetables for Christmas; also dried meat, rather surprisingly, for his chickens. I had just picked my first crop of cucumbers, which seemed the very thing for vegetarians and didn't grow at Frido, because it was too warm and dry there. On the other hand, it was very good for bananas and various other things we didn't do well with. We quite often made some exchanges, and on these occasions Ritter showed himself a pleasant and reasonable sort of person.

When Heinz went up to Frido with his produce, he was astonished to find Ritter carving up a big bull in a most workmanlike fashion. He realised that whatever vegetarian ideas Ritter

50

might have arrived with, they had definitely been discarded by now, probably a good long while ago.

'I've just shot the brute,' said Ritter, sounding a little embarrassed, and added hastily: 'He's been plaguing me for weeks, knocking down my fence time and again.'

Some pieces of the dead bull were already sizzling in the pan, Heinz could smell the aroma wafting over from the stove.

'Care for a steak?' asked Ritter. 'You've come just at the right moment.'

Heinz accepted with pleasure, deciding it was just the fitting punishment for the wretched bull to land up in a supposed vegetarian's frying pan.

* * *

Our first Christmas on the island, and it was still 82 in the shade. We tried hard to think of a pine forest deep in snow, but instead there were gay butterflies—all wrong at Christmas. Still, I made a Christmas cake—it smelt marvellous when I was baking it—and Heinz shot a boar, so we had our Christmas roast pork. I managed to produce some home-made liver sausage, and even a kind of salami I had smoked in the chimney. Our entire Christmas fare was made from ingredients provided by the island, and even in our cave there was a good seasonable atmosphere.

Except of course for the heat. 'When you think of the cold winters in Europe,' Heinz began.

'I'd rather be celebrating Christmas on the Galapagos,' I finished the sentence for him. 'Even if the weather's like the height of summer. Anyhow I feel really well here—and happy. How about you, Harry?'

'Oh, I'm happy all right,' he answered, 'particularly with your present.' We had given him a fine mouth-organ, brought out from Germany without his knowledge, something we knew he had long been wanting. 'I'll be giving you a recital soon!'

'Well,' said Heinz, 'after all that food I think we ought to go for a good Christmas walk. Coming?'

'Listen,' I told him, 'I'm going to have a baby any day now, and you want me to go climbing over rocks. Oh, all right, but don't expect me to walk very fast.'

'Do you good, Mother,' said Harry. 'You've hardly been out of the estate'—we always called it that very grandly— 'since we moved in here.'

Nor I had. And I found this half hour's walk at least as tiring as our six hours' march with packs up from the coast to the caves. But when we reached our destination I was very glad I had come.

Heinz and Harry had brought me to a cliff-side, with a little spring gushing out of it, and a fine wide view across a broad strip of pampa to the sea. A big herd of cattle and their calves moved peacefully over the pampa, pigs and donkeys mingling with them in easy familiarity. It was an idyllic scene, perfect for the first Christmas on 'our island.'

Chapter 5

Our house was ready at last, the essentials at least: the kitchen and my bedroom. And the rooms were under a roof thatched with sugar-cane—thatched the right way this time. It was a laborious business, because sugar-cane is very brittle when dry, so that you have to keep on moistening it while it is being handled. No rain had seeped in so far, but how the roof would hold up in the rainy season only time would tell.

In comparison with the cave this was a palace. We built low foundations from stone—the lava stones which lay around in great quantities. Strong tree-trunks were rammed into the ground at the four corners, and the walls between were also made of logs. I scraped the moss off old lemon trees, using it to fill up the gaps between the wall poles and thus stop the wind whistling through them. We were proud of our log-cabin, small as it was, which had taken so much hard labour to build. Every log was the trunk of a small tree, mostly from the strip of bush we had cleared, so Heinz and Harry had to trim the trunks to size, then cart them on their shoulders to the 'site,' which was very near the caves.

They had long worn out their shoes, in clearing operations, hunting, and walking over the rough jagged lava boulders. 'I simply must buy a new pair,' Heinz said. 'Think I'll drop over to Guayaquil.'

'Good idea,' I said, 'it's only a few hundred miles. Make sure you go to a good shop.'

'Oh yes, I'll see where there's plenty of choice. I'm pretty particular about my shoes.'

'Perhaps you could get me a pair of evening shoes while you're there,' I suggested. 'In case Dore asks us to dinner for a joint of vegetarian beef.'

All three of us had got into the habit of making this sort of silly joke; it was a useful antidote to the depression we sometimes felt at all the things we couldn't have—except by making them ourselves, as we did with the shoes. The island offered us cowhides, so we should have to make shoes out of those, which meant curing and tanning and cobbling and much else besides. We didn't know how to do any of this, but necessity is the mother of invention, and we learnt by trial and error, by guess-work and growing experience.

We didn't in fact tan the hides, we only let them dry in the sun whenever it happened to be shining. Then we cut them up into pairs of soles and a lot of straps, and cobbled ourselves sandals. They weren't too bad to start with, and were at least a protection against stones and thorns; but they were no good when it rained. The rain made them sodden, they swelled up shapelessly to twice their size, like sponge in water, and fell off the wearer's feet. When that happened, they were just left lying —to the delight of the rats, who had a great fancy for cast-off cowhide sandals.

I lined the walls of my bedroom in white material. The room was about six feet by six, with the bed along one wall. The bed was a 'four-poster' with crossbars; the mattress, made of strong fast-coloured linen, was stuffed with straw. With thick woollen blankets on, it made a good bed at night, while in the day we used it as a divan to sit on. Along the other wall went a shelf with a curtain over it, where I could keep clothes; and above the bed, the whole length of the wall, was another shelf, for our books. I could at last take them out of the crates, where they were starting to moulder. The bedroom door would lead into the living-room, only that wasn't there yet—and wouldn't be before the child was born.

It was quite a respectable kitchen, with a proper stove made from stones, an oven, and a wide chimney above them, in which a whole lot of meat and sausage could be smoked. There was also a sideboard, several shelves, a table and two chairs—all home-made, of course. We caned the seat part of the chairs with raw cowhide. This was by way of experiment, and if it worked well, we were going to do the same with all our chairs, seats and also the beds.

We cut straps from the cowhide before it was dry, then made

them wet again and stretched them between trees to pull them quite straight. We bored holes in the crossbars of the chairs, then drew the still wet straps through these holes in lattice-work, as you darn socks. We drew them as tight as they could possibly go. Then we put the chairs out in the sun, and the moist straps became hard as steel in the sun. It all went as planned, the chair seats were as taut as tennis racquet strings.

The table was a terrible labour. Heinz said he would rather build three houses than have to produce a firm, non-wobbly table. The windows were provisionally of wire mesh, for of course we had no glass. As a matter of fact, if my memory served me aright, glass was a bit of a luxury in Ecuador itself and none of the old houses in Guayaquil had glass windows.

We had begun bringing our things from the cave to the new house, when the flaxen-haired Lorenz suddenly turned up, asking: 'Can I give you a hand?'

I had just lit our first fire in our highly civilised kitchen. The stove drew splendidly, with no smoke or smell, and I was brewing some 'house-warming' coffee. 'No thanks,' I answered. 'It's very nice of you, but I think the baroness might make trouble if she found out. Would you like some coffee, though?'

His eyes beamed. 'Thanks ever so much,' he answered. 'I'm from Dresden, you know'—we had already guessed from his accent that it was somewhere in Saxony—'and we Dresdeners can't do without our coffee.' He took the cup in both hands, and began to drink. It loosened his tongue at once. 'I was up at Frido yesterday with Dr Ritter, trying to find out about getting away from here. I just can't stand the way things are at present.' He swallowed some hot coffee, which must have scalded his throat, then continued: 'The baroness treated me all right in Paris, you know, I wasn't always a sort of manservant like you've seen me here. I mean, we went into partnership together, and I put up a lot of money too, though you might not believe it, seeing me now. I gave her all my savings before we came out here, and how does she treat me? I'm just about good enough to herd her cows and fetch water. All the better work is left for Philipson and Valdivieso.' He took another long gulp, savouring it to the full. 'I say, this is marvellous coffee. Do you know, the baroness can't eat any rice without milk, so every day I have to go down to the hut on the coast with fresh milk for her ladyship. She only gives me the bare necessities to eat, and the other two have a fine time with her down there. Because she's brought a lot of stores, you know—most of it with my money too. Only I don't get any of it, I'm treated worse than a dog . . .'

He went on in this vein for a bit, and I sympathised politely, but there was nothing I could do to help him, and in any case I felt his worries were comparatively small compared to mine. For it could only be a matter of days now before the child came. Surely it would be born before 1932 was out.

The first labour pains began the next day, December 30th. Dear God, I prayed, let it all go well. There was such a vast amount to do outside the house. Heinz couldn't waste hours on end just sitting with me. I knew that only too well, and hid my pains as much as possible. He and Harry mustn't be worried till it was really necessary.

Everything was ready in my bedroom in the new house: linen, bandages, cotton wool, scissors, nappies, and a tin of talcum powder. Would it be enough, I wondered feverishly. I only had this one tin, I ought to have brought two, or even three—but it was too late to think of that now. My bed was prepared. We had put thick layers of paper over it, and covered them with pieces of linen sterilised by boiling.

The pains were very violent by now, but the day passed, and so did the night, though I scarcely slept. Heinz made a support for my back so that I could sit up a little; the pains weren't quite as bad then. I felt alternately burning hot and freezing cold. Dawn crept on into morning, and still nothing happened. Heinz made me some strong coffee, and I got up, walked around a bit. The pains abated. I could even get meals ready and bake a New Year's cake.

Heinz and Harry worked very hard that day, and when night came, they dropped off to sleep at once, leaving me alone with my agonising pains. I had to bite hard into the pillows so as not to scream. But I kept in control, I didn't scream, and that night passed too. It was New Year's day, and surely it couldn't go on much longer. I was desperate, and couldn't eat any of the food Heinz lovingly prepared for me. I could only drink and drink, I was feverishly thirsty and felt as if my throat were burning. Heinz sent Harry out with the dog, thinking by the time he returned the child would have come. But nothing happened, and the pain was driving me mad.

The third night went by like an age. It was seventy-two hours since the pains had started, they were more than flesh and blood could stand. That night Heinz and Harry hardly slept either. They got up while it was still dark. I heard them going out. I was so weak I couldn't even say anything, anyway they would be back soon. They had gone out, I didn't know why. Perhaps they had heard a bull breaking into the garden. They might shoot it. I shouldn't even hear the shot.

It was still dark. I felt as if the air had left my lungs. Air, air, I must have air. I couldn't stay in bed any longer. I got up, dizzy with fear and pain. 'Heinz!' I tried to call, but could hardly hear my own voice. I went out of the house, Heinz and Harry might have gone to the caves. I staggered over towards the caves, half fainting. There was no one in the main cave.

'Heinz!' It was more of a squeak than a scream, it wouldn't have reached outside the caves. There were a few things still left in the cave, I saw a crate, two crates. They were open, and there were books in them. A book—yes, this was the time to find a book and read, it might calm me down a bit. The rickety table was still there, but there wasn't a spark of fire in the fireplace. Had they let the fire go out? I couldn't remember where I was, didn't realise the house was twenty or thirty yards away from here. They must be in the bush. Perhaps they were following the spoor of a bull. In the bush. Yes, I'd go into the bush as well, just to find them, not to be alone.

There was a straw pallet on the ground. I nearly tripped over it. Straw . . . but I had a bed, a real bed. With white linen on it . . .

For a moment everything went black. My legs wouldn't hold me any more, then all at once I felt as light as a feather. The straw . . . I let myself drop down on it, I felt the straw under me. I lay there, unable to move. 'Heinz! Heinz!' this time I screamed so loud that I started in terror at my own voice. It echoed back through the cave, loud and empty. There was no answering call.

I lay quite still. There was a rustling at the entrance to the cave, an eerie rustling. It was still dark outside. An owl hooted.

57

I heard a bull bellow, the bellowing came nearer and nearer. He must be heré by now, somewhere very near me.

He gave another bellow, a bellow of rage and pain, as if he were mortally wounded. He was less than three yards away from me, I broke into a cold sweat, tried to call out, call for Heinz, but no sound came, I was too weak even to open my lips.

Then I heard a cry. It didn't come from me. A short, shrill, squeaky, penetrating cry. It didn't come from me, nor from Heinz—it was the first cry of our new-born child. The child was there. I couldn't realise it, I was too weak, too helpless. I didn't hear the steps of people hurrying up to me, I didn't see my husband standing by me. I was past seeing and hearing.

Harry was close behind his father, and Lump dashed in with them, barking happily (they told me afterwards) to see me lying on the straw. Then he became very quiet, because I was so quiet.

Heinz and Harry brought me carefully over to the house, me and the child. 'It's a boy.' Was that Heinz? I was so weak I couldn't take in even those few words.

Heinz laid me gently on my bed, bathed the child and wrapped it in a big towel that was lying ready. Then I and the child fell into a deep sleep. Heinz and Harry also slept the last two hours of the night.

When daylight came, I woke. I couldn't speak. I drank the coffee which Heinz brought to my bed, drank it greedily. I ate the two beaten up raw eggs and stewed pumpkins. Then the pains returned. I knew I was far from out of the wood yet. The child was there, thank God, that had gone off well. It lay near me, the pink fists pressed against the face, and slept with eyes tight shut. I saw the little face and tried to raise my arm to stroke it, at least to feel it for the first time; but the pains were so fearful I felt incapable of the slightest movement. The birth was not yet over. It was over for the little creature that lay near me, but not for me. The after-birth was still not there, after so many hours. Though almost drugged with pain, I could see one thing quite clearly: my life was in danger. The danger was growing every minute, something must be done about it, and at once. I couldn't do anything myself, nor could Heinz. Only a doctor could help in this. 'Dr Ritter,' I muttered. 'Get Dr Ritter.'

'Harry!'

'Yes, Papa.' Harry was dashing out, when Heinz called him back. 'Take Lump with you.'

'Right. Come on, Lump.'

The dog barked joyfully, I could see him wagging his tail, Harry going out of the door.

All at once I was quite lucid again. Harry's eyesight was still very bad, he would miss the way to Dr Ritter, he would get lost. It might take a day before he reached Ritter, if he got there at all. I beckoned to Heinz, who bent down to listen. I whispered my fears.

'Harry!' I heard Heinz calling after him. Harry was already some way off. 'Come back!' Heinz called, and a minute later : 'I'll go myself, I know the way better, so I can go faster than you.' Then he raced off, down to Dr Ritter.

For the first time I had a good look at our new islander. He had very fair hair and brown eyes. To judge from his crying his lungs were quite in order.

Three long hours passed before Heinz returned—with Dr Ritter, thank heavens. Ritter examined me, and was now a doctor pure and simple. He seemed to have forgotten everything else.

'Have you still got pains?' he asked.

'Yes. Very bad ones.'

'I must operate.'

I didn't care if only he helped me.

Suddenly he seemed to have changed his mind. 'No, I'll try first with quinine, and hot and cold compresses.' He told me to do the compresses myself, then left, saying he had to speak to the baroness. They must have made up their quarrels somehow, I registered faintly.

After a good hour Ritter was back. He washed his hands a dozen times with antiseptic soap. Then he performed the operation, without rubber gloves and also without an anaesthetic. The pain was so cruel I could have screamed my head off, but somehow I managed to bear it in silence. Anyhow it was fairly soon over, leaving me with only a soothing weakness. He *had* helped me, I could breathe again, could even bring out a faint smile when he proceeded to congratulate me on my son. 'You've been very brave,' he went on, 'I congratulate you on that too.'

I smiled again, inwardly regretting that when Heinz and I were talking about him I had once called him a heartless brute.

59

'All that wasn't exactly a picnic for you,' he said thoughtfully, and I wondered whether now for the first time he really grasped that it might have gone wrong; if it had, he would have carried a heavy burden of responsibility, at least morally, for having refused to give me the help I had asked for beforehand. But however terrible it had been, it was all over now, and I did not want to remind him of such things—I was too grateful that in the end he had helped me in time. I asked him what I should do now.

'Stay a few days in bed,' he told me, 'and get over all you've been through. See you're properly looked after.'

It occurred to me that this was somewhat superfluous advice. I should have had to be more or less crazy to have tried to get up at once. However, it might be a way of saying there was no special treatment needed.

He looked at the child for the first time, and nodded appreciatively. 'A fine strapping boy,' he said at last. 'Well built. Don't go feather-bedding him. The harder his mattress the better. That's the way to get worth-while characters.' This sounded like a bit of his special philosophy, though I didn't quite see what the softness of the mattress had to do with someone's future worth.

'We do appreciate your coming very much,' said Heinz. 'May I ask what we owe you?'

'Money—you want to give me money?' Ritter shook his head. 'What can one do here with money? It's no good to one at all. And besides, I want to live without money, live only off what nature offers us. But I'd be pleased if you could bring down a pig some time. And my chickens are extremely fond of your dried meat. If you'd let me have a sackful every fortnight . . .'

I turned my face away to hide my amusement at a professed vegetarian asking to be paid in pork! He was asking quite a hefty fee too, but I didn't care. He could have had twenty pigs, for after all he had saved my life. What an extraordinary fellow, though! I should always remember him saying: 'I didn't come to Floreana to practise as a doctor,' refusing to help me beforehand and then turning up at last quite willingly when it was almost too late.

I had a few days sick-leave, which I felt had been well earned. I dreamed away the time, while Heinz acted as cook and nurse. Harry spent a lot of the day fetching and chopping wood. We couldn't agree on a name for the boy, till Harry suggested Rolf, which we all thought was just right: nice and short, Rolf Wittmer, it went very well.

Of course Rolf ought to be baptised—like any Christian child, even if he's born on Floreana; but how were we going to get a pastor? Perhaps we ought to put a letter in the barrel, announcing the happy event to the world. Then a pastor might one day come with some ship and perform the christening. We could only wait for that, but in the meantime I couldn't get over the miracle of my first baby. Another new personality had come into our midst, we were a family of four, not three. A simple, ordinary fact, but one I found very hard to take in.

On the third day after the birth I got up for the first time, and tried to walk. But my head swam, and I had to hold on to the table. I managed to reach a chair, and sank into it, exhausted. Just then I heard footsteps outside, strange ones—in this island solitude the ear learns very quickly to distinguish between noises. Those steps didn't belong to one of us anyhow, and Lump barked in a different way. No, he was announcing visitors; as it happens, the visitors I would least have expected—the baroness, with Philipson and Lorenz. She had no revolver in her belt today, and altogether seemed in an unusually genial mood.

'Congratulations on your son,' she said with effusive cordiality, taking both my hands and shaking them hard. Then she presented me with clothes for the baby and a tin of Quaker oats, and kept expressing amazement that I was up again so soon after the birth.

Remembering the rice episode, I found this abrupt change to *grande dame* benevolence rather hard to take. However, we could do with the gifts, and I certainly did not want to spoil the peaceful atmosphere, so I accepted with proper gratitude.

All three of my visitors were in high spirits, rather too high for my condition. I was chiefly wanting rest, but it seemed they had a great deal to tell me.

'Valdivieso is no longer in our Hotel Company,' the baroness reported. 'He's been fired, and he means to leave the island with the next ship that puts in. Till then he's living down in Post Office Bay. Lorenz has to go down every day and take him his food . . .'

'Really?' I said, feeling profoundly disinterested in whether Lorenz took Valdivieso food or not. As for the Hotel Com-

pany . . . but the baroness was continuing. I made an effort to
listen.

'. . . All differences of opinion between the management of the
Hotel Company and Dr Ritter, and in the last resort with yourselves too, were due to the trouble-making of this Valdivieso.
But now he's out of it, we can undoubtedly live together in
perfect harmony . . .'

'I hope so, of course,' I murmured, and then gave up the effort,
switching off my attention while the baroness talked about herself and her plans. At last the visit ended, I hoped she was not
hurt, but she must surely understand that I tired quickly.

The next day both Ritter and Dore appeared. I was far from
clear now what their practice was on the eating of meat, so I
offered them rice pudding and fruit salad to be on the safe side.
Dore gave me useful advice about bringing up the baby, and she
too seemed very well-disposed, considering I had not seen her
since that first visit we paid to Frido Farm. Then she said: 'Well,
we must be going now. We want to drop in on the baroness,
and have a look at her hotel plans.'

How very odd, I thought: first the two women abuse each
other, and now they're paying each other friendly visits. Changes
were evidently occurring in island 'society,' though I wondered
vaguely how long this harmony would last.

Soon I forgot about them, for we had our own worries, in
particular the roof, which was obviously not going to be watertight after all. A day or two after this the rain pelted down so
hard that rain and bits of roof broke into the room together.
Everything was swimming, all our clean clothes and linen were
drenched. But the next day the sun was so strong that everything
dried out again very quickly. The disaster was only temporary.

Gradually one great weight was taken off my mind: the lack
of a 'nanny' for little Rolf. I no longer had to keep my eyes on
him all day or carry him around with me when I went out and
worked in the garden. For ordinary life had to go on, and the
birth had already put us back quite a lot. But now, while Heinz
and Harry worked in the bush or the plantation, and I was
occupied among my vegetables or with the chickens, Lump was
a perfect baby-sitter. At first the dog had been rather jealous of
Rolf, and barked fiercely when I took the child on my arm. But
in no time he got used to the new member of the family, and

soon never left his side. When I was outside, Lump would sit by the chest in which I had bedded Rolf, and I could rely completely on my nursemaid Alsatian. If the baby cried, he would listen for a bit, and if it stopped, well and good. But if Rolf went on crying, Lump would bark until I heard him and came in. If anyone or anything approached the baby too closely, even if it were only an inquisitive chicken, Lump would growl angrily and chase it away. Later on, when Rolf could crawl, he often slept in the dog's 'arms.' Sometimes a piglet would be lying against Lump's tummy when Rolf crawled his way up; he would simply push the piglet away and use Lump as a pillow. On these occasions Lump sometimes gave a slight moan, but he never moved, even if Rolf slept 'on him' for an hour or longer.

Lump had, in fact, grown into a splendid house-dog. He was a bit too fond of pork, and sometimes pinched a bit here and there, but we had enough meat and could easily forgive such minor offences in view of his many virtues. I even taught him to run errands.

One day when Heinz and Harry were somewhere in the bush I thought of something very urgent I wanted to ask, and they wouldn't be back till evening. I wrote out the question on a piece of paper and called the dog. 'Listen,' I said, 'listen carefully.'

He sat in front of me, looking at me with those intelligent eyes of his, his ears pricked as if he could understand every word.

'Run to Master as quickly as you can,' I told him, 'and take him this paper.' I tied it to his collar. 'Now go to Master.'

He ran off, ran through the thick bush for almost an hour, and found Heinz. In two hours he was back, again with a piece of paper on his collar. Better than bush-telegraph—he had brought me my answer.

Chapter 6

We could see the sea. from a small hill near our house (which we christened Olympus), but not Post Office Bay or even Blackbeach which was much nearer; the 1,800-feet Sierra de Paja (Straw Ridge), highest hill on the island, blocked our view in that direction. We therefore had no warning when ships called, and were quite unprepared for our next visitors—a whole platoon of them, it seemed—even though it turned out as agreeable a visit as the first visit had been disturbing. They came in February in the pleasure yacht *Velero III* owned by G. Allan Hancock, Los Angeles oil magnate, railway king, multi-millionaire—and patron of science. Every year he placed his luxurious yacht at the disposal of a group of scientists, and himself went with them on a two or three months' cruise to whichever part of the world they were visiting. He had been to the Galapagos Islands in 1932, and of course had called on the celebrated Dr Ritter. He did so again this year, and while at Frido Farm heard about the island's new inhabitants. He was most interested, so Ritter later brought him up to us—with all his party.

Our log cabin was complete by now with a healthy-sized living-room, but even so I didn't see how they were all going to be squeezed in so that I could offer them refreshments. I managed somehow, though it was a tight fit, and they all seemed very content with our hospitality. Luckily I was feeling quite fit again myself, and able to cope with the invasion. Heinz and Harry took 'time off,' so we could all enjoy a wonderful break from our normal routine. Luckily too, some of the party spoke German, one of them particularly well. We felt greatly drawn to this man, Professor Waldo Schmitt, at that time head curator of biology at the United States National Museum. As it turned out, the friendship we formed with him proved of special consequence to us in a few years time: it 'saved our life' on Floreana.

Our friendship with Mr Hancock was also of the enduring kind, in fact it has lasted to this day. He was full of admiration for all we had made out of the bush, a flourishing plantation which was already bearing ample fruit; and he was even more astonished when I showed him Rolf, a lusty babe of six weeks. 'And you had that baby here?' he gasped incredulously.

He was interested, but less impressed, on seeing my poultry. My five hens were not doing very well, it must be admitted, they gobbled up most of the eggs they were supposed to hatch.

'Oh, so you keep chickens?' said Hancock.

'Do you?' I asked.

'Well, I've got a bit of a chicken farm, you know. Brings me in about twenty thousand eggs a day.'

'Twenty thousand!' It was my turn to gasp. 'And I'd be glad if I got twenty. Still, I suppose you have to start in a small way. But perhaps you can give me some advice . . .' I told him about the cannibal hens, and he suggested what I should do.

We felt greatly refreshed and revived by the visit of Hancock and his party, but it had an unpleasant sequel. Hearing about this both from Ritter and from Lorenz, we were able to picture quite vividly the scene which took place at Frido Farm after the *Velero III* had gone.

Hancock had brought generous presents for Ritter, things which we islanders considered among the treasures of the earth: shoes, clothes, tins of food and milk, tools. When the baroness heard about these presents, she came up to Frido with Philipson to arrange for a 'fair distribution.'

'My dear baroness,' said Ritter coldly, 'these things were given to me, and I have no intention whatever of "distributing" any to you, as you call it.'

'You scrounger!' she hissed.

'Scrounger yourself,' Dore Strauch retorted. 'I've often wondered where you picked up that title. I for one don't believe you're a real baroness.'

The baroness shouted back that Dore was just a common schoolteacher, who should not dare open her mouth in front of a lady honoured by a gracious sovereign—and she and Philipson soon went off in high dudgeon. The friendship between the two households had evidently been as shortlived as I had expected.

Ritter told Heinz that the baroness had also been visited by Mr Hancock, who had invited them on board his yacht, and had apparently given them presents for us as well. 'Among other things,' said Ritter, 'there was a whole crate of tinned milk for your wife, so that she should have a good reserve for herself and the baby.'

Even after the rice incident Heinz was astonished at the combination of meanness and high-handedness which had inspired this behaviour. When he politely enquired about the milk given by Mr Hancock—we had talked it over, and decided once more that it was futile to make a fuss—the baroness, out of the goodness of her heart, presented me with one tin of milk. That was all we ever saw of the crate.

One day two or three weeks later Ritter asked Heinz: 'Were the Johnsons at your place?'

Heinz was puzzled. 'Johnsons?'

'You know, the American ship that came here after Hancock's party.'

'We didn't know there'd been one.'

'That's funny, Mrs Johnson expressly told me she was going up to see you, in fact you were the chief reason why she'd come here. Or rather little Rolf was the reason. His birth on our island has caused quite a sensation according to her. I expect Philipson has been sending off articles about it.'

'Ah,' said Heinz, light dawning. 'He and the baroness will have seen these Johnsons down at Post Office Bay, and told them it wasn't worth a four hours walk up here. No doubt the baroness promises she'll bring us all the presents they leave, and again that's the last we see of them. Meanwhile it's all good publicity for the "Hotel Company," though I don't see much of a hotel going up. I wish they'd start building—somewhere as far away from us as possible.'

'I don't see them building in a hurry,' Ritter forecast.

'Nor do I.' Heinz shook his head gloomily. 'If the tent in our orange grove is going to be their marvellous hotel, I think we'll have to move ourselves.'

As a matter of fact, we had seriously been thinking of moving. Not only because of our unwelcome visitors. We were no longer content with a log cabin, we wanted a real stone house far solider for the next rainy season. Beebe's book about the Galapagos Islands said that the east of Floreana was the most suitable place for settling, with plenty of fresh water, and Heinz therefore decided to make a reconnaissance trip, walking east round the coast from Post Office Bay.

As it happened, the results of this reconnaissance were negative, proving only that Beebe must have meant the part of the island where we actually were; so we should not be moving in order to build our stone house. But an interesting sight met Heinz's eye when he reached Post Office Bay, his first visit there for five months. The hut built by the Norwegians and occupied by the baroness was completely closed, but outside stood a board with a pencilled notice fastened on it:

'Friends, whoever you are! Two hours from here lies the Hacienda Paradiso, a lovely spot where the weary traveller can rejoice to find refreshing peace and tranquillity on his way through life. Life is such a tiny fragment of eternity, shackled to a clock—let us be happy in it the short time we can. In Paradiso you have only one name: Friend. We will share with you the salt of the sea, the produce of our garden and the fruits of our trees, the cool spring water that trickles from the rocks, and all the good things friends have brought us when they passed.

'We would have you spend with us a few moments of this restless life, we would bestow on you the peace with which God endowed our hearts and minds when we left the turbulence of great cities for the tranquillity of centuries which has thrown its cloak over the lonely, romantic, miraculous Galapagos.
Baroness Wagner-Bousquet.'

Near the chalet lay a mass of empty whisky, beer and liqueur bottles, the sad remains of the 'good things' friends had brought. The way up to the hills was signposted with big red arrows, so that the 'friends whoever they were,' could more easily find their way to the Hacienda Paradiso.

That very day, as it happened, some of the prospective friends came to the island—in a big American yacht, which anchored outside Post Office Bay. But her owner, Mr Vincent Astor, went visiting Ritter, and despite the notice showed no signs of wishing to spend any moments in 'Paradiso.' He returned to the yacht without calling there, much to the baroness's chagrin. She commandeered one of the motor-boats still on the beach, and sent Philipson over to the yacht with a special invitation for Mr Astor. Without even answering, Astor had Philipson taken back to the beach—leaving the baroness still more furious against Ritter, who she swore was behind it (as Lorenz assured us afterwards and as we could well imagine). Taking Philipson in tow, she rode straight up to Frido Farm, to find him unpacking the presents Astor had brought him.

The tough-looking Philipson was also spoiling for a fight, but Ritter was stronger than he appeared, or else his own anger had lent him extra strength. After a short and acrimonious interview, he took Philipson by the scruff of his neck and threw him out. The baroness hastily retreated, as he threatened to apply the same treatment to her.

Two or three weeks later came a real red-letter day: we at last had more mail from Germany, the first to show that our letters from Floreana were being received at home. The schooner *San Cristóbal* called, a privately owned boat, which we gathered toured the islands more or less regularly from Chatham. She brought us not only a sack full of mail, but two crates full of presents from our friends and families in Germany. I began pulling out letters in batches, couldn't stop to read one before I had to look at the next envelope and guess who it was from. Meanwhile Heinz and Harry were opening the crates; then we all fell on those and snatched at the contents.

'Books . . . seeds . . . a razor!' Heinz shouted. 'Everything we ever wanted,' I shouted back. 'Materials, curtains, kitchen knives, an iron . . .'

'And chocolate and Quaker oats,' Harry joined in, not to be outdone in the general jubilant foraging.

'And a whole outfit for Rolf,' I went on, examining it. 'A bit small perhaps, but then it's been about six months coming.'

'But it's come, it's all come!' cried Harry. 'It's come today, hooray, hooray, hurrah for the things from home.'

That was it: the things from home. You believe you've struck roots in your new home, a tiny island in the middle of the Pacific, but there is still so much that ties you to the old home, thousands of miles away. You long to hear from people there, and when you do, you don't know whether to laugh or cry. As we finished sorting the contents of the crates and began reading the letters, I found tears running down my cheeks.

Heinz sat on the table, lit a cigar, and glanced through some of the newspapers that had been sent. Suddenly he gave a soft whistle, and bent forward, frowning. I could see big red lines scoring the page he was reading. 'What is it?' I asked curiously.

He put down the paper, and picked up another, then looked at me, puffing at his cigar. 'Well, well, well, what remarkable news! And we should never have known though we were right on the spot!'

'Oh, come on, out with it, you beast,' I laughed. 'Don't keep me in suspense.'

'All right. Listen to this. "Revolution on Pacific Island . . . Woman Proclaims Herself Empress . . . Local Opposition Imprisoned . . ." '

I snatched up another newspaper, and met the same glaring headlines: 'Baroness Seizes Control of Galapagos Island.' 'An Austrian baroness,' I read out for Harry's benefit, 'with her private army of aristocratic freebooters, has established her rule over the small Pacific island of Floreana. Dr Friedrich Ritter, the former Berlin dentist, who opposed her reign of terror, has been captured and put in chains . . .'

'Ritter in chains?' exclaimed Harry with a puzzled grin. 'It sounded a bit different the way Lorenz told us—when Ritter threw the baroness and Philipson out of his house.'

'Well anyhow, Floreana's in the limelight all right,' said Heinz. 'Look at these pictures of the baroness dressed as a pirate.' He ran his eye down the columns of one paper. 'I'm glad they don't seem to have anything about us. I wonder if these picturesque reports were put out by Valdivieso out of spite, or whether they're friend Philipson's idea of publicity. Even the London *Times* has got something about it, I see, and here's a Copenhagen paper: "Sensation on Floreana." '

'But if it's a publicity stunt, what's the point?' I demanded. 'A reign of terror doesn't sound very like a peaceful paradise. Won't it put people off coming here?'

'You don't know the Americans yet, Grete dear,' Heinz answered. 'It'll draw them here like a magnet to see the mysterious empress. Then they'll find out it's all nonsense, but even so they'll be pleased to stay with a baroness in her "hacienda." ' He chuckled. 'What strikes me, though, is that there may be trouble in Paradise when they find the luxury hotel is only four stakes holding up a tent. How will they explain that away?'

'Oh, it's still in the planning stage, I suppose, and meanwhile what did the advertisement say—all the good things friends have brought us when they passed? From now on they're going to get all the "good things" first instead of Ritter.'

A thought struck Harry. 'Lorenz was talking to me the other day, and he said something about the baroness wanting to get to Hollywood. So the hotel business might be just a sort of blind, mightn't it?'

'It might indeed,' his father agreed. 'Empress of Floreana in sensational new picture—I can see the posters already, in her imagination anyhow!'

Quite soon after this the governor of the Galapagos Islands came over from Chatham with seven soldiers and an interpreter, a Dane by the name of Knud Arenz. The Ecuadorian papers had apparently not had anything about the 'Empress,' so the governor was not coming to learn her dispositions for her new empire. On the contrary, the purpose of his visit was to investigate the complaint which had been laid against her some months before by Ritter and Estampa after her smashing of Estampa's landing-raft. (Since then, incidentally, Heinz's dinghy had also come to a violent end, as he found on his visit to the coast.)

Rather surprisingly, instead of going to Frido Farm, the governor decided to hold his 'court of enquiry' in the 'Hacienda Paradiso,' where the baroness evidently put down a red carpet for him. She had probably sent her own version of the Franke-Estampa affair, and from the confidences of Lorenz, by now our usual informant, we learnt that less was said about that than about her future plans. South Americans are easily impressed by a European baroness, and she could be charming enough when she chose. At any rate the governor granted her a title to four square miles of land—for her hotel.

Afterwards he came to us, and we offered him the same hospitality as we should to any other visitor. He granted us a title too, but only for fifty acres: we were only simple settlers, not budding empresses. The same applied to Ritter, who was naturally furious about the outcome of this official visit; and to add spice to the baroness's victory, the governor invited her to Chatham for a few weeks' holiday.

As the boat sailed away, we breathed a sigh of relief and went back to the normal rhythm of our lives, hoping during her absence to recover some of the peace and solitude for which we had come to Floreana in the first place.

We still had our own cares. One was the wild dogs, which were worse than the cattle and had already stolen several of our precious pullets. They attacked other animals as well, stalking in packs of up to eight, their merciless teeth tearing to pieces a donkey, a pig or a calf so that the unfortunate creature died in agony. We found several of their victims in the bush, lying helpless and lacerated and still living. It was high time for a campaign to end this plague and shoot the predators.

Another of our worries was the damp in our log cabin—and the cold. It was strange that we should find it colder and wetter here than we had done in the cave; but the wind blew through all the cracks and joints, bringing in the damp with it, and every now and then water trickled through the roof. It was probably impossible, we decided, to make a roof so watertight that it wouldn't let in rain during the rainy season. The cold season was beginning, and we had to keep a fire going day and night, or the cold in the house would have been almost unbearable. The transition from great heat to great cold was so abrupt that we felt the latter as particularly severe. Extraordinary indeed that we should suffer from cold when we were almost on the Equator!

Rolf had cried a good deal when cutting his first two teeth, but on the whole he was a cheerful, healthy child, a great joy to his parents and elder brother. 'Only what are we going to do about school and all that?' I asked Heinz one day. 'The nearest school's about six hundred miles away, if I remember rightly— so I don't suppose the school bus will call for him.'

Heinz gave one of his disarming laughs. 'My dear girl, he can't even walk yet, and you're already thinking about his higher education.'

'All very well for you to pull my leg, but you wouldn't want him to grow up without any schooling, would you? When he's six at latest, he ought to . . .'

'Let's talk about it in a few years' time,' he interrupted.

71

'I wish he'd stay as small as he is now, I love them at this age. But he won't, you know, and in a few years time I'll be asking you just the same question.'

'Listen, dear,' said Heinz. 'We came out here of our own free will, we knew what we were letting ourselves in for. We'll find a way of solving these little problems when they arise.'

'And have you got a nice solution in view for when Rolf is five or six?'

He laughed again. 'I rather think you might be teaching him yourself. You'll do it splendidly, I'm sure you could have been a schoolmistress yourself. Unless you'd like to ask our friend Dore.'

'Sooner have a shot myself,' I said. 'All right, you win. Anyhow, we've got plenty of other little problems as you call them. What are we going to do for soap? We're almost out of it.'

'Make some, I suppose.'

'And how do we do that, may I ask?'

'I haven't any idea so far, but we can do some experimenting as usual.'

So we experimented, and found that a combination of wood ashes, clay and cattle fat produced a mixture reasonably like soap, though it reminded us depressingly of the *ersatz* stuff we had known in wartime. But my soap had fewer stones in than that, the clay was washed better, and the main thing was that it did its job of cleaning satisfactorily. What more could one ask?

After this we did more experimenting with the bark of the guava tree (a sort of alum) which we were eventually able to use for a complicated process of tanning hides. Then we turned to the problem of how to extract the sugar from its cane. The inventive Heinz made a real sugarpress—well, it worked anyhow —a kind of mangle the peeled canes could be turned through. The juice that came out was caught and boiled down for several hours, producing a syrupy sort of molasses which in Ecuador was called *miel*. We used it as a sweetening, it also tasted delicious spread on our bread or poured over the various puddings I made.

So with nature helping us we gradually found things becoming easier. We had our own vegetables now. All the seeds we had brought with us and planted had come up magnificently and were thriving even beyond our expectations.

There was still heaps to be done, of course. Heinz and Harry cleared a new piece of bush, which was to be our new maize field. For our new house they had already felled eight hundred trees and planed the thin trunks. Besides this they squared off stones, vast quantities of stones, some dragged over from considerable distances and all needing to be dug up. If everything went well, we hoped to move in by October.

About the end of July the baroness returned from her holiday on Chatham, bringing with her the Dane, Knud Arenz, who had acted as interpreter at the 'court of inquiry.' 'He's been engaged by the baroness for a salary of ninety sucres a month,' Lorenz informed us in confidence. 'He's to be her gamekeeper.'

Besides Arenz she had brought back a she-donkey with foals and ten hens. It looked very much as if she were going to settle here for a long while, perhaps for good.

The next time the *San Cristóbal* called, in September, she brought yet another German—Floreana seemed to have an attraction for Germans—a journalist called Werner Boeckmann. He was probably following up the stories about the Empress of Floreana, and he made his first call on the Empress herself. Later on he came to us, and when we asked if he was staying for long, he said this was only a flying visit, but he would be returning the following month with his brother-in-law for a longer stay. In fact, he went off again with the ship a few hours later.

After this visit remarkable and mysterious activities began at the Hacienda Paradiso. By day not the slightest sound came up to us from there, but as soon as it was dark everything sprang to life. Trees were felled and wood chopped under the faint light of lamps, to the accompaniment of singing and laughter. Then dawn brought silence again, the same strange silence which lasted all day.

'I bet she's looking for buried treasure,' Harry speculated. 'After all, there's supposed to be some all over the island, isn't there?'

'Well, that's what the inhabitants of the other islands say,' his father agreed. 'The stories of buried treasure have gone on for hundreds of years, and I dare say there's something at the bottom of them. But vast quantities of pirate gold—that's the sort of legend you get about any island like this.'

'All the same,' Harry went on eagerly, 'I expect Herr Boeckmann showed the baroness some secret map giving just where the treasure lies.'

'Could be,' I said. 'Your guess is as good as mine for anything to do with the baroness. Only if it *was* treasure, why didn't she start searching before? We'll just have to wait for the next instalment, eh?'

The next instalment was, that the mysterious nocturnal activity suddenly stopped—on the very day Herr Boeckmann turned up again, accompanied by his brother-in-law, Herr Linde. The *San Cristóbal* also brought a soldier sent by the governor for the two men's protection. Protection against whom, we wondered, who on earth was supposed to be harbouring designs against them? We hadn't any idea, but then we also didn't know what stories the baroness might have told the governor about the dangerous characters inhabiting the island (excluding herself, of course). This bodyguard even had a gun and ammunition, so he must have been sent for some specific purpose; what it was, remained a riddle which in fact we never solved.

Curiously enough, the two men took up residence with Dr Ritter, who had by now expanded his quarters a bit, rather than with the baroness. She was naturally furious that they preferred the hated Ritter to her Paradiso, the delights of which she had presented in the usual glowing colours. 'Perhaps *you'll* stay with us anyhow, Herr Linde?' she asked hopefully. But Herr Linde still declined, so she invited them to go shooting with her, and this they felt unable to refuse. The whole company, including the Ecuadorian bodyguard, went off next day to the pampas, where according to Gamekeeper Arenz there was an abundance of game. I had a funny feeling about this shooting party, perhaps a sort of premonition such as I sometimes get.

I had little Rolf in the bathtub, and was just finishing giving him his bath when I heard loud excited footsteps outside. Then Lorenz came panting in. 'Can I have the water-bag at once, please?' he asked breathlessly.

'What on earth for?'

'There's been an accident on the shoot.'

'Is someone badly hurt?'

'Yes, Herr Arenz. The soldier shot him, and he's in terrible pain. The baroness thinks the water-bag might help to reduce the pain.'

I fetched the water-bag. 'Where's he been hit?' I asked.
'In the stomach.'
'Oh my God!'
'Dr Ritter's already there and has examined him.'
'And says . . .?'
But Lorenz had already snatched up the water-bag and dashed off again.

In the afternoon we heard a fuller and very different story from Werner Boeckmann and Linde, his brother-in-law. 'The baroness was firing at a calf,' Boeckmann told us, 'at the same time as the soldier fired at a pig. In both cases they missed, but one of them hit Arenz in the stomach. It all happened in a flash, so that at first we didn't even notice anything—till suddenly Arenz was lying doubled up on the ground, groaning. We tried to make him as comfortable as possible, and my brother-in-law and I ran off to get Dr Ritter. Ritter returned with us at once, and examined Arenz. He found the bullet mark going in, but no mark of its coming out; so it's still in the stomach. To judge by the hole it must have been about a 6-millimetre bullet.'

Heinz opened his eyes in surprise. As he told me afterwards, he knew that the Ecuadorian soldier only had a service rifle with a bigger bore, so it could not have been his bullet which hit Arenz.

'I can't get something out of my mind,' put in Linde, who had so far been silent and very thoughtful. 'I was with the baroness when we were on our way to the pampas. We were talking about shooting, I think, and she suddenly said: "You know, I've got a terrible habit. I prefer to shoot animals in the leg, then I catch them and nurse them till they're all right again, the poor creatures." '

We stared at each other, aghast at this perversion. 'And you think,' said Heinz, 'that she was actually aiming at Arenz, meaning to hit him in the leg and then nurse him?'

Linde shook his head slowly. 'No. I don't think she was aiming at Arenz. If I try to think exactly what happened, then I really can't avoid the conclusion that she meant to hit me with her bullet, not him. I know he was standing very near me and then jumped in front of me in a crouching position. That was the moment when the baroness fired. The bullet, so I imagine, was meant to go in my leg, but went into poor Arenz's stomach

75

instead. If he'd been only a second later jumping in front of me, it would have got me.'

We didn't need to say out loud what we all realised: that she had tried to shoot Linde in the leg and then nurse him better in Paradiso—where he had refused to stay of his own free will. It was fantastic—yet it seemed all too plausible. In any case we had no proof, so we had to keep our strong suspicions to ourselves.

Five days afterwards the *San Cristóbal* returned to pick up Boeckmann and Linde. Arenz was taken down to the coast on a stretcher and put on board. Philipson was to accompany him to Guayaquil, where the bullet would be removed.

Only Ritter dared say openly that it was the baroness who had shot Arenz. From his examination of the wound he had conclusive evidence that the shot must have come from her gun, not the soldier's; and he also knew her possible motive for shooting at this 'human game.' Drawing the obvious deductions, he sent another letter to the governor, in even stronger terms than before, reporting what had happened and demanding that the baroness be removed at once from the island, on the grounds that she was clearly insane.

The baroness looked quite ill when Heinz met her a few days after the 'accident.' She had heard of Ritter's charge, and did not even fly into a rage when Heinz referred to it. Her voice, usually so hard and domineering, sounded very weary. 'I'm tired of Floreana. It's wearing me out, this constant battle with the Ritters, and the woman not recognising my status as a baroness. If I could, I'd leave here at once.'

Anyhow we had a cheering piece of news: Arenz's condition was not so serious as we had feared, for the small-calibre bullet had not done any great damage. The operation at Guayaquil went off successfully, he recovered quickly and was soon discharged from the hospital. He never returned to Floreana, and I doubt if he ever accepted another job as gamekeeper.

Chapter 7

The last few months we had had no rain at all, and the island presented a dismal sight. Dead animals lay around; when you got near them, you could see flies swarming round the bodies. The spring had only enough water left for bare essentials, and would give out altogether if the drought persisted much longer. The blazing heat dried everything up; we tried to keep at least our vegetable plants alive so that we should have some fresh food in the immediate future. Things looked even grimmer at Frido Farm, Ritter told us he was thinking of distilling sea-water and bringing it up to his plantation, if rain did not come soon.

To make matters even worse for us, Heinz developed a painful and dangerous tooth abscess, and had to stay in bed. I went up to see Ritter, but was met by Dore, who sent me packing in a most unfeeling way. 'Dr Ritter can't do anything for that. You must just see how to cope with it yourselves.'

The baroness seemed to be making good her setbacks by taking it out of poor Lorenz; Philipson was beating him, his groans and their shrill abuse sometimes penetrated to us from Paradiso. Once he came running to us crying like a small child. 'She blames me for everything that goes wrong with her,' he whimpered. 'When there was a yacht here lately, she begged the captain to take her to the South Seas, and she again asked Mr Hancock to take her to Hollywood. Both times she got snubbed, and afterwards she screamed at me, saying I was behind it.'

At least we had distractions from the drought and the sadistic baroness, because for once we had plenty of visits. It seemed to be a feature of Floreana life that either no ships put in for months, or else they came one after the other, as if the island were a favourite retreat for millionaires and a sort of Pacific travellers' rest. Mr Hancock came twice in *Velero III*, and Professor Schmitt was again in his party; they were both old friends by now, we put them up in our new stone house, and spent some wonderful days with them.

The day after their second visit, the *Velero* was joined outside Post Office Bay by a Norwegian pleasure yacht, the *Stella Polaris*, which under the name *Hohenzollern* had been owned by the former German Kaiser. She left the same day, but while she was still there, the two yachts were joined by a third ship which looked a mere cockleshell behind them, the *Monsoon*, a forty-year-old fishing boat now rejuvenated and commissioned by a party of young Danes, who were paying for a pleasure cruise round the world by purchasing ethnographic rarities which could be sold to museums and private collectors. One of the party, Haakon Mielche, wrote an entertaining book about his travels called *Let's See if the World is Round*, in which there is a brilliant chapter on Floreana and its inhabitants.

The governor at Chatham had asked Mielche to act as postman, so before coming to us he visited both Paradiso and Frido Farm. As a collector of curiosities, he found both households highly rewarding, if less congenial company than ours; and being an excellent mimic, he made us laugh uproariously with his rather malicious descriptions.

'She took me by the hand,' he wrote of the baroness in his book, 'and led me into Paradise, a tent hut in the middle of a vegetable garden, where a powerfully built fair-haired youth gave me his paw and was introduced to me as "my Sonny-boy." With watery blue eyes, curly hair and a sickly-sweet smile, "Sonny-boy" resembled a gigolo in a rather cheap Berlin night-club. A German cook, who looked tubercular and almost at death's door, also smiled wanly in the background and brought tea. The interior of the Hacienda Paradiso hardly lived up to the promise of the notice on the shore . . . The walls were decorated with photos of the baroness as South Sea princess and as Parisian society lady . . . Nestling with dreamy, half-closed eyes on a corner of one of the divans, she told me, quite unasked, her romantic life-story, while Sonny-boy stroked her hands and arranged the cushion behind her . . .'

As to Ritter, Mielche wrote: 'Ritter was a philosopher, rather small . . . with a long pointed nose, protruding eyes and the hair of a prophet. His disciple, Miss Dora, smiled a toothless welcome, for the couple had at their disposal only one pair of false teeth, and when I visited them it was Ritter's day . . .'

Having so many other things to do, we were accustomed to making some excuse if Ritter tried to launch into one of his high philosophic discussions, but Mielche had listened with determined interest, and told us: 'When I got there, he was sitting on a rough chair, frowning furiously; you could see he was absorbed in some exacting philosophical activity. It soon transpired that he was mapping out the human brain. But this work was only in its early stages, he was making a preliminary survey. Alas, I shall doubtless never see the completion of his life's work, for by living according to nature he means to stay alive till the age of a hundred and forty. He therefore has a good ninety years' time. I have not.'

Mielche's visit to Floreana was all too short for our liking, but soon all the ships had gone, and we were back to our solitude and daily cares, including the drought, for it was the dry season. It was not long after this that Lorenz came up to our new house, begging us to give him shelter. 'I just can't bear it there any more,' he groaned. 'The baroness and Philipson have beaten me till I collapsed.'

Poor Lorenz did look a pitiful sight, but we were unwilling to take him in, for fear of concentrating the baroness's malevolence on us. Ritter also refused, and when Lorenz told us this, we saw we should have to give him the asylum he asked for. We just couldn't leave him to perish in the bush, and he told us: 'Philipson's threatened to kill me if he ever sees me again.' Grim prospects indeed; with Lorenz in the house I found it hard to sleep that night. The baroness and her 'husband' must both be insane, there was no telling what they might not do against the protectors of their chief victim.

But strangely enough, the baroness was not annoyed at Lorenz living with us. The next day we saw her come up the path, and were flabbergasted to hear her call out enticingly at the garden gate: 'Lori, do come out a moment please. Please come, dear Lori, I've got something I *must* say to you.'

He let himself be enticed, and disappeared with her down the path. Hours later he returned, looking cheerful and relaxed, but quite soon afterwards sat down at the table and began crying.

79

He was a very sick man, it was plain, and all we hoped was that another ship would soon come to take him off the island.

While he was with us, however, the baroness performed the same little comedy almost every other day. He went with her time and again, but he never told us what they did or talked about. We assumed she had half made it up with him—or could still be kind to him as long as he was not under the same roof. Perhaps it was really Philipson who was his chief persecutor.

'Lori!' Once more I heard the melodious cooing call at the garden gate. But Lorenz was not in the house, he was out somewhere with Heinz and Harry; despite being such a sick man, he had insisted on working to pay for his keep. I was alone with Rolf.

The baroness was in her riding costume: shirt-blouse, breeches, high boots, and a scarf tied smartly round her head.

'Lorenz isn't here,' I told her.

She looked me up and down. 'Then please tell him that friends of ours have come, and we're going to Tahiti with them. I hope that'll be a better place to realise my plans. Lorenz is to look after the things I've left behind, till I either return or send him word.'

'Then I wish you a successful journey,' I said.

'Thank you, Frau Wittmer. *Auf Wiedersehen* or perhaps good-bye.'

Many ships called at Blackbeach or Post Office Bay which we knew nothing about, so I naturally accepted her statement that a ship had come in. But when the men returned and I gave Lorenz the message, he refused to believe it. 'It's a trap to lure me down there,' he said, 'and when I get there, they'll bump me off. I know too much about her.'

He had talked before of Philipson threatening to kill him, but we regarded it as a little far-fetched, and here again were the fantasies of a sick man. He stayed for a meal with us, and only then summoned up the courage to set off for Paradiso.

We did not see him again for two days, but assumed the baroness had not left after all and he was still with her. When he came back, he told us a strange story. He had stood outside the 'Hacienda Paradiso' for a long time, then ventured inside at last to find it empty indeed: deserted. The donkeys were gone. So were most of the baroness's and Philipson's things. He went down to the Norwegian chalet in Post Office Bay, and found some footprints in the sand. Otherwise he had found no trace of them on the island, despite two days' search.

I accompanied him to Frido Farm. 'The baroness has gone,' I informed Ritter. 'Did you know?'

He shook his head incredulously.

'You don't believe it?'

'I've not seen a ship,' he replied. 'If there'd been one here, I'd surely have seen it . . . Dore!' he called. 'Dore, come out here, there's some interesting news.'

When she heard, she danced for joy, almost forgetting her bad leg. Then she made us some hot chocolate and fetched all sorts of delicacies from her store-room. We had never seen her so cordial, but Ritter was strikingly silent, and seemed far from his usual self. We were spared all philosophical discourse.

Suddenly he turned to Lorenz. 'But as for you, my good Lorenz, the sooner you get away from here, the better. Sell what you don't want to take with you, and then make tracks to get yourself back to Germany as quick as you can.'

Lorenz evidently accepted this advice, and afterwards went down to Paradiso with Heinz and Ritter. Ritter opened up the crates and boxes with complete assurance; he seemed quite sure the baroness and Philipson had gone for good. Whatever he may have been like as a philosopher, he was certainly a good business-man, and excelled in bargaining, paying far less for his purchases than Lorenz asked. So he had money after all, I commented later, and could find a use for it!

'Are you sure you can sell it off just like this?' Heinz asked at first.

'It's all been bought with my money,' Lorenz claimed, and Heinz remembered his telling us something like this before; so although it seemed surprising he let it go, and bought what Ritter had left, including the corrugated iron.

Afterwards they all came up to me, and Ritter drew up a formal report about the baroness's sudden departure. It struck us again what a hurry he seemed to be in, to put in writing what was after all far from proven fact. I remarked mildly that she had told me she might come back, but he merely shook his head and said with conviction, almost as if he had private knowledge he was not going to give us: 'She won't come back. Take my word for it.'

'What about the ship, though?' said Heinz.

He seemed to have changed his mind about that. 'Well, I wouldn't have seen a ship unless it came round to Blackbeach. Anyhow they're gone—gone for good,' he repeated.

We had no objection to her departure being recorded, though it dawned on us later that he was decidedly anxious to set himself up as the island's legal authority, guardian of law and order.

After this life went on undisturbed for several weeks, and by July the long drought was over at last. The rain came down in real cloudbursts, swiftly reviving both animals and plants, if nearly drowning them at first. It had been a struggle, but we had brought our garden vegetables safely through, and now we could harvest our own produce again. We could certainly live on our own produce throughout the year—there would be more than enough for our modest needs—if only (but it was a big 'if') there had been some way of catching and storing the rainwater from the short rainy season. The clayey, stony soil, of course, did not hold the moisture, which would have watered the island for a whole year. As it was, this just evaporated.

Still, we were very ready to count our blessings. The island had kept us fed, the drought was over, we had no special cares, and even had leisure and energy to start reading again in the evenings. We gave ourselves English and Spanish lessons, and were making good progress, though it was much harder for Harry, poor boy. His eyesight, unfortunately, had not improved as much as we had hoped. He had an extraordinary 'feel' for practical tasks like chopping trees—he never cut himself, and the work was as well finished as anybody could wish; but reading and writing were still a very great strain for him. We had to repeat words to him over and again, which also helped to fix them in our own minds.

I went on with my home-made 'teach-yourself-English' and 'teach-yourself-Spanish' during the day. I kept a small dictionary with me when I was working in the garden, and every now and then looked up the objects I saw round me: earth, stones, trees, bushes, blossoms, fruit, chickens, goats, donkey (we had now got our own donkey). I would make a mental note of some new or old word, then put the dictionary away, and the next time I saw one of the chickens would mutter: 'That's a chicken'—first in

English, then in Spanish. Three minutes later: 'The dog is in the house.' I dare say anyone who didn't know me and had heard my trilingual monologue would have thought me crazy.

In the middle of July there was at last a boat—a boat for Lorenz! The *Dinamita*, described by Mielche as 'a small cigar-box,' was a fishing vessel owned by one Trygve Nuggeröd, a Norwegian living on the island of Santa Cruz. On board he had the Danish writer Rolf Blomberg, who wanted to have a look at Floreana. We liked both men very much.

Lorenz was very excited when Nuggeröd agreed to take him. 'Only as far as Santa Cruz,' said the Norwegian. 'The *Dinamita* isn't up to much any more. But you can soon get to Chatham from there.'

'Then I'll sail for the mainland,' he told us eagerly, 'get my papers in order at Guayaquil, and contact my brother in Germany. But I'll come back and say good-bye to Floreana before I sail for home.' His eyes could still shine when he thought of his native land, of seeing the spring in Germany; and his excitement was infectious, even reviving some of my own home-sickness—but Floreana had made a better new home for us than it had for poor Lorenz. We gave him a packet of letters to post for us from the mainland.

So off he went in the little *Dinamita* with Nuggeröd and Blomberg. A month later there was a letter for us in the barrel from Blomberg. He had written it in haste from Santa Cruz when the *San Cristóbal* called there, as he knew the boat would also be calling at Floreana.

'The three of us got here safely,' he wrote, 'and Lorenz kept begging Nuggeröd to take him on to Chatham, he just couldn't wait to continue his journey home. In the end Nuggeröd agreed, and sailed for Chatham with Lorenz and an Ecuadorian. But the *Dinamita* never arrived there, so the *San Cristóbal's* been sent out in search of her. It's assumed they've been stranded on one of the islands, but so far there's no trace of them or the boat, and it's feared she must be lost. She had no sail, and if the engine had a breakdown, as it easily might, she could have drifted anywhere. The currents round this time of year are very strong, of course, as you know . . .'

We were shattered. Poor Lorenz—and Nuggeröd too, doing Lorenz a good turn in a boat that was no longer really seaworthy.

A minor cause for distress was that our letters were presumably lost too.

For two months we heard nothing more. Then the *San Cristóbal* came again, with Blomberg on board. He had no further news, but said he still hoped the three men might be keeping alive somewhere on one of the smaller islands and would some day be found. There was no news either from Tahiti, where the baroness and Philipson were supposed to be going : they also had disappeared without trace.

Then Dore Strauch announced that she was leaving Floreana, and we wondered if Ritter would too, for he told us in a tone of quiet resignation: 'The island has not given me what I hoped.' Dore had fallen ill, and he confided that they were always quarrelling now, it was getting on his nerves. 'The poor woman's not herself, I know,' he said, 'but she's become extremely difficult. Oh well, we'll have Hancock here again in January, the *Velero III* can take her to the mainland, and from there she can travel back to Germany. But it's three months till then, and I don't know if I'll . . .' He stopped in the middle of the sentence, and gave a heavy sigh. We were still left in doubt whether he too meant to leave the island which had so sadly disappointed him.

Chapter 8

14th November, 1934 was another memorable day for me. For the first time since we landed on Floreana, over two years before, I left the island, and again in a small boat. Not for six days and nights, as we had done then, but at least out to sea. It was a motor-boat bringing me to a four-masted cargo schooner—the vessel used by Mr Phillips Lord on his radio programme, 'The Cruise of the schooner *Seth Parker*.' This cruise brought him to the Galapagos, he visited us on Floreana, and now we were making a return visit to the *Seth Parker*. I had never been on a big private ship like this, so it was a particular thrill for me.

We were having a meal in one of the saloons when another motor-boat returned to the ship with some officers who had been visiting Frido Farm. 'All Dr Ritter's chickens were found dead,' one of them reported, 'seems they got meat-poisoning.'

'Always thought he was meant to be a vegetarian,' said another.

'Well, he's not now,' Lord commented. 'He asked me to a meal yesterday and opened a jar of potted pork. But it had gone bad, it was quite uneatable, so his wife threw it to the chickens. And there you are, today they're dead.'

Ritter had given a message to the officers, if they saw us on board the schooner, to ask if we could let him have a couple of hens and a cock so that he could start raising a new lot. Two days later Heinz and I took them up to him, and he came out to meet us. We listened to the story again from him, and as we went into the bungalow, he remarked: 'Wasn't it bad luck!'

I stood in the doorway, unable to speak, staggered by the sight that met my eyes: he was busy potting chickens, the very birds which had died of food-poisoning. A medically qualified man, and a supposed vegetarian into the bargain—it was incredible. 'But will they be all right to eat?' I heard Heinz ask.

'Oh yes,' came the assured answer. 'It's not as bad as all that, you know. All the poison will be boiled out of them. I'll let you have a jar if you like.'

'Thanks very much,' Heinz said hastily, 'but I don't think we will.'

He did not press us.

I always seemed to be alone when something unpleasant happened—as I was six days later, when I heard excited footsteps at the garden gate. Through the door I could see Dore Strauch coming, and I went to the garden gate to meet her. I was already apprehensive, for she had hardly ever been to the house before: it was an hour's difficult walk from Frido, and with her bad leg she went out very little. All I could think of to say was: 'Why didn't you come on the donkey?'

Instead of answering, she said in great agitation: 'Something terrible's happened, Frau Wittmer. Dr Ritter has got meat-poisoning. He's extremely ill, in fact I think he's dying.'

I took her into the house, and she sank into a chair, exhausted. I sat down myself, feeling quite dazed by this news. She began to give me details: 'The day before yesterday we opened some of the jars, with the meat from the dead chickens . . . We realised at once the meat was bad, but Friedrich said I only needed to give it a good boiling, then it would be quite safe.'

'And you ate some of that? You both did?'

'Yes, I had some too.'

I didn't know what to say to this. Two people had eaten poisoned meat, and one was supposed to be dying, while the other had come all the way over to our house and still looked perfectly normal. 'How long has he been ill?' I asked eventually.

'He didn't feel well yesterday morning, and put it down to the meat. But the worst of it is that he can hardly see, which makes him sure it's a form of poisoning.'

'And you didn't have any ill effects yourself?'

'Oh yes, I was sick directly afterwards, and haven't felt anything since then. But Friedrich got worse and worse . . .'

Then why on earth didn't you come here yesterday, I felt like asking, but she seemed too agitated for such questions at the moment and was pouring out her story very fast: '. . . During this morning his tongue swelled up so badly he couldn't talk properly any more, only a sort of mumbling it's impossible to make anything of. About the last thing he said more or less comprehensibly was that it would be very funny indeed if he as a vegetarian was going to die of meat-poisoning . . . I know I should have used a stomach-pump at once,' she moaned, 'but we hadn't got anything that would make one.'

I guessed that every minute might be vital, so I wrote a hasty note for Heinz, telling him to come to Frido Farm as soon as he got back. Then I found a thin rubber tube which I thought might do for a stomach-pump, and went off with Dore. She could only walk very slowly, so that it took longer than usual to get to Frido. When we did, I saw that it was probably too late—it was certainly too late for any stomach-pump efforts. Ritter could not speak at all, and wrote what he wanted to say on a piece of paper; but he could still hear, and evidently understood everything we said.

He looked as if he were in excruciating pain, but would not take the morphia injection Dore tried to give him, and she did not even succeed in sucking out a clot of mucus which had lodged in his windpipe.

Heinz came at last, about five o'clock. By this time Ritter was too apathetic, or too far gone, even to write messages on the paper by his bed. But soon afterwards he made an immense effort, felt for the pencil and wrote his last sentence: 'I curse you with my dying breath.' Then he looked up at Dore, his eyes gleaming with hate. Even at that horrible time I was startled. Here were two people supposed to have been living together in spiritual harmony, despising all worldly things, and now when one of them was dying his last emotion was hatred for the other.

The next few hours were unbearably painful. Dore tried to act as if she had not noticed the hate-filled eyes, but whenever she came near him, he would make feeble movements as if to hit or kick her. There was nothing we could do to help him, except perhaps to pray for him. He grew more and more restless, but became quieter towards nightfall when Dore left him to get a little rest herself. While Heinz and I were alone with him, he suddenly put his hands together and lifted them towards me.

'You want to pray?' I asked softly.

He shook his head, and made the same gesture, once to me and once to Heinz. We could make nothing of it at all.

Beads of sweat gathered on his brow, which I periodically wiped away with a towel. I had just done this and shaken up his pillows, when Dore came in. It was nearly nine. Hearing her voice, he sat up, looking like a ghost as he tried to pounce on her. His eyes flashed with a wild feverish flame. Dore shrieked, and drew back in horror. Then he collapsed soundlessly, falling back on the pillows. He had gone.

When Heinz had satisfied himself that Ritter was dead, we decided that he should go back to the children, leaving me to spend the night with the distraught Dore. I did not get much sleep, for she talked almost incessantly, though much of what she said was half delirious. She kept on referring to some secret which Ritter had with Lorenz, but I could not get out of her what it was supposed to be.

I had told her about Ritter holding up his hands, and this surprised her. 'Why did he do that?' she asked me two or three times, and I could only repeat that I had no idea. Then she suddenly found an explanation. 'He was begging for your forgiveness,' she whispered mysteriously.

'Forgiveness. What for?'

'I don't know. I only know that's what he meant.'

'What did he think he'd done to us?'

Again the mysterious whisper: 'I don't know.'

All through the night the rambling talk went on, and once she started up, crying: 'I shall be murdered here, I must get away, I must.'

'Come now,' I said soothingly as I could. 'There's no one on the island who would want to hurt you. Try to calm down and get some sleep.'

'No, no, I must get away from here,' she screamed again. Then she spoke more quietly, with a sort of grotesque solemnity. 'I must spread Dr Ritter's fame through the world. They would not acknowledge him during his lifetime, but now he is gone, his writings will be ranked among the great masterpieces of philosophy. It is my task to see they are.'

At last the morning came, and Heinz was there to take me home. I was worn out, but the relief at leaving that bungalow of death and delirium was so intense that I almost sang in the morning air.

The next day Heinz and Harry dug a grave for Ritter amidst the stones he had removed with such labour to build his little settlement. We brought flowers from our garden and threw them into the grave, as we prayed his soul might rest in peace. We did not bring Dore out for this, for her nerves, always bad, seemed to have been shattered completely.

After this I felt obliged out of common humanity to spend a good deal of time with her up at Frido. She recovered very slowly from her near breakdown, and was full of dark hints about murders, forgiveness, her need to flee from the island. In some way it all seemed to be connected with the disappearance of the baroness and Philipson.

That remained as great a mystery as ever. The day I last saw the baroness, she said a ship had come, but Ritter said he had seen no ship, there was no mail left or any other evidence of a ship's having called. It was out of the question, of course, that the two of them could still be on some remote corner of the island. For one thing they would have had no earthly reason to go there, and for another their supplies wouldn't have lasted out so long, they couldn't have kept alive making no contact with the outside world. Yet it was certainly most strange that nothing had ever been heard of the baroness in Tahiti or anywhere else; she had not been a woman who seemed likely to retire into obscurity. Sinister suspicions long pushed to the back of our minds began to come to the surface. What was Ritter's secret with Lorenz? That day last March they had both taken it for granted very readily that the baroness would not be coming back; Ritter had told Lorenz to get away from the island as quickly as possible; and as we knew, they both had good reason for hating her.

She had been a thorn in Ritter's flesh from the first, stealing his limelight, collecting all the publicity about Floreana in the world's press which had formerly been his; and perhaps even more important, she collected a large proportion of the gifts brought by curious and admiring American tourists. As to Lorenz, he had once been her favourite, then he was superseded by Philipson: beaten, degraded, treated as drudge and scapegoat. Yet he knew the facts about the accident to Arenz, he knew many other unsavoury details from the baroness's past, and she would be ruthless in suppressing a potential blackmailer, who she knew was trying to leave the island. Lorenz had obviously been aware of this very possibility, he had expressed to us quite openly his fear of being killed by Philipson and the baroness: a man with such fear might well strike first, especially if he had an ally.

But Lorenz was a sick man, I pointed out, he couldn't have overpowered Philipson and the baroness together.

'Perhaps,' Heinz conjectured, 'he got into the chalet when they weren't there. He would know where she kept her revolver, he could have waited to trap them on their return.'

'Yes, or sneaked up on them somewhere,' I suggested, recalling how Lorenz had often scared me with his way of creeping through the bush followed by sudden jack-in-the-box appearances. 'But you never found any traces afterwards apart from those footsteps in the sand. I mean, there weren't any bloodstains or dragging marks. And what about the bodies?'

'No difficulty about that. High tide twice in twenty-four hours, and then the sea comes within a few yards of the chalet, and would carry anything back with it on its way out. Plenty of sharks waiting in the bay. After all, fishermen on the other islands get rid of their rubbish by throwing it into the ebbing tide. Still, the lack of bloodstains rather suggests that if there *was* foul play, it took place on the beach, not in the chalet. I suppose you still can't get anything lucid out of Dore?'

I shook my head. 'She wouldn't tell me even if she could. But at present she isn't fit to be dragged through all this, and of course we haven't any proof of anything. I wish Mr Hancock would come, but he isn't due till January.'

In fact Hancock arrived in the middle of December. I was up with Dore when we sighted his yacht outside Blackbeach Bay. We went down together to meet him. 'Where are your menfolk?' he asked in surprise.

'I'm afraid there's bad news,' I answered. 'Dr Ritter died three weeks ago. It's been a great shock to Miss Dore, and I'm looking after her a bit.'

'My God!' Hancock exclaimed. 'And he said something terrible might happen. What a series of tragedies!'

I asked him what he meant, and he explained that he had

received a letter from Ritter, written in the autumn, telling him briefly of the baroness's disapppearance and asking him to come quickly as things had happened and might happen which were too terrible to be put in a letter. Hancock set out at once for Floreana, but on the way here horrifying news diverted him to the small island of Marchena, in the far north of the Galapagos group, almost directly on the Equator: an island consisting only of sand and stones, with the sun blazing straight down on it.

Four months after Lorenz left Floreana in Nuggeröd's fishing boat, the crew of an American tunny-fisher passing Marchena saw a white rag fluttering in the sand on the flat beach. On the beach itself they found a small rowing-boat, two dead bodies, and a case near one of them containing a packet of letters all destined for Germany—with our names on the envelopes as senders. The tunny-fisher took off the case with the letters, but left the bodies and notified Chatham. A radio message went out to the world, the papers seized eagerly on the news and embellished it with highly imaginative conjectures. Several of them, making deductions from the senders of the letters, wrote to the effect that: 'As one of the two deceased has long fair hair, this may be presumed to be Frau Wittmer.'

Mr Hancock reached Marchena before arrangements had been made to collect and bury the two bodies. They had not yet begun decomposing, he told us, having been preserved in the sun like mummies. 'I recognised Lorenz at once,' he said, 'you could still make out his features. He was lying stretched out in the hot sand, all his clothes worn to shreds. The other man, Nuggeröd, lay quite near him. They must have died of starvation and thirst, there isn't a drop of water on the island.'

'And the third man?'

'I didn't see any third man.'

What had happened then to the Ecuadorian—an Indian called José Pasmino—who had sailed with them (as we knew from Blomberg's letters) in the ill-fated *Dinamita*? We could only guess. She was an old boat with no sail, and her engine had failed before this. If it did so again, the boat would be helpless, and could have drifted anywhere, carried by the dreaded Peruvian current, which was particularly strong at that time of year. Coming from the far south, from Antarctic waters, this current had driven many a becalmed ship into the vastness of the Pacific.

With a crew crazed and soon dying from starvation and thirst, she might wander for months, a ghost ship to be fearfully avoided by any other ship that passed her. If this had happened even to big four-masters, it was all too easy to imagine for the *Dinamita*. Perhaps José Pasmino had stayed aboard her, while the others landed on the desert island in the skiff, because he thought there was more chance of being rescued. If so, she might still be drifting somewhere in the Pacific with the dead Pasmino on board, or more probably she had already broken up and was at the bottom of the sea. No trace of her, in fact, was ever found.

Soon after Mr Hancock left, taking Dore Strauch with him Floreana was invaded by American newspaper reporters, seizing on every word we could say about the chain of tragic events and building them up into a magnificent 'Galapagos drama' for sensation-hungry readers. Much of what we told them they garbled unmercifully, and what they didn't know, they mostly invented: truth was strange enough here, but nothing like so thrilling as the fiction based on it. In the circumstances we should perhaps have been prepared for an unpleasant visit we received early in January 1935.

Luckily I was not alone this time. Harry was out in the bush, but Heinz and I suddenly saw a handful of soldiers marching up with fixed bayonets. My conscience was clear, but we were not used to seeing armed soldiers, and I admit my heart stood still for a moment. They were followed by the governor from Chatham with an interpreter from Santa Cruz.

'What do you want with us?' Heinz asked. There was no answer. The soldiers gathered round us in a circle, the governor said something to the interpreter, who asked Heinz to go into the house with them: they were investigating a crime, and would examine him first.

After what seemed an age, it was my turn. They brought me in to be interrogated. 'Tell me exactly what happened about the baroness's disappearance,' the governor asked me through the interpreter.

I told him what I knew, and what he must long have known himself. But he was not satisfied. 'You're hiding something from me,' he insisted. 'You're hiding the most important thing. Let's have the truth at last.'

I looked at him blankly.

'Your husband killed the baroness,' he said: a statement not a question.

'What!' I cried. 'Who on earth do you get that from?'

'Dr Ritter.'

'But Dr Ritter's been dead six weeks.'

The governor smiled patiently. 'I know. This was before his death.'

I shook my head incredulously, and he explained that an Ecuadorian paper had published an article which Ritter must have sent off shortly before his death, and which expressly accused Heinz of shooting the baroness. The reporters who had come seemed to think we were somehow connected with the baroness's disappearance, but we put this down to idle rumour, and none of them had mentioned Ritter's charge. The gist of what he wrote was as follows: 'There was no ship anywhere near Floreana on the night the baroness is supposed to have left the island. But during the night I heard shots and a woman's scream. It could only have been the baroness. And the only person who could have fired the shots is Heinz Wittmer.'

When we heard about the screams, I began to laugh a little hysterically, and Heinz pointed out to the governor that this would have needed superhuman hearing on Ritter's part since Frido Farm was three miles away from the baroness's Paradiso, with the 1,800-feet Sierra de Paja in between the two places. He also commented that if the baroness and Philipson were shot, it could equally well have been done by Ritter himself or by Lorenz, both of whom had strong motives for the murder.

After the interpreter had translated all this, the governor only had a few more questions put to us, and his tone had changed completely. Our manner was no doubt also evidence of our innocence, and if he had ever believed the fantastic story, it was clear that he had now mentally acquitted us. His stern face relaxed, he became polite and friendly, and the soldiers too looked less forbidding. As we seemed to be 'leaving the court without a stain on our characters,' I invited the governor and his interpreter to lunch, which I quickly prepared. While he was enjoying a leg of chicken, he had the soldiers bring up our post. There turned out to be half a sackful of post from all corners of the globe, most of them from complete strangers wanting authentic details of the 'Floreana Tragedies,' and some offering good advice for our future if we stayed on the island.

The governor had finished his meal, and was about to depart. '*Caramba!*' he cried suddenly, jumping up from the table. 'I nearly forgot the most important thing. Here, Señora Wittmer!' He pulled a form out of the cuff of one sleeve of his uniform coat. This form proved to be a cable from a German newspaper, asking if we were alive and if we would be ready to write about the events which had taken place on the island. The reply was paid, up to seven words.

The governor was anxious to get back to the ship, and there was no time even to consult Heinz. I had to decide quickly, but what could one say in seven words? I scribbled something down on a bit of paper, showed it to Heinz, who grinned and nodded; then I gave it to the governor, who took it with him to the ship and at once signalled off my seven words. Seven hours later, as I afterwards heard, this brief message was shown on a huge poster outside the offices of the German newspaper: 'We are alive Ritter dead will write.'

When Dore left, she had asked us to look after Frido Farm till we heard from her. I had stayed there and cleaned it up, but after this we decided to let the place go completely. Heinz put a simple cross over the grave, on which he carved Ritter's name and the date of his death; we did not know his birthday. We did this for him, but that was the end of an ugly chapter: from now on we hoped to forget about the late Friedrich Ritter, and be no more involved with his affairs.

In the course of time Dore got his *Life and Letters* published, a pretentious outpouring of pseudo-scientific 'philosophy.' Little progress had been made on it in the last months of his life, and there is hardly anything about us, I am glad to say. But the egotistic and boring book sparks into brief animation when he writes about the baroness. His deep hatred for her is thus well documented, and he may well have at least encouraged Lorenz to carry out the crime; perhaps more, we shall never know. Nor shall we know whether he spread the horrible lie about Heinz to shield himself or to try to get the Wittmers also off 'his island' and be the only possible recipient of American gifts.

But now we certainly saw very clearly the meaning of those hands held up to us from his deathbed: he was pleading for our forgiveness. It was hard to forgive him then, there are some things you cannot forgive—not at once anyhow. It was only very gradually, through long lapse of time, that I managed to think more dispassionately, without resentment or hatred in my heart, of the man who had tried with such meanness and malice to drive us out of our beautiful island.

Chapter 9

We had been on the island two and a half years now, and felt a sense of great happiness and achievement when we contemplated our flourishing 'mixed farm,' with animals, poultry and crops, where there had formerly been a wilderness of stones and bush. It had been a terrific test of endurance for all of us, and the 'delicate' Harry, who the doctor in Cologne thought should have gone for two or three years to a sanatorium, had shown a toughness and resilience we could never have hoped or demanded of him. Heinz too, who had a slight heart condition from the 14-18 war, had stood up to the gruelling work amazingly well. We had grown trees and shrubs and plants, and made them thrive by the sweat of our brow. This, as we could have told the earlier settlers, was the only 'fertiliser' that would work on Floreana.

Occasionally we reminded ourselves that we had only come out for those two or three 'sanatorium' years, but there was no talk now by any of us about returning to Germany for good. What we had done here so far was only a beginning. Now we were the island's only inhabitants, we could hope to get on with our lives in peace, and we should never have had the heart to leave all we had built, to let it revert to wilderness again.

Nevertheless, I had to admit that I was sometimes afflicted with acute nostalgia for my family and friends in Germany, to whom I had said good-bye when I was only twenty-eight. Heinz was much older, of course, when we left, and had already lived forty years of his life in Germany; but by temperament he was much less liable to this sort of homesickness. In any case it was obvious that we could not all go on 'home leave' together. However, the Cologne newspaper for which I had undertaken to write about our experiences was offering to pay what seemed to us very large

96

fees, and I should probably be able to supplement these with lectures and articles elsewhere. For the first time, therefore, we could afford my making such a trip, which would also be useful, Heinz suggested, in case Dore should start putting out stories about us which needed immediate refutation.

So all was prepared for my long journey and absence, and on 17th February I stood on the beach of Post Office Bay with my luggage, while two-year-old Rolf crawled round near me in the sand. We were going home, my old home, which he had never seen. A small boat took us out to sea, away from the new home, to the *San Cristóbal*, which was on her way back to the mainland. Among other passengers on board were the retiring governor of the islands, who had now completed his period of service, and the new governor, his successor. I did not exactly meet the latter, for we neither of us spoke to each other, but once he was sitting opposite me and kept staring at me most disconcertingly with his pitch-black eyes. Afterwards, when he had gone, I asked the captain who this was, to which he only replied: *Comandante . . . no bueno*. That's a pity, I thought, but soon forgot about it. His name, I discovered, was Carlos Puente.

In Guayaquil I was pestered unmercifully by reporters, it was harder to keep them away than the bulls on Floreana. Then I was given another interrogation about the 'missing persons' in the German consulate, which lasted several hours. Two days later, on 1st March, the packet-steamer *Cerigo* sailed for Panama, where I got on another steamer bound for Germany. At the end of April, after a pleasant but uneventful voyage, we were in Hamburg, and of course I went straight to Cologne.

There I had a distressing reminder of recent tragedies: the return of all the letters we had given Lorenz to post. The American tunny-fisher who discovered the bodies handed in the case containing the letters to the customs authorities at San Diego, California, who sent them to the German consulate in Los Angeles, which sent them to the foreign office in Berlin. They thus arrived in Germany in February, .before I had left Floreana; but as it was known that I was coming to Germany, they were forwarded to me care of the Cologne newspaper. After travelling all this way they came back to me nine months after I had sent them off.

97

They added nothing, of course, to the solution of the island's mysteries, which have remained unsolved till this day. It is true that years after this, during the war, rumours reached us that the baroness had been seen dancing for a third-class night-club in either Tahiti or Panama—reports varied—but we could only discount them as improbable embellishments of the legend which had grown up about the former 'Empress of Floreana.'

Dore Strauch, I learnt, was living in Berlin, and she now attributed Ritter's death to pneumonia or other natural causes. No doubt it was hard for her to admit that the great philosopher had died from eating spoiled meat, but I still wondered on hearing about the pneumonia whether there was more to the 'inexactitude' than that. We only had her word for it that she had also eaten the meat and vomited directly afterwards, and there was her inexplicable delay in coming to us for help when she must have seen he was very ill. Did he beg her to come the day before, did she refuse, leaving it till she guessed it was too late?

No, that was too horrible, though it might have accounted for the strange intensity of hatred he had shown in her presence during his dying hours. A volume of Nietzsche lay open on his desk with a passage scored in red about retribution for one's actions. I remembered his confiding to me shortly before his death: 'You never know what she might not be capable of.' Perhaps he thought she was acting as retribution because she knew he had a hand in the baroness's death. Yet he told me himself that he was intending to eat the poisoned chicken, that the meat would be all right after boiling. But in the throes of his agony he may have wrongly believed that she had poisoned him, and accused her of it while he could still speak: hence her terror afterwards, though innocent of the crime, and her talk of fleeing at once.

All this was mere conjecture, of course, and I did not refer to such suspicions when writing my account of the last year's happenings. I tried to keep this as sober and objective as possible, but it was no surprise to hear from the editor of the Cologne paper that she was writing him angry letters. As, however, I stuck to facts she could scarcely dispute, these protests soon dried up. She was probably editing Ritter's papers and preparing her own version of events: I willingly left her to it. As a postscript

I must add that when *Satan Came to Eden* appeared in America two years later, it caused a minor stir but was not very successful; and that she died in 1942, the last person who could have cleared up the mysteries which had surrounded our island.

My own report was serialised in the Cologne paper, which then wanted to make it into a short book. For this, however, it had to be submitted to the Propaganda Ministry, whereupon it turned out most inconveniently that the baroness had a brother who was a big shot in the Nazi party. My book therefore had to be 'expurgated,' much to my disgust, and I was obliged to stay in Germany much longer than I had intended—so as to see it through the press as little damaged as possible. Mr Hancock sent me a film he had taken of the Galapagos Islands which I could use when giving lectures, and in this way I was able to earn my keep for the extra weeks, which dragged into months. But I had no word from Heinz and Harry all this time, and was missing them very badly.

There was another thing too. It was wonderful to be back in Cologne, looking at the great cathedral and watching the Rhine flow majestically through. It was wonderful to see my father again, hale and hearty; he had remarried, a widow with three children—I liked her and them very much. But after the first excitement of homecoming, I found myself very uneasy at political and social developments in Germany—even before they interfered with my literary efforts. When we left the country three years before, Hitler had not yet come to power, and it was both painful and alarming to see the Nazi régime in action, ruthlessly suppressing all possible opponents—Adenauer, Heinz's respected former chief, had even been put in prison for a short time—and already persecuting harmless Jewish citizens. My sister, who had had many Jewish clients in her hairdressing saloon, hated the Nazis and had already emigrated to England the year before. Admittedly many of my fellow-countrymen seemed very optimistic, talked of a better future for Germany, rejoiced in its expanding power and prestige. It would be dishonest hindsight to pretend that I fully appreciated what an abyss of crime and disaster the country was being led into, but I did feel 'something was rotten,' and this feeling made me all the readier to leave 'civilisation' again, to return to our primitive island. I stayed in Germany till the end of October.

Just before I left, I had a most unexpected offer from a man I hardly knew, one of the mass of people who had written to or visited me in curiosity about our life and attitude and plans. He was full of admiration for what we had done, but insisted we could not keep going indefinitely in our long isolation from the 'civilised world.' We had shown what we were worth, and now we should cut loose from our remote island, we should come back and manage his estate! He had full confidence in us, he needed us, and he would not only pay for our return journey to Germany but would settle some money on us while we built another new life for ourselves 'in a less back-breaking and heart-breaking environment.'

As far as I could judge, he seemed genuine enough, a wealthy philanthropist who honestly believed we should come to a bad end on Floreana. But I was longing to get back there, back to the life we had chosen for ourselves, and although I appreciated this kindness, if he really meant it, I somehow did not take him seriously. Truth to tell, I hardly thought about the thing at all, my mind was too full of good-byes, packing and last-minute preparations. A few days later I was in Hamburg and went aboard the *Rhakotis*, which was to take me to South America. On 5th November she put in at Antwerp, where I found a telegram from our well-wisher in Cologne: 'Hope to see you back here very soon with all your family. Feel sure you will come and am shortly sending cheque to Floreana for passage money.'

I stuck the telegram in my pocket, felt deeply touched, remembered the man and his offer for a few days, then gradually let the matter slip out of my mind. There had never been any question of my accepting. We had only just got going on Floreana, we must make many more acres of wilderness blossom. I had not heard from home—from our island—all the time I had been away, but if Heinz and Harry were well, as I prayed I should find them, then I knew all four of us were happy staying where we were. Where we *should* be, that is, if Rolf and I survived this frightful Atlantic crossing!

By the time we were approaching South America, the wind had reached hurricane force, and the two heavy locomotives we had on board for Chile began to work loose from their wooden plankings. A gigantic wave tore through these like a piece of paper, the captain was desperate, and almost let the locomotives roll into the sea.

However, we reached land at last, and soon Rolf and I were in Guayaquil once more, only to find that our good old Galapagos schooner, the *San Cristóbal*, had cleverly arranged to leave for the islands just before our arrival. Heaven knew when the next ship or boat would be going there. It might be weeks or months, and I had dearly wanted to be 'home by Christmas.' There was little hope of that now.

'Why not go and stay at Ambato?' an acquaintance in Guayaquil suggested. 'There's a good hotel I know there, the Villa Hilda, where you can live cheaply and well till you get word of the next boat. You don't want to stay in this terrible Guayaquil heat, it's nice and cool at Ambato.'

This last was a big point, and I thought it a good idea. Ambato is about 200 miles north of Guayaquil and about 80 miles south of Quito, Ecuador's capital. There were trains to Quito every other day from a place called Duran, to which you took a ferry from Guayaquil across the Rio Guayas.

The trains were always crammed, but besides first- and second-class carriages had a special 'observation car' at the back, on which, having been warned in advance, I had reserved our seats. This carriage had swivel-chairs and huge glass windows, allowing a panoramic view of the breath-taking scenery we passed through. I did not have to worry much about Rolf, who luckily slept most of the time, and this first journey on the Guayaquil-Quito railway was one of the unforgettable experiences of my life.

The railway was started in 1897 by two brothers from Virginia, the Harmans, and is a great technical triumph for its engineers, though its completion after immense labour was attended by great loss of life from fever. It was built on a narrow track, blasted out of the rocks. For the first four or five hours it went through tropical forests, then it began climbing steadily to about 5,000 feet where the fruit and crops became less tropical and more European. Later on it reached nearly 8,000 feet, where instead of the eternal snow you would find in Europe at this height, there was a scent of peaches and apricots, and a riot of colour from millions of flowers—geraniums, for instance, blooming in whole bunches.

Then we went even higher, and as the train wound up the steep slopes, we sometimes saw the same landscape beneath us six or seven times from opposite windows. At one point it stopped abruptly, on the side of a precipice, and began hurtling backwards into a valley. I could already picture us being hurled into the abyss below. Then it stopped just as suddenly, and moved forward again with a jerk. This happened several times, and the train conductor, seeing me turn pale, explained that it was quite all right, we were just passing the Nariz del Diablo (The Devil's Nose). We were now some 9,000 feet above sea-level, and it was bitterly cold even when we had wrapped ourselves in all the coats and extra blankets we could lay hands on; the hot cinnamon brandy obtainable at stations was very welcome indeed.

It was quite a relief to begin travelling downhill after this, and about 5 p.m., amidst a glorious sunset on Mount Chimborazo, we reached the town of Riobamba, capital of the province of Chimborazo and at the foot of the mountain. After dark, almost exhausted by all the magnificent views, I dozed off most of the rest of the way, till about ten at night we arrived at Ambato. With Rolf and all our baggage, I made my way to the Villa Hilda, where the manageress, a pleasant Swiss woman, received us with great friendliness. We were given a fine room and a splendid supper, and when next morning I saw the beautiful garden and grounds, I had already decided that if we must be stranded away from Floreana, this was not at all a bad place to possess one's soul in patience.

Ambato is the capital of the province of Tunguhagua, and a great fruit and wine centre. Monday is Feria (market) day, and extremely colourful with farmers from all over the province bringing in their produce, consisting of European vegetables and fruit like potatoes, apples, pears, apricots, peaches, strawberries, gooseberries, cherries, morello plums, nuts and grapes. There was also a market for the horses, sheep and pigs. The food at the hotel was excellent, and although I was longing to get back to our island, this was a real rest-cure after the strenuous 'home leave' and disagreeable Atlantic crossing.

It was only at Christmas that I felt really sad, cut off both from my family on Floreana and those I had left behind in Germany. I missed the strong, quiet, solemn emotions of a German Christmas, amidst the wild gaiety of the 'public holiday' at Ambato, with dancing in the streets and outside the Church doors, more like a carnival in my native Rhineland than any religious festival. But praise be, it was not many days later I heard that the *San Cristóbal* would be sailing again on 4th January. Soon I was once more standing on the quay with all my luggage, trying to keep Rolf amused, stop him wandering off and falling into the sea. We sailed down the Rio Guayas, a good forty miles to the mouth of the river and the open sea. From there it was seven days and six hundred miles, another severe ordeal for a bad sailor like me and for my long-suffering stomach.

But then at last the coast of Floreana lay ahead of us. We dropped anchor in Blackbeach Bay, and the captain sent a man up to the house with news of our arrival. It was seven o'clock in the morning. I had given the man precise instruction how to get there, but the hours passed and no one came. I knew it was a long way, but suppose something had happened to them? By the evening I was almost hysterical with anxiety, and then I suddenly heard barking from the bush. 'Lumpi, Lumpi, good old Lumpi!' I yelled joyfully as I saw the dog racing down the beach in wild excitement to bark and bark at the ship. Then at last I saw Heinz coming out of the bush, leading the donkey. The landing-boat was lowered at once, and was soon speeding towards the shore.

'Papa, Papa, come and fetch your little boy,' Rolf kept shouting across from it as we got nearer and nearer. This was a sentence we had taught him in Cologne, and he remembered it splendidly.

'You look well,' was all I could think of to say as I jumped ashore, then I was locked in my husband's arms. For minutes we stayed in a silent embrace overflowing with happiness, while Rolf pulled picture-books and toys out of a little box he had with him, and put them all round us in a circle.

'How's Harry?' I asked at last, as we began walking towards home.

'He's all right—up there looking after the animals, and longing to see you. Actually he hasn't been too well lately . . . I don't think it's anything much,' Heinz reassured me, 'perhaps he's been working too hard.'

Before we got to the house, Harry rushed out to meet us. Perhaps he did look a bit pale, though it was hardly noticeable in his excitement—and in mine. I had only just got over this new joyful reunion, when we reached the house. But what on earth . . .? I was flabbergasted. While I was away, our house seemed to have grown.

'Yes, Mother,' said Harry, 'we've built on a new bedroom, just to surprise you.'

They had certainly surprised me. It was a fine big room, about twelve feet by fifteen, with concrete floor, six windows, a big wardrobe, a carpet on the floor and a desk by one of the windows: more comfort than I had ever dreamed of finding on Floreana. But what a mass of work had gone into this one room, it must have taken weeks and weeks, no, months and months. Then I grasped properly for the first time how long I had been away.

'Eleven months,' said Heinz, and I could see how hard those months had been for him.

'Did you get my letters?'

'Yes.' He smiled wryly. 'The first lot of mail came in the middle of November.'

I had left in February, and he hadn't heard a word from me till November—by which time I was already back in South America.

'I had no idea what might be happening to you in Germany, or how long you'd be staying.' He gave me an apologetic look. 'So I killed most of the chickens. The work would have been too much for me.'

Twelve hens and a cock were left, my fine chicken farm was reduced to a few remnants. But I had learnt a lot about poultry breeding, I could soon build it up again. I was not sad at this confession by Heinz, I was much too happy to be back home, nothing else was of any importance.

Nothing except of course Harry's health, and that did cause us great anxiety. We insisted on his taking more of a rest, and I gave special care to his diet. But he was still far from well, and in April he had to stay in bed with a strange fever. I thought at first it might be malaria, but then the symptoms were wrong. Whatever it was, it passed gradually, and after a fortnight he was able to get up. Even then he was not really fit.

Apart from this we had no major worries, and the small daily ones were amply made up for by the peace and tranquillity we now had in full measure. We were the island's only permanent inhabitants, no one disturbed us. It was one of those periods when no ship called for weeks and weeks, we even began to think it would be nice to have our solitude disturbed once in a while, to have visitors again. They came, most suitably, on my birthday: 12th July, 1936.

We had seen to the animals and were sitting contentedly having our coffee with my birthday cake, when we heard aeroplanes. Two English planes were circling above our heads. While we were still trying to puzzle out what this might mean—it was surely something important—six British naval officers turned up at the garden gate. One of them introduced himself as Admiral Best.

Since the 'court of enquiry' with the Galapagos governor and his armed guard, we felt a bit 'allergic' to men in uniform. But this time there was no interrogation about a supposed murder; instead we received a most charming invitation. 'His Majesty's Cruiser *Apollo* is lying at anchor outside Post Office Bay,' said the admiral. 'We have come to invite you to dinner on board.'

We accepted with pleasure, but first insisted they came in and had some birthday cake and coffee. Then Heinz showed them over the house and estate, on which they said some extremely kind things. Meanwhile I collected fresh fruit from our trees and loaded them on the donkey for the officers to take back to the ship. I was still in my working shorts, but when we all got down to the old Norwegian hut I changed into a dress, after which I felt ready to board the ship. But before the festivities began Admiral Best put his bathroom at our disposal; to lie basking in the hot water was an unusual treat for us.

We went into the reception-room to find all the officers assembled wearing their gala uniforms. But there was a black ribbon on the white coats, in mourning for King George V, who had recently died. After cocktails had been served and drunk, we were shown into the wardroom. Before we sat down at the gaily decked table, the German national anthem was played in our honour, followed by the British national anthem. The wine sparkling in the glasses was Rhine wine, a pleasure indeed for former citizens of Cologne.

I was seated next to the admiral, with Heinz opposite him. There was a painful moment early in the meal when the admiral, amidst one of those sudden silences that sometimes occur, leaned over towards Heinz and asked: 'Tell me, Mr Wittmer, what do you think of the Hitler régime?'

The bit of bread I was eating stuck in my throat. How was a German to answer such a question? I had, of course, told Heinz my impressions of Germany the previous year, and we knew from my sister that the Nazis were already very unpopular in England. He threw me a glance of enquiry, but I could hardly whisper across the table to help him, even if I had been able to think of something appropriate. But my husband showed his usual presence of mind, and after only the briefest hesitation came out with: 'We love our country, sir. We do not always like its government.'

The admiral looked at Heinz, then at me. Then he stood up, raised his glass, and with a slight bow towards each of us said: 'I respect your attitude, and may God's blessing be on your work here.'

We thanked him, deeply moved, and the atmosphere cleared at once. After this no word of politics was spoken which might have spoiled a wonderful evening. It was dark but starry over the sea when we went on deck towards midnight. All the crew had taken up their positions on deck, and when we arrived, at a signal from the admiral, the band played *The Last Post*. Then one of the motor-boats took us back to Post Office Bay.

The whole ship was gaily illuminated, her lights were reflected in the dark waters below. Then her floodlights flashed on, making the bay as bright as daylight.

The motor-boat returned, and almost immediately afterwards the cruiser's engines began to run. We sat on the steps of the old chalet, watching her go. The lights grew fainter and fainter, the ship smaller and smaller. In half an hour there was nothing left of the *Apollo* in sight.

'Was it all real?' Heinz asked softly.

Yes, the whole evening had been almost too good to be true. What a birthday!

It was one o'clock when we eventually started homewards, and it took us four hours walking through the still of the night before we reached our house. We got back in the first light of dawn, just as Harry was putting on the water for early morning coffee.

Chapter 10

Nearly four years old, Rolf loved going up 'Olympus,' the hill at the end of our garden, and looking out to sea. You couldn't see Blackbeach Bay, but you could see ships going to it from Isabela —if there had been any ships to sight. But alas, since the *Apollo* we had had no visitors at all, and there hadn't been a boat from the mainland all the eight months I had been back. So we hadn't had any mail either, and although I said little of this to Heinz or the children, I had to admit to myself that I felt a little homesick for Germany. In other words, I had still not 'settled down' in the loneliness of our island even after four years. Heinz had, Harry had—they often said they had no wish to go back to Germany—and Rolf's six months there were rapidly fading for him into a pleasant but remote dream. He could look at the sea for hours on end, but he had no longing to cross it again, as I had in that autumn of 1936.

'A ship, Mutti, come quickly!' he called excitedly from the hill. 'A ship, a ship!'

I rushed up to join him. Yes, at last: a boat coming into Blackbeach. I couldn't wait for Heinz and Harry to get back from their work, but took Rolf with me and rode down to the coast on the donkey as fast as I could go. It was only a fishing boat from Chatham, but her *Capitano*, Manuel Guitierez, was an old friend of ours, and we waved a welcome, for he had already landed.

'*Señora! Señora!*' he cried. '*Tres sacos llenos de correo por Usted! Tres sacos, Señora!*'

Three sacks full of post: I was laughing and crying at the same time, as happy as a child looking at a Christmas tree full of presents. Old Manuel, our Santa Claus, invited me on board for

107

lunch, but kind as it was of him, I felt too eager to get home and look at our 'presents.' He sent a man up with me to the Asilo de la Paz to help out my donkey, for whom three sacks were too heavy a load. When we got there and I had given the man some coffee, we settled down to the important business of exploring the sacks' contents. As usual, it took us days to read all the letters, not only from Germany but from the United States, and also from my sister in London. And besides the letters and newspapers, there were the packages to undo, full of all the things which might seem commonplace anywhere but on an isolated island, but were of tremendous value to us. It was almost ridiculous how delighted we were to receive a set of sewing needles, they were just as precious as the tins and foodstuffs: more so in a way, because I had a lot of sewing to do before next April. That was when we expected another addition to the family.

Deep down inside, I was a bit scared about having this second baby. We were alone on the island now, there was no Ritter to perform an emergency operation if anything went wrong. My mind was not eased till we had our next visitors, men from *Dar Pomorza*, a Polish training ship. There was a doctor among them, he examined me and told me everything was all right, I had no need to worry. I confided to him that I felt homesick. 'That's bad,' he said, 'and not even very sensible, I'm afraid. Things look rather black in Europe, you know, it's a bit like sitting on top of one of your Galapagos volcanoes. There's a lot of rumbling underneath, and one feels it may erupt any time—so if I were you, I'd be glad you're on a nice peaceful island.'

I sighed. 'We don't know much about what's going on in Europe, and if you're right I suppose we *should* be grateful to be away from it all. All the same, it's a little frightening to know you're going to have a baby in the spring with no doctor or midwife if things aren't plain sailing. I told you about my first baby.'

'Yes, I can understand very well how you feel,' said the Polish doctor, 'and I'll tell you what we'll do. We'll send a message to Panama giving the likely date. Then surely some yacht which is in the vicinity at the time will put in to see you're all right. Does that help?'

'Oh, if you *could* do that, it would be wonderful.'

'Trust me,' he said. 'We'll send out the message this evening.'

His promise reassured me greatly, and to complete my recovery from anxiety and homesickness, we suddenly had plenty of callers in quick succession. We greatly enjoyed having them, though it gave me twice as much work. But that kept me from brooding, and there were no unpleasant incidents such as we had experienced in our first two and a half years.

One day in January, it is true, we were reminded for a troubled moment of the baroness and her revolver. We heard a shot in the bush, then another very near us. Heinz went out with his gun to meet the disturbers of the peace.

They turned out to be no disturbers of the peace, but extremely welcome guests, whom we had missed seeing four years before : Captain and Mrs Irving Johnson from the brig *Yankee*. These were the Johnsons Ritter had told us about, who had heard of Rolf's birth and wanted to come up to the Asilo de la Paz, but the baroness put them off. This time there was no one to put them off, and they had fired the shots to signal their arrival— with all their crew. The *Yankee's* second voyage round the world was to last eighteen months and she had on board about two dozen youngsters who were 'working their passage,' seeing the world and incidentally getting a fine training in seamanship.

They came up to our house three days running, and when they left Mrs Johnson declared: 'We'll be with you again in three years' time. Expect us the same day!'

I laughed, though a little wryly. At home you sent a card saying you'll come next week-end, while here you announced a visit for months or even years ahead—even if it was 'to the day,' as the Johnsons promised.

Meanwhile there were only a few weeks to wait before the island's next inhabitant arrived, and the Polish doctor had been as good as his word. On 17th March the yacht *Nourmahal* arrived with Mr Vincent Astor. He brought up the ship's doctor, who examined me and told me my condition was excellent. 'The baby should be born within a fortnight,' the doctor said, 'and you won't have any trouble, so don't worry. Anyhow, we'll drop round again at the end of the month, and see how things are with you. Is that good enough?'

'And how!' I answered.

Punctually a fortnight later Mr Astor returned. 'No baby?' he asked, when he saw me.

'No baby.'

'Don't worry,' he told me again. 'I'll be back again soon. And then there's the *Meta Nelson*, Calvin Bentley's yacht. I've had a word with her ship's doctor, who's promised to call in. All part of our mobile maternity service, what!'

It was certainly comforting to know that complete strangers were so far concerned for my welfare. I was less pleased, at the beginning of April, to receive a call from three men who were not doctors. They had rucksacks on their backs, and one of them, who told us his name was Charles Hubbard, said they had a lot of time to spend on Floreana. They wanted to shoot and fish, also to study the island a bit.

I was huge by now, and felt in no mood or condition even to have them in the house. But Heinz insisted we could not turn them away without even offering them a meal. How like a man, I thought, realising that of course he was right, bother him.

They soon went back to their boat, and I did not see the other two again. But Hubbard fixed up to go out shooting with Heinz the next day, and naturally he came back to our midday meal. I could see Heinz liked him, but I still felt there was something rather strange about him, and couldn't quite make out why he had come here. The third day he came, while we were sitting over coffee, I decided to have it out. 'What exactly are you studying on Floreana?' I asked. 'The plants or the game or the stones—or what?'

'None of those,' he answered with a smile. 'I'm studying people.'

'People?' Light began to dawn.

'Yes. People like you.' His smile became rather sheepish. 'You and your life on the island. I've already done that the last two days without your knowing. But I've got to tell you now before I impose on your hospitality any more.'

He waited for me to say something, but I was speechless. He went on with his confession: 'To come right out with it, I'm from the American magazine, *Liberty*. There's been a book published in America called *Satan Came to Eden* . . .'

'What!' I exclaimed. I had forgotten about Dore's book. 'I thought all that business was over and done with long ago.'

'I'm afraid not,' he said. 'You see, the book is full of contradictions, and *Liberty* have sent me to find out on the spot exactly what is true in the lady's story and what is false. You can help me—if you're willing to.'

'But now of all times, Mr Hubbard . . . I mean, the baby might come any day.'

'I know.' He nodded sympathetically. 'But I'll make you a suggestion. I'll come up here early tomorrow morning, and if there's still no baby we can talk about the Ritter business. It'll take your mind off the waiting, and besides you wouldn't want this Dore dame to get away with a lot of lies, would you? How about it?'

I didn't refuse outright, but I didn't agree either. Hubbard wasn't easily discouraged, however, and when he arrived the next morning, I felt it was quite a good idea after all. 'Good morning. No baby?' he asked me to start with. 'No baby,' I replied, and we settled down to talk about the households at Frido Farm and the 'Hacienda Paradiso.'

He came every day after that, his greeting and my answer became a ritual formula: 'Good morning. No baby?' 'No baby.' Then we got to work, laboriously understanding each other through a combination of German and English with a few words of French and the aid of various dictionaries. Hubbard wrote notes and asked me questions, which I answered as best I could, sitting in an easy chair with my feet up and cushions at my back. Heinz periodically refreshed us with brews of good strong coffee. These were very welcome for me, because I was feeling dreadful, at my lowest ebb. In those days I was incapable of any effort, and Heinz had to do the cooking as well as everything else, while Harry looked after Rolf.

But that period passed too, I recovered some of my energy; but the baby still did not come. Mr Astor's yacht again returned, and the doctor shook his head on finding no baby. '*Paciencia, paciencia!*' he admonished me. 'It can't possibly be later than the 15th.'

A few days later the big yacht *Meta Nelson* put in, and the ship's doctor came up to us at once, as he had promised Mr Astor. But there was nothing he could do or say after examining me except: 'Don't worry, it can't be long now.'

I tried not to worry, even though I had twenty-three guests in the house that day (including Charlie Hubbard). For the owner of the yacht, Mr Calvin Bentley from Miami, had also brought his wife and all his party. But so as to avoid giving me extra work, he had also brought the ship's cook, who made sandwiches and coffee which the guests ate sitting outside on the stone veranda. I found Mrs Bentley very interesting to talk to, and in spite of my state I greatly enjoyed the day. When they all came, I had thought it extremely inconsiderate of them; but by the time they left, I felt ashamed of this, and made a mental vow! 'Anyone who comes here, rich or poor, white or black, shall always find this an open house.' I believe I have kept that vow through all the years, and hundreds of people who came to the house as strangers have left it as friends. Indeed many of them helped us wonderfully in return, especially during the war.

But the *Meta Nelson* left, and on the 12th April, an unbearably hot day, there was still no baby. Nor the 13th nor the 14th. That morning when Hubbard gave me the ritual greeting, I couldn't answer him, the joke had gone sour. We had finished our work, and although his continual questions had quickly tired me, I was pleased that between us there was now a decent account of the whole Ritter-Baroness story. For my part in its preparation (which was quite an important point for us) *Liberty* were to pay me a large fee. I had been furious with Hubbard at first for his deceit about 'studying the island,' but I soon found that we got on very well together. We were all good friends, and I felt sad when he had his last meal with us before leaving. 'What's it to be, Greta?' he asked, standing on the steps with his rucksack on his back.

'A girl, of course, Charlie,' I answered with complete conviction. 'I've got enough boys in the house already, I need feminine reinforcements.'

I looked after him for a long time as he started on the path towards the sea. I did not guess then what a loyal friend he would prove, how he would stand by us in the long war years when he was a Squadron Leader in the American Air Force. We were very sad to hear in 1950, when he was head of a meteorological station in the Arctic, that he and eight others had been killed in a plane crash.

April is always the hottest month on Floreana. The damp heat is oppressive enough when there is any rain. When there is none, it is almost unbearable. That 1937 April seemed even hotter than usual, and there wasn't the smallest shower. Everything was parched and withered, there wasn't a spot of green anywhere, and in the daytime not a sound could be heard from the game in the bush. They were lying somewhere dozing in the shade of the algerobo trees. The bush only wakened to life when darkness came. Then the squealing, grunting, bellowing and mooing penetrated right to our house.

The two doctors and everyone else had counselled patience. I felt I was a master of this art, or perhaps I was too weak to be even impatient. But on the 17th April the pains were so severe that I knew the long tormenting wait was nearly over. Water was boiled, and everything was set out which I might need, even drugs and medical appliances in case anything went wrong, though I hoped of course that these would not be needed. The night began, dragging on interminably, but at midnight I heard a cry. Automatically I grabbed one of the diapers I had piled within reach near my bed, wrapped the child up, and laid it down by me. That was the last small effort I was capable of, after that I collapsed on to the pillows exhausted.

A few minutes later I was shaken by convulsive shivering. Heinz was quietly and skilfully doing all that was necessary, but when he saw my violent shudders he had a bad shock. In this emergency, as in so many other of life's stresses and strains, he quickly brewed some coffee—our own home-grown coffee—the universal panacea. It was incredibly strong, but my teeth were chattering so much he could hardly get a few mouthfuls down my throat with a mouthful of whisky. 'Any better?' he asked anxiously.

'S . . . s . . . till fr . . . freezing,' I stammered.

He fetched blankets and eiderdowns from all over the house, and heaped them on my bed. I could hear the child whimpering near me, but its voice sounded so remote I couldn't grasp where it came from. The temperature in the room was somewhere round a hundred, but I still felt chilled to the bone. After an hour, when I was still as cold as ever, Heinz filled a large water-bag with hot water, and put it at my feet. This home-made hot-water bottle did the trick, for at once I felt a slight, comforting warmth, and had soon fallen into a leaden sleep, oblivious of all around me, including the child I had brought into the world.

The boys had woken, but Heinz had got them to go off to sleep again, and in the morning he sent them off on a long walk.

When I woke, they were still out, but then Rolf rushed into our bedroom, ahead of Harry, eager to show me something he had found on the walk. 'Mutti, Mutti, look what I've got . . .' He stopped short and looked in amazement at the bed, and me submerged in blankets. 'Are you ill?' He stole right up to the bed. 'Or has the little sister come at last?' He was dead sure it was going to be a sister, a brother was out of the question. 'Can't I see her?'

I felt just then like telling him to keep quiet and go away, but of course it was quite natural for him to want to see her. 'I've got to bath your little sister and dress her,' I told him. 'Then you can see her. But you're both hungry I'm sure, go and have something to eat until I'm ready.'

Rolf had a good appetite, so this suggestion at once found favour. Forgetting his little sister, he dragged Harry off with him. While they were away, Heinz brought a bowl and water. My hands shook as I bathed the baby, but I managed it. 'Well, you've got your heart's desire,' said Heinz. 'A girl.'

I nodded, and for the first time had a good look at my daughter. She looked sturdy enough, she had very fair hair and dark brown eyes.

Rolf charged back into the room. I showed him his sister, and was expecting whoops of joy. His mouth turned down. 'What? That's the little sister you've been talking about all the time.'

'Of course.'

Rolf drew a deep breath. 'But she's so terribly small. *She'll* never be able to hold a *machete*.' He looked at me disapprovingly. 'Can't we swop her for something bigger?'

'Yes,' I admitted, 'she *is* a bit small. But isn't she a lovely little thing! It won't be long before she's as big as you are now and can hold a *machete*. You were just as small once yourself, you know.'

This argument made no impression on him. It was not till I told him I might some time get a bigger little sister as well that he expressed moderate satisfaction. 'Yes, I could do with two little sisters on my farm.' He thought a moment. 'As long as they get big enough to use tools, like you've told me.'

I had to stay in bed for five days, the strain of the last weeks had taken its toll. I was worried too about the baby, who brought everything up. The sixth day I felt strong enough to get up, but only for a short time. When I was lying down again, we had a round-the-bed conference of the whole family on what to call its new member. Each of us suggested five names, and from that selection we made our final choice. In the end we gave her two names, Ingeborg, and Floreanita after our own dear island. In the family she was always called Inge, but for our Spanish-speaking friends she was and remained Floreanita.

My strength slowly returned, but Inge went on vomiting, and I wished again, as I wished for myself in the hour just after her birth, that one of the doctors who had turned up before would come now, when we really needed them. But both the yachts had left the islands, and there was no guarantee another ship would call. If one did, she might not have a doctor on board, and if there were a doctor, he might not know how badly we needed him. 'We must send word out somehow,' I told Heinz.

'Right,' he said. 'I'll go down to Post Office Bay tomorrow and fix a notice on the post-barrel. Then anyone who lands is bound to see it.'

That meant his being away all day, four hours there and four back, but it seemed our only hope. The next morning, while he made a good breakfast, I wrote out the notice in big letters, found a handful of drawing-pins to stick it on to the barrel, packed it away in his shirt pocket with a safety-pin attaching it to the shirt so that it shouldn't get lost. 'See you fix it so that it can't be missed,' I admonished him.

'Yes, of course . . . Right, I'll see you this evening.' He set off on the journey, with Lump at his side as usual.

About five, I wrapped Inge in a blanket, took her on my arm and went out to meet him; and it wasn't long before Lump came dashing up to greet me, wagging his tail hard, his tongue hanging out. Then Heinz emerged out of the bushes, looking rather bright despite his day's march. I saw that he was carrying a small parcel under his arm. 'Nice of you to come and meet me.' He stopped a moment for a breather.

'Where was the buried treasure?' I asked, pointing to the parcel.

'A little yacht passed and put this in the barrel for us. It's got cigarettes and cigars in, and some chocolate for the children. They wrote a note saying they imagined we'd find it one day.'

One day—that was good! I was still half amused, half irritated, by the Galapagos idea of time, which seemed to be reckoned not in minutes and hours but in weeks and months. You certainly needed *paciencia*.

Heinz was ravenously hungry, and I hadn't the heart to disturb him with questions till he'd at least got some food inside him. But after a bit I had to make sure. 'You managed to fix the message on the barrel all right?'

'Message?' He stopped his fork in mid-air. 'What message? Good Lord!' Gradually it dawned on him. 'I expect it'll still be where you fixed it this morning. Oh, Grete darling—I just don't know what to say . . .'

Of course it was still there. In his shirt pocket. So was the safety-pin with which I had stuck it to the pocket so that it shouldn't get lost. It hadn't got lost. Heinz looked so remorseful I thought he was going to get up then and there and go down to Post Office Bay again, but that I couldn't let him do. A whole day had been wasted (except for the parcel!), but accepting that was also part of Galapagos *paciencia*. At home you say: 'Just go round the corner and post this.' But when 'round the corner' was a walk of four hours each way, and the collection might be next month—well, you had to alter your ideas, that was all. Heinz could go down there again tomorrow, or the day after. A ship might come this week, next week, some time . . . Mañana, mañana —it was a difficult lesson to learn.

The weather seemed to be all topsy-turvy. We were supposed to be in the middle of the rainy season, and half way through May not a drop of rain had fallen. The whole island, stone and tree and bush, seemed to be wearing the same colour, a parched brown which hurt the eye. The sun was still scorching, but it was nearly the *Garua* time when it was cold by Floreana standards. The nights were already much cooler, we had to cover up well to keep warm. There was heavy dew on the ground in the mornings, and the dried-up grass began to recover. During the last few days of the month the dismal scene had brightened a bit, we could here and there see traces of green again.

On the 31st, when we were sitting at breakfast, Lump suddenly started barking his head off.

'Callers, so early in the morning?' I looked at Heinz in amazement. 'They must have spent the night in the bush if they're up
here already.'

'Perhaps it's a doctor . . .' he began, but before he had finished
the sentence I was up and out of the door. I saw four people
standing at the garden gate, Lump was still yelping at them
furiously. There was a middle-aged man with a rather younger
woman, a girl and a boy: judging by their looks they were either
from the mainland or one of the other islands. As I went to meet
them, I saw that the man was very tall and very thin, which made
him seem even taller, and had a yellowish-white face that looked
almost Chinese. He was wearing an immaculate white suit, perfectly creased and without a speck of dust. His brown shoes
also were gleaming with polish, no trace of damp to be seen
although the grass was soaking with dew. This model of elegance
bowed deeply and introduced himself as Don Ezequiel Zavala.
Despite his exquisite politeness I soon felt rather uneasy with him,
whether because of his unusual height or his exuberant gestures
or a slightly shifty expression in his eyes.

The woman was his wife, Maruja, and she too was elegant,
though not quite to the same degree. This was as it should be,
since he was clearly the master of the house, which had to be
reflected in their external appearances as well. In fact she never
left his side, and looked as if her main concern was not to let
Don Ezequiel soil his beautiful clothes. She was plump and very
short, only about five foot, with a very well-cut face, a very dark
skin, black eyes and lank black hair. She had two front teeth
missing, but her smile was warm and attractive.

Zavala then introduced Marta, a daughter from his first
marriage. She was about sixteen, and her complexion was honey-
coloured. She was tall for her age and well developed. Her
features were not so fine as Maruja's, but she still made a very
pleasing impression, even if her conversation on this first day
was confined to 'sí' and 'no.'

Finally, with a condescending gesture, Zavala introduced the
black-eyed young Indian boy as José, *nuestro compañero de
trabajo.* 'Our companion in work,' I translated to myself, but
Señor Ezequiel seemed to stress the '*trabajo*' and clearly placed
less importance on the '*compañero.*' I shook hands with him,
realising at once that Zavala did not approve of this, while for

117

José it was an unusual honour which turned his face into one enormous grin.

I asked my early callers into the house, and the series of introductions began over again. Zavala addressed Heinz simply as 'Mister,' which besides showing that he knew some English was evidently intended as a signal courtesy. We squeezed up to make room for our guests at the breakfast table, but when Zavala noticed that I was laying a place for José, he made a vigorous protest. No, this young man was only *compañero de trabajo*, it was quite out of the question that he should sit at one and the same table with Mister. Such a system of etiquette was new and rather strange to me, but I fell in with his wishes and put José at a small side table.

So then everything was all right—everything except our ability to communicate with each other. For after the opening gambits of politeness, which were spoken fairly slowly, the Zavalas broke into a torrent of Spanish which was far beyond me and too rapid for my dictionary to keep up with. We tried to give the impression that we were getting the gist of what they were saying, but after half an hour of animated speech and gesticulation we still had only a glimmering of why the Zavalas had come to Floreana. First of all I thought that some boat from one of the islands had put in to Blackbeach and they were just paying us a brief visit. Gradually, however, it dawned on me that they were proposing to live here.

Don Ezequiel pulled some papers out of his breast pocket and handed them to 'Mister' to read. But it was all in Spanish, and Spanish was not Mister's strong point. 'If we're to read these,' I said, 'it will take us the whole day. Would you mind explaining them, Señor Ezequiel, but please speak a little slower, we can't quite follow you when you talk so fast.'

He resumed his discourse, and now we began to understand, with the help of his eloquent gestures, what it was all about. Don Carlos Puente, the *Jefe territorial* or governor of the Galapagos Islands, had decided that some of the indigenous population should live on Floreana besides the *gringos* (foreigners). It had come to the governor's ears that there was a 'mass of cattle' on the island, and the hides would be very valuable in Ecuador for making leather, which was in short supply. Zavala had lived for fifteen years on Isabela, where he had a small coffee plantation, and now Puente had transferred him to Floreana to shoot the excessive numbers of cattle, dry the meat, cure the hides, and send both to the governor's residence at Chatham. What would be done then with meat and hides Zavala did not know.

In return for the services he was shortly to render to his country, Zavala was taken on to the governor's military payroll, with a hundred sucres a month and extra allowance for food. He was also to receive a title to Frido Farm; but Zavala was unwilling to accept this billet, since besides being gamekeeper he was Floreana's Harbour Commander. He therefore preferred to live near the coast, 'the better to control marine traffic.'

Floreana would see great improvements, he told us, very conscious of the dignity of his two new posts. 'A lot of ships will be coming to Floreana to take off the meat and hides.'

We were a little dubious about these 'brighter prospects,' but refrained from saying so, not only because of the language difficulty. And when the Harbour Commander and family had departed, I sighed deeply. 'Our wonderful undisturbed existence on Floreana is over.'

Heinz nodded sadly.

For three years we had been the island's only human inhabitants, living as good neighbours with the wild cattle and donkeys and pigs. Now Puente had sent Zavala here with a death sentence pronounced on the cattle.

'Oh well, let's wait and see,' Heinz suggested. 'Things often turn out differently from the way these people expect.'

Chapter 11

In the months during which we were the only inhabitants our efforts to learn languages had rather fallen by the wayside. Now the Zavalas had come, I decided to work seriously again at my Spanish, so that at least one member of the family should be able to communicate with our new neighbours more or less easily. I gave myself exercises whenever I had a quiet half hour, and while I was breast-feeding Inge I would talk Spanish to her!

For the next weeks we didn't see much of the Zavalas, who were busy installing themselves at Blackbeach Bay. But one day Maruja came rushing up to our house, eager to impart her big news: 'A marvellous yacht had just gone past. Isn't it a pity, though? She's sailed on to Post Office Bay, so my husband has had to go all the way there to check the ship's papers.'

I was glad that our new Harbour Commander was at last having some work; nothing had been done so far, it appeared, in the 'game-hunter' sphere. Maruja stayed for a chat, and she admired the progress I had made in her language; but we did not hear any more of the yacht till the next day. Then her owner came to see us, a Dr Holcomb from California with his wife and two children. A doctor at last, our enforced *paciencia* had been rewarded.

He examined Inge, and took a terrific weight off my mind by assuring me that the vomiting would stop in two or three weeks, and then she would be perfectly all right—this prognosis proved correct. When I told Holcomb about my uncontrollable shivering immediately after the birth, he looked very grave. 'Even in what we call civilisation, such births don't often turn out well. You must both have been under a lucky star.'

After we had been talking for a while, Mrs Holcomb pulled

a letter out of her pocket. 'By the way, the governor of the islands asked us to give you this, he said it was very important.'

'Thanks very much,' I said. 'I wonder what Señor Puente can have to say to us that's so important.' I was going to postpone reading it till our guests had gone, but then I noticed the peculiar way the envelope was addressed. Instead of our name, which was perfectly well known, it said in English: 'To the German citizens on Floreana.'

I opened the envelope. The letter was also in English. I read it out: 'You are requested to leave the island at the earliest opportunity. You are permitted to move to Chatham, Isabela or the mainland. You are also permitted to return to Germany.'

Heinz could not follow this in English, and when I translated it into German, his first reaction was to roar with laughter. 'The man's off his head!' he exclaimed. 'Big of him to permit us to return to Germany. Well, well, well—I wonder if this has anything to do with Zavala's hide business. Perhaps Puente meant to start it on Isabela where Zavala's been all these years, but thought there were too many people there who'd see what was going on.'

'I see what you mean,' I said. 'Floreana looked the best island for their little partnership, but now they'd rather have no one else on the island at all, so we're being thrown out. This is frightful.'

'I shouldn't be too upset,' Mrs Holcomb advised. 'Write to the German Embassy at Quito, and see if they can help you. By the way, the governor gave us another letter for the Conways, the American couple on Santiago, addressed in the same odd way.'

We had heard of these Conways, who had been living on Santiago for the last three months. It was an island which had probably never had any long-term settlers, though when Darwin visited the Galapagos Islands there were some forty or fifty people on Santiago. Officially there was not enough fresh water there to maintain life, but it was also said that a supply of fresh water existed, if you knew where to find it. Perhaps the Conways had found it, and perhaps they would find some way of escaping eviction. Whatever they did we certainly meant to put up a struggle before letting ourselves be turned out of house and home—which we had built with our own hands, with no assistance from anyone outside, let alone from Governor Puente.

After the Holcombs had gone, we drafted a letter to Puente, enquiring why we were being asked to leave Floreana, since no reason had been given, and pointing out that we had two children born on the island who therefore had Ecuadorian citizenship. Most of the letter was polite and restrained, but Heinz could not help a note of sarcasm creeping in at the end: 'In case Your Excellency should be willing to pay for our return to Germany, so generously permitted, we should be ready to leave the islands, after due compensation for all the work we have carried out on Floreana.' As Mrs Holcomb had suggested, I also wrote to the German Embassy at Quito, enclosing a copy of our letter to Puente, and to the Foreign Office in Berlin, with an urgent request that they should intercede on our behalf.

Heinz and Harry were just clearing a new strip of bush, but after Puente's communication they decided to stop work until this miserable business was settled one way or the other. But we had not even managed to send off any of our letters so far, and unfortunately it was one of those times when no ships came. For nearly two months we were kept on tenterhooks, under constant threat of being driven out of Paradise.

Then at last a ship did call, heralded by young José, Zavala's Indian 'companion of work' or more simply, houseboy. He arrived after sunset, an unusual time for a visit, for there is no twilight on the Equator, it gets dark very quickly as soon as the sun is down. 'A ship!' he shouted from outside our gate. 'A ship!'

I came to meet him in great excitement. 'What sort of a ship?'

'Oh, a beautiful ship, white all over, and with beautiful white sails. She's flying a German flag, Don Ezequiel says, and she's much finer than any yacht I've ever seen. The sails are *so* white.'

Most of the ships which came to the Galapagos Islands had sails that were off-white at best, so José's enthusiasm was understandable. When he had got over it a little, he went on to tell us that 'all Germans from the ship will be coming up to you to-morrow. Señora Maruja said to me, we must let Señora Margarita know about the Germans coming.'

We were still sceptical. Why should a German ship stray so far afield? We hadn't had a single German ship calling here in all our five years on the island. I would like to have dashed down to the beach at once, but it was pitch dark by now; and besides,

poor José gave me a gentle but unmistakable hint that he hadn't
even had any lunch today. So first I had to feed him, as well as
fixing him up with somewhere to sleep, for I couldn't send him
him back to Blackbeach in the dark.

By what he said, the Zavalas sounded as excited about the ship
as I was. I couldn't sleep that night, and was up before sunrise
preparing a festive reception for our first German visitors in
years. I had a fine joint in a casserole on the stove, and all the
morning I was in a fever of impatience. This infected Lump,
who crawled round sniffing and whining as if there were thunder
in the air. Suddenly he lifted his nose, pricked up his ears, listened
a moment, then shot out of the house towards the gate, barking
loudly and joyfully. We didn't yet hear anyone coming.

Then we saw him: a tall man in naval uniform, his broad
shoulders a bit hunched, the blue cap pushed to the back of his
head. He stood at the gate, and introductions were unnecessary.
He knew all about us, and we knew from countless photographs
who he was: Count von Luckner, the famous naval commander
of the 14-18 war.

'Hullo there!' he boomed cheerfully, big laughter lines crink-
ling up his eyes. 'Had to drop in and see how you Cologne old-
timers were doing. Mighty nice place you've got here, I must
say.'

He gripped my hand so hard and shook it so violently that I
felt as if it were dropping off.

'If we'd had any idea it was you, we'd have come down to you
last night,' said Heinz. 'As a matter of fact my wife wanted to
when we heard something about a German ship.'

Luckner laughed. 'Yes, women are like that, aren't they! By
the way, I've brought my wife with me too. Only she'll be a
little behind, she's riding a donkey.'

'How did you come by a donkey?' I asked curiously. 'Did you
bring one with you?'

'Oh no, that family on the coast were very nice and lent us
one. It takes a bit longer than walking, but my wife preferred it,
and the woman is coming up with her.'

They arrived, Maruja leading the donkey. Luckner introduced
us to his wife, also the chief engineer and the first mate of the
Seeteufel. We went into the house, talking away merrily. Poor
Maruja, of course, couldn't understand a word of what we were

saying, but when there was laughter, which was frequent, she joined in with the greatest goodwill.

My special lunch was much appreciated by all, and afterwards, to Maruja's intense admiration, Luckner entertained the company with one or two conjuring tricks and feats of strength for which he had long been celebrated. Then he began regaling us with some of his recent experiences and a fund of delightful anecdotes. The hours passed in a flash, and soon Maruja timidly suggested that she ought to be taking the party back in case the donkey should not find its way in the dark.

Before they went, I told Luckner about the Puente business, showed him the letter and our answer to it. He roared with laughter at both. 'Don't get any grey hairs about that,' he told us, still chuckling. 'We'll have your governor all right. Just leave it to me.' He turned to Heinz, and gave him a terrific thump on the shoulder. 'Come on down to the boat, Wittmer, we'll have a good old evening together. Don't suppose a drop of the hard stuff will hurt you, will it!'

Heinz had wilted slightly under the assault on his shoulder, but was most willing to fall in with this plan. The donkey was saddled, and Luckner's wife kissed baby Inge, whose name was the same as hers, a particularly fond farewell. Then the procession moved off, with her at the head, Maruja leading the donkey once more, then the officers of the *Seeteufel*, and Luckner in the rear with Heinz. 'You will remember to do something about Puente, won't you?' I called after him.

For the last time I heard his great booming laugh. 'I'll take care of that little matter, Frau Grete, don't you give it another thought. I'll radio out a message from the ship tomorrow morning, and pull a few strings in the right places . . . *Auf Wiedersehen*, dear lady, but don't expect your husband back too early—eh, Wittmer?'

Soon they had disappeared from view, and Heinz went to one of the longest evenings of his life. There was a good deal more than a drop of the hard stuff, as we had all guessed, and the next morning when he returned, he was somewhat below par. But it had been very well worth it, he declared emphatically, and indeed the memory of the Luckners' visit kept us going for weeks. It was touching to think they had planned their round-the-world voyage to fit in a call on a solitary German family on a remote Pacific island. Everything seemed brighter somehow, although it now rained almost ceaselessly to make up for the past months of drought.

We felt reassured by Luckner's promise, and thought less about Puente's plans, until one evening in the middle of September. It was pitch dark outside, the rain was beating against the window-panes, and suddenly the dogs began barking furiously. They went on and on in a most menacing way, so that you remembered the wild blood in the veins of Lump's offspring.

Yes, Lump, the sworn enemy of the island's wild dogs, had found a lady friend among them, who had given him a fine litter. We kept some of the puppies, and Lump had brought them up very firmly, so that they were now well-trained house-dogs loyal and devoted with an even keener nose and ear than their father. Sometimes they were almost too good as watch-dogs, so that visitors on their first visit to the Asilo de la Paz often found a rather unpeaceful welcome, and had to retreat up a tree, out of range of the sharp teeth, until we called the dogs to order.

At any rate, they were all barking so hard that September evening, that I eventually went out into the darkness. There stood José, soaking wet and shivering with cold, but almost as excited as he had been a month before when announcing the arrival of the German ship. This time his news was less agreeable. 'El Calderón is here, the government ship from Ecuador, Señor Comandante Puente is on board, el Gobernador del Archipiélago de Galapagos.' He reeled it off in one sentence, like a ritual incantation.

'Come on into the house and warm up a bit,' I told him, and he accepted gratefully.

'The Gobernador himself sent me up here,' he went on, mopping the rain from his face. 'The Señores Alemanes are to come down to Blackbeach Bay at once, the Gobernador has to talk to them urgently, he says.'

We looked at each other, and shook our heads. No one, not even our worthy Gobernador, could make us go down to Black-beach on a pitch-dark night like this. We told José we wouldn't think of it.

'Comandante Puente will be very angry indeed,' he said nervously, no doubt fearing for his own skin if his mission was not accomplished.

'We'll come down tomorrow morning at daybreak,' Heinz then declared. 'That should be quite soon enough.'

José gave us a disapproving look from his black eyes. 'Muy malo, muy malo!' he commented. 'Very bad, very bad!' He quickly became reconciled, however, when I gave him a nice big supper. He ate voraciously, and half an hour afterwards was fast asleep.

At daybreak next morning we were already on the way down to Blackbeach. Of course the governor was an important personage who must not be kept waiting indefinitely. But it seemed that he had waited long enough already, for when we were about half way, near Frido Farm (now more or less wild), we saw the *Calderón* steaming off. We went on down even so, in case Puente had left an answer to our letter or the *Calderón* had brought mail for us.

The first thing we saw was a lot of people, obviously landed here by the *Calderón*, who were rushing about in some confusion or agitation. When the Zavalas saw us approaching, they hurried to meet us and give us a first-hand report of events on the coast. Don Ezequiel was full of pride that his lord and master had deigned to spend the night under his roof—the thatch for which, incidentally, had been made from sugar-cane out of our garden. 'Señor Comandante Puente was very displeased,' he rebuked us, 'that you did not obey his order to come down here last night. But he will be returning to Floreana quite shortly, and then the matter he wrote to you about will be settled.'

We asked about the crowd on the beach, and heard that Puente had followed our island's historic tradition as a penal settlement by sending us a convict. Captain Goyorico had made a bomb in Guayaquil, the thing had exploded, causing a man's death, and he was now to serve his sentence on Floreana, with his wife and eight children to keep him company. It was then the custom in most parts of South America for convicts to be left to fend for themselves as far as food went, unless their families could provide it for them. Puente had fallen in with this custom, believing no doubt that there was a plentiful supply of fruit and vegetables on Floreana, which only had to be picked, not to mention the cattle and pigs. He was even generous enough to tell Gamekeeper Zavala that some of the game shot might be used to provide meat for Goyorico and his family, as no arrangements had been made for them to bring any provisions along. It was easy to see that the convict and the gamekeeper would very soon fall out with each other.

A little way off we saw two other people, a man and a woman. They were carrying crates and luggage from the bay to a bit of high ground a little inland.

'Americanos,' Zavala informed us. 'They want to settle here. They were living on Santiago, but it wasn't a good island to settle on, because there isn't enough water. So Comandante Puente has brought them here.'

Ah, the Conways! We remembered Mrs Holcomb telling us how they had had the same sort of letter as we had, ordering them to leave Santiago. We went over and introduced ourselves, and took a liking to this couple at once. Elmer Conway was tall and powerfully built with a clean-cut open face and twinkling eyes. He was a year younger than Heinz and both had been officers in France during the war, fighting on opposite sides. Frances Conway made quite a contrast with me, for whereas I am on the short and stout side, she was tall and slim, with broad cheekbones, very fair, rather lank hair, light-brown eyes, a straight nose and flashing white teeth of which you saw a lot when she smiled. Our husbands also had this in common: each of them kept a pipe in his mouth almost all the time, which was continually going out and being lighted again throughout the conversation, carried on in a wonderful medley of English, German, French and Spanish. Indeed a strange babel reigned among the international island we had suddenly become. The Conways spoke English and French, we spoke German and a little English and Spanish, Zavala and the Goyoricos were rattling away in Spanish, and José's mother tongue was Quechua, the old original language of Ecuador's Indians.

It was certainly an exciting day for us—in fact, a bit too much all at once. We were rather disturbed by the arrival of a convict with such a large family, but we could only wait to see how things developed; and besides we had a further, more immediate excitement. The *Calderón* had indeed brought us mail, a whole sack full: parcels, letters, postcards, and a pile of newspapers and magazines. It was the first mail for five months. We spent half the night and most of the next day reading it all.

The day after that we had our first visit from the Conways, a visit much enjoyed on both sides. As the original 'island stock,' we were able to give them useful inside information about life on Floreana, and Heinz showed them a good place to settle, quite near us, which was called 'Alta Hacienda,' because there was a regular orchard there planted by former settlers. The matter of food came up over and over again, as was only natural on an island where nothing except perhaps oranges dropped straight into your mouth. Everything had to be worked for, and besides other difficulties you were contending with a rhythm of drought for months at a time followed by immense cloud-bursts. We advised the Conways on the basis of our own experiences, and told them how to avoid some of our early mistakes; where there were language difficulties, we reached a good understanding with miming.

As far as Puente was concerned, their story was pretty much as we expected. The letter he sent them was similar to the one we received, though it did give a reason for their being asked to leave Santiago: the inadequacy of fresh water supplies on the island. They admitted that there was something in this, but told Puente they had received permission from the Ecuadorian government to settle on any of the islands they wished. Therefore, if they were not allowed to stay on Santiago, they refused to move to Chatham or Isabela, but would go to Floreana. Puente was obliged to bring them, and as it clearly upset his plans for our island, he decided to land Goyorico here as well. What with our approach to the German authorities and the fact that we and the Zavalas were no longer the only inhabitants, we felt rather hopeful that Puente would give up trying to remove us.

Right from the start the Conways buckled down to work just as we had done when we arrived five years before. They accepted the conditions they found, did their best to improve them, and it was good to have them on the island. Goyorico and Zavala, however, were at loggerheads as soon as we expected, with Goyorico demanding fruit and vegetables from the Zavalas' garden, saying he and his large family could not live solely on meat; and Zavala telling him to go out into the bush and look for fruit there. The argument was continued incessantly, with no give-and-take on either side.

We did not let their quarrels bother us, especially as we had a new and serious anxiety of our own: Harry was very ill again.

He had not been feeling well for some time, and complained of a heavy feeling in his arms and legs. It might, I thought, be some germ the Goyoricos had brought on to the island. Then he got terrible headaches, and pus started coming from his nose. He had to stay in bed most of the day, and could only get up for an hour or two at a time. He was blinder than ever, though his other senses, always very acute, became extraordinarily strong. He sometimes heard people coming to the house even before the dogs had, and would inform me, for instance, if it was one of the Conways, because he could smell their American cigarettes. However, his illness did not pass, as I had hoped, but got worse and worse. His temperature reached 106, and he could no longer move or feed himself. I had to feed him and stay with him much of the day and night, just when there was so much else to do.

Inge needed a lot of looking after still at eight months, and although Rolf was nearly five, he could hardly give his father much help with the harvest, which now had to be gathered in. It was going to be a fine harvest too, the potato tops were six feet high, and had to be cut down with the *machete* to get to the tubers at all. We were expecting about four tons of potatoes, but we were obliged to pick them in the worst conditions, for the rain was incessant, and we were always getting soaked to the skin and freezing cold.

The rain upset everything. We couldn't afford to sit at home and wait till it was over, and if we wanted warm, dry rooms, we had to fetch our own firewood. With the rain this was always so sodden that it had to be dried out first in the oven if we were not to be almost suffocated by the smoke. But the oven wasn't big enough to dry out the wood we needed, so sometimes we had to put up with the smoke.

Then there was the lack of sleep. I would get up at five in the morning, having sometimes spent most of the night at Harry's bedside. If only a ship would come, I thought, a ship with a doctor—just as I had thought earlier in the year after Inge was born. But the months passed, and no ship came.

'Don't you worry, Mother, there'll be one by Christmas,' Harry assured me one day when he was feeling a little better. 'You know I've got a good sixth sense.'

I laughed. 'Only hope you're right. What'll you bet?'

'I'm not betting—but you wait and see.'

Chapter 12

Rolf was an intelligent and lively little boy, but he did not seem to possess much ear for music. I had been teaching him, trying to teach him, some carols and little songs for Christmas, but one evening a few days before Christmas, as we were all singing them in the boys' bedroom, I was appalled by my lack of success. He was horribly out of tune, but sang so loud it drowned the rest of us. There was such a din, in fact, that we did not even notice the dogs barking uneasily outside. Then we heard loud knocking on the door, our singing broke off in mid-note, and Rolf cried in delight: 'It's Santa Claus!'

It was not Santa Claus, but two officers and some ratings from the American destroyer *Charleston*, which was lying at anchor in Post Office Bay with another destroyer, *Babbitt*.

It was Santa Claus after all, though, for one of the officers said: 'Tomorrow all the officers and some of the crew will be coming up here, and the ships' doctors will be coming too.'

'What did I tell you, Mother?' Harry smiled faintly from the bed.

This was indeed a Christmas present. I was so overjoyed that I emptied out on to a large tray the whole stock of honey-cakes and biscuits I had somehow found time to bake, and offered them to my guests.

The next morning the increased number of guests came as promised, and the path up to the house was thronged with people. I couldn't count them all, but there must have been over sixty. 'Here comes Santa Claus!' one of the leaders called out: they all had rucksacks on their backs, full of presents for us. Heinz's and my bedroom filled up more and more, till there was no longer a bedroom but a small warehouse.

130

Rather incredibly, as it seemed afterwards, I managed to feed this multitude! We had started preparing for the meal the night before, boiling and peeling half a sack of potatoes, and now I had ready a huge dish of potato salad mixed with tomatoes, cucumber, beetroot, slices of egg and pork. For dessert there were enormous piles of pineapple slices, coffee flowed like water, and I had hung up on the veranda three immense bunches of ripe bananas, which our guests had only to reach for. They did so with a will.

Three doctors had come, the ships' doctors from the two destroyers, and Dr Mueller, a leading Panama physician. Unobtrusively, they went into Harry's room and made a thorough examination. When they came out, I could see from their grave and anxious expressions that they were not happy about him. 'Like to show me your spring?' said Dr Mueller, as an excuse to get me on my own. We went out towards the spring, and after a minute or two he began to say what he had to.

'I'm afraid I have very bad news for you. Harry has a form of rheumatic fever, for which no effective drug or treatment has so far been found, even in the United States. Moreover, his heart has been seriously affected, and although I hope he will recover from this attack, and may even be able to work a little again, you will have to be very careful that he does not have the slightest shock or extra excitement, for that might have the very gravest consequences. I think it's only fair to warn you of this now, and I wish I could hold out more hope of a complete cure. But I'll give him some drugs which should put him on his feet again.'

This was grim news indeed, but I had been half expecting something like it, and anyhow it was better than the long uncertainty we had been in before. A partial cure was much better than nothing, and at least Harry would have the best drugs available. Heinz must go down with Mueller to fetch them. At this a thought struck me: how to tell Heinz? 'My husband's heart is also not very strong,' I said to Mueller, 'it's an old trouble dating from the war. How much of what you've told me shall I tell him?'

'He'll have to know sooner or later, won't he?' Mueller replied. 'But of course he too should be spared unnecessary shocks. Break it to him as gently as you can.'

This conversation, on top of entertaining so many people in our house, left me feeling dead tired by the early afternoon. But I kept going until our guests had departed—accompanied by Heinz, poor man, who had to face the seven or eight hours trek to collect the drugs. Mueller had promised that he and the other doctors would spare Heinz as much as possible over what they said to him about Harry.

The next day I broke the news to Heinz as gently as I could, but even so his face turned ashen and he took it very badly. The next few days he was silent and withdrawn as he went off to work, and when he came back in the evenings there was nothing I could think of to restore his cheerfulness. He did not even enjoy the good cigars which had emerged from among the mountain of presents we had been brought by the destroyer. One night I had a long talk with him, insisting that for Harry's sake we must make this a specially happy Christmas. I had been bustling about decorating the Christmas tree and preparing for our festivities. Heinz saw the point, and made a big effort; soon he seemed more his normal self again. Harry was already benefiting from the drugs, so the whole family looked forward to the Christmas celebrations almost as if our troubles were forgotten.

It turned out a happy Christmas after all. For one thing Baby Inge spoke her first words on Christmas morning. 'Mama! Papa!' —We really heard them distinctly for the first time! She looked at us with her bright little eyes, and gave one of her rare little gurgles of laughter. They were rare with us, that is, for she would smile and laugh all the time when she was with Maruja, who would carry her around on her arm to the delight of both. I rarely had leisure for this, though I sometimes took her on the left arm, for instance, when I was making pancakes, stirring the mixture and putting it into the pan with my right hand. However, there was no denying that she adored Maruja, and later that morning we saw a happy beam spread all over her face, as Maruja and Marta appeared.

When I was in Ambato, I had discovered how different the Ecuadorian Christmas was from ours, and the Christmas-tree custom, though it was just beginning to come in, was completely unfamiliar to most of the population. It was not surprising, therefore, that both Maruja and Marta marvelled at our gaily decorated Christmas tree. *Qué lindo! Qué bonito!* they kept

132

repeating. We had put it in the boys' bedroom, so that Harry could enjoy everything with us from his bed.

Soon I had made some coffee, and while we sat at the table, Maruja poured out some of *her* troubles, notably all the insults her noble husband was receiving from the contemptible Captain Goyorico, and the failings of young José, her husband's *'compañiero de trabajo.'* 'He's such a lazy devil of a boy, and won't work at all,' she was complaining for the third or fourth time, when we had a diversion from the arrival of more callers : about fifteen people poured through the gate.

They were from the *San Cristóbal*. I was not too pleased about this invasion on Christmas Day, but true to my secret vow I invited them all in, brewed some coffee and brought out more cakes. My reward came sooner than I expected, for they told us they had come to take the Goyoricos off the island again, which was extremely good news for all concerned, possibly including the Goyoricos themselves.

Directly after the people from the ship had gone, we had another visitor, Mrs Conway. She staggered a little as she came into our Christmas room, and looked as if she had had some sort of shock. But she said nothing about it till she had handed us our presents. Rolf was thrilled beyond measure when he received an airgun, which the Conways had brought with them from the United States. He pressed it lovingly to his chest, declaring proudly: 'Now I can shoot a bull just like Papa can. May I go out and shoot one straight away?' We laughed and were happy with him, but said he should wait till our visitors had gone. Mrs Conway had turned pale again at the word 'bull'; now she began to tell us about her encounter.

'I met a bull on the way here. There he was all of a sudden, standing right in front of me, not moving at all. He was like a statue. I didn't move either. I was paralysed with fright and couldn't even run away. We just stood gaping at each other . . . for what seemed like hours.' Evidently one of them had made way for the other in the end, for Mrs Conway appeared to be unscathed. But she was so agitated at the memory of it that for the moment she couldn't go on with her story. 'What did the bull look like, Mrs Conway?' Heinz asked abruptly.

'Well, he was pretty big, that's the chief thing I remember.'

She thought a bit. 'Oh yes, he was white with black spots, I'm almost sure of that . . .'

She was interrupted by a burst of laughter from the whole family. 'That was Caspar!' cried Harry from the bed.

'Caspar?' Mrs Conway looked bewildered.

'Yes, Caspar. Go on, Papa, you tell her.'

'All right,' said Heinz, 'Caspar and I first met last Christmas. I was coming up from the coast thinking of other things when I was pulled out of my thoughts by a whole lot of bellowing going on rather near me. I crept cautiously forward, and saw three big adult bulls stamping around in a circle. Sometimes when one of them grunted, it looked as if he were telling the others something; and when they bellowed, it was like bullish laughter. Well, as it was Christmas and I remembered the three wise men, I christened the bulls Caspar, Balthasar and Melchior. I'm afraid Balthasar and Melchior went the way of all flesh, which in the case of Floreana bulls meant into the pot. But Caspar and I became good friends, you know, and whenever we meet in the bush, I say hullo to him, he gives me a friendly grunt, then goes on through the bush. The dogs know him now, and don't do anything to him.'

'What about Zavala?' asked Mrs Conway.

'Oh, he leaves Caspar alone too. I suppose he thinks the meat would be too tough. Anyhow, the old boy's quite one of the family now. During the drought this year he used to come up to the fence and drink the water we put in the troughs for our donkeys.'

'Well, thank heavens you've told me all that,' said Mrs Conway. 'It's true he was the first to make a move this morning, but I must say I'd rather lost my nerve after he'd gone. In future I'll always be very polite to him when we meet.'

She kept to this, and both we and the Conways met him very often in the next weeks. 'Hullo, Caspar!' you would call out, at which he would lift his massive head, gaze at you for a moment with his great glassy eyes, grunt a brief acknowledgment and pass on into the bush. But one night he presumed on his friendship too far, breaking into our garden and eating up half our cabbages. The live-and-let-live policy had broken down, so with reluctance we decided that Caspar must follow his friends to become Floreana beef.

Meanwhile we had celebrated Rolf's fifth birthday, and to our great joy Harry was able to get up that day for the first time for weeks and join us at table for the birthday dinner. He was still far from well, but it was a great thing to have him up again. Rolf was already taking an important place in the house, chopping wood, attending to the chickens, and keeping Inge amused. Brother and sister adored each other, we were still the most united of families, and the only thing missing at the birthday party was some greetings from Germany or England. We had not had any mail since the Conways came in September, and we began repeating the same old silly jokes about how lazy the postman was getting and how the post-van must have broken down.

The ship that came at the end of January certainly did us proud. Among the letters in the three sacks of post was an official-looking one from Quito. We opened it at once, and it turned out to be the all-important answer to our appeal from the German Embassy there. This informed us: 'We have made representations on your behalf to the Ecuadorian Government, which has now formally stated that you may stay in Floreana as long as you wish, living in the area of land you have cleared and cultivated.'

We never knew what was the biggest factor in bringing about this splendid reprieve, but the influence exerted by Count von Luckner's personality had probably played a decisive part. We found a letter from him too in one of the sacks, sending us greetings from Australia. He had sailed half way round the world, while we were still on the same little island, an island where we could stay, unmolested, as long as we liked. To complete our joy, we found another letter, right at the bottom of one of the sacks, which told us that Puente himself had been replaced as governor. His successor was already on the way to Chatham. Better and better: Heinz decided we must celebrate the occasion with some of our home-distilled brandy. We didn't make large quantities of it at the moment, but this was definitely an occasion to bring it out.

Zavala was now without his great patron, but this seemed to worry him less than the escapades of the work-shy José. The Indian boy's latest habit was to disappear into the bush, where he could find plenty of fruit and at least as soft a sleeping-place as the bare boards chez Zavala (though the Zavalas were now build-

135

ing a proper house). José would roam round the island for two or three days, living free and unrestrained as his ancestors had done before Europeans came to the Americas; and although Zavala kept on catching him and locking him up, José became more and more clever at absconding. Soon he was away for ten days at a time, the bush had swallowed him up completely; and we noticed that every morning some papaws were missing from our garden.

This was no irreplaceable loss, but it irritated us and was rather a mystery. We couldn't be sure it was José at first, and we thought he would have been afraid of the dogs. But dogs themselves could hardly be the culprits, nor our cat, Puchito, for all the thieving habits which had earned for her the surname of Ladrón. It was the custom in Ecuador to give your animals surnames, and we really didn't feel like calling her Puchito Wittmer. She would pinch meat from a frying pan or eggs from a nest, anything that came within reach of her long paws and sharp teeth.

I had found her wild in the bush while she was still a kitten, and although I got badly scratched, I brought her home to protect our garden from the depredations of sparrows and doves. They would come in swarms and almost steal grains of seed out of our hands. Once when we carelessly left a sack of sugar outside, the sparrows fell on it and quickly riddled it with holes, each picking his own, which was evidently a point of honour among Galapagos sparrows. At any rate Puchito (we called her that at first, and only added the derogatory name later) was tolerated as a sworn enemy of the sparrows despite her own delinquent tendencies; and to return to our present problem, she would hardly take papaws off trees. It must be a human delinquent after all.

We informed Zavala, who came with his daughter to keep watch on our garden. Marta hid in the sugar-cane field, while Zavala climbed an orange tree. As it began to get dark, José came strolling into the garden. He was obviously familiar with our habits and knew we should be in the house having our evening meal. He walked up and down, feeling the pineapples, picking those he felt were ripe enough, and putting them in a sack he had brought. Then he turned to the bananas, looking over the single bunches, pushing the leaves aside with a long stick to see if he had missed any ripe bunch, and again harvesting whatever his connoisseur's eye deemed fit. Then he went on to the papaw trees, where the fruit was all ripe, and began filling his sack. This was the moment Zavala had waited for. He leapt down from his orange tree and dashed towards José. The boy at once dropped stick and sack and papaws, and fled, but the long-legged Zavala soon caught up with him, tied his hands behind his back with a strap of cowhide, and dragged him back to the house in triumphant pride.

We asked Zavala and his daughter to stay for some supper, which he accepted with alacrity. But when I wanted to give the weeping José something. Zavala insisted: *No una bocada!*— not a single mouthful. With his coffee he smoked his usual cigarette, which was tobacco rolled up in newspaper, then his donkeys were saddled. He rode first, then Marta, while José was to walk in between tied to the head of Zavala's saddle.

When they got down to Blackbeach, as we heard later, José was first thrashed, then made to bathe in the sea where the salt water would get into the weals. Then his shirt and trousers were taken away so that he shouldn't escape again. But a few weeks later he managed it nevertheless, and this time Zavala did not catch him. Eventually he was taken away from the island, and was sent to the Ecuadorian equivalent of a reform school. He may have been 'a bad lot,' but we did not care for Zavala's repressive methods of discipline.

After the loss of José Zavala decided to go in for fishing, and he got over a boy of about twenty from one of the other islands to act as his mate. He had no boat himself, but used a boat of ours which a friend had obtained for us and we kept at Black-beach. He did not ask for permission to use it, but perhaps regarded this as one of the Harbour Commander's 'perks': not very friendly of him, but there seemed little point in making a fuss. Sergio seemed a pleasant youth, and it was he who brought us news of our most important 'caller' yet.

At the end of July, 1938, I was working in the garden, with Rolf playing near me, when I heard a zooming noise overhead. Leaving everything, I rushed up to 'Olympus,' and from the little hill could see two big aeroplanes heading directly, as it seemed, for the Asilo de la Paz, in other words for us. Heinz and Harry had also heard them coming, and joined me on Olympus. They wheeled a few times right above our heads, then flew off in a wide arc, to come back and circle over us again. Then we saw something being dropped from one of them.

For five minutes or so we could hear the roar of their engines. They were still somewhere over Floreana, though soon there was only a faint rumbling in the distance, as when they had come, and then nothing but a vibration in the air, which scarcely penetrated to our ears but which we imagined we could still hear long after all was silent again. The silence was deep and oppressive. For a long time we stood on the hill looking in the direction from which the planes had come, wondering what they had come for and what they had dropped. Unfortunately we had been too fascinated to take our eyes off them, and so had failed to mark the exact spot where the package must have come down. Despite frantic searching we never found it; and we spent a restless evening speculating on solutions to the mystery without any real clues to help us.

The next morning, just as we were finishing breakfast, Sergio came panting in waving two letters. He was too out of breath to divulge his news, but kept the letters in his hand, and I saw his eyes going towards a joint of cold pork on the table. 'I'll find you some breakfast, Sergio,' I told him, getting up from my chair, 'but for heaven's sake tell us what you've come about and what those letters are. Are they for us?'

'Yes, they're for you.' He put them down on the table, and Heinz and I snatched up a letter each. I tore open my envelope with trembling fingers, and collapsed into the chair with shock. The letter I was holding was signed 'Franklin D. Roosevelt.' 'What is it, Mutti?' cried Rolf. 'You look all funny, are you all right?'

'Yes, thanks, Rolf,' I gasped, 'I think I'm all right, as long as I'm not dreaming. Just pinch me, will you, so that I can be sure I'm awake.'

Rolf obliged. I was not dreaming. This was a letter from the President of the United States of America.

'I am on board the United States cruiser *Houston*,' the President wrote, 'and we were anchored outside Post Office Bay. I radioed two of our escort planes to fly above your farm with a signal that we would cruise off Blackbeach, so I hoped you would come down there and we could take you out to the *Houston* in a launch. But she was there two hours without your turning up, so I'm afraid we had to go on to Isabela. However, I shall hope to make your acquaintance some other time, and as a little souvenir of my visit I have had two crates left at Post Office Bay, the contents of which I expect you will find useful. Sincerely yours, Franklin D. Roosevelt.'

I looked at Heinz, who was staring across the room as if stunned. He handed me the second letter, the one he had opened; it was from our old friend Professor Waldo Schmitt, Curator of the United States National Museum at Washington. I tried to compose myself in order to read it.

'My dear Wittmers,' it read, 'I am here with the President aboard a large American cruiser, the *Houston*. We have been collecting specimens on the islands—we have already got a lot of fine things for the Museum, including a number of different animals we hadn't managed to get on any of the Hancock cruises. I am so sorry I had no opportunity to warn you of this visit, but when I told the President about you and your life on Floreana, he said he would like to meet you, and then it was too late to give you any notice.

'Then we saw a big cloud of smoke at Blackbeach as we were passing on our way to Post Office Bay, and I was very worried, thinking something might have happened to you. Some of the officers and the ship's doctor and I went ashore in a launch and tried the trail up from Post Office Bay. But it was not well enough marked—you may recall I suggested your doing something about this when I last saw you—so we went round to Blackbeach in case you should happen to have seen the ship and gone down there. But we found nothing but a heap of ashes and one small house which was all locked up—no sign of life at all. We returned to the cruiser, and the President ordered two planes to fly over your farm, while the *Houston* herself sailed round Blackbeach, and we landed there in the launch. This time we saw Mr and Mrs Conway and a young Ecuadorian, who explained to us about the smoke. Unfortunately, we couldn't wait any longer, so I had to go off without seeing you, which is a real shame. However, I was very much relieved to hear from the Conways that you were all well, and perhaps I'll be able to get over to Floreana again quite soon. All the supplies are a gift to you from the President, who wanted to leave a little something . . .'

'A little something!' I exclaimed. 'A little something from the President of the United States.'

'You two aren't being fair,' Harry protested. 'What on earth is it all about?'

'Quite right,' I admitted, and gave the children the gist of the two letters.

'And he waited there two hours just to see us!' marvelled Harry. 'Oh, if only we'd found that signal they dropped out of the plane! What a terrific opportunity wasted.'

'Yes, it's infuriating,' Heinz agreed. 'Still, he said he hoped to see us some time, and anyhow he's left us a souvenir.'

I nodded. 'Talking of that, isn't it about time somebody went down to Post Office Bay and saw what he *has* left us?'

'It certainly is,' said Heinz. 'I'll go and get Hannes at once.' Hannes was our donkey.

'Can I come too, Papa?' Rolf demanded eagerly. 'Oh, please let me. I've never been to Post Office Bay.'

'All right,' said his father. 'You can ride on Hannes going down there—but you may have to walk some of the way back. I don't suppose Hannes will be able to carry you *and* the crates.'

So Heinz set off, with Rolf on the donkey. About an hour from the coast they found on the track a bunch of sticks tied together, stuck between some rocks, from which waved three white sheets of paper, like small flags. They could not miss the sheets, which had messages written in large black letters with a thick pencil. One said: 'Supplies in tank for the Wittmer family. Compliments of the President of the United States—U.S.S. *Houston*.'

The second, with a letter-heading from the United States National Museum, said: 'Mr Wittmer, in the large tank uphill from . . . (this word indecipherable) are some supplies that the President of the United States directed us to leave for you. Greetings Commander Callaghan and party.' At the bottom were the familiar initials W.S., and on a third sheet Waldo Schmitt had written in German, in case Heinz's English should not be up to the first two messages: 'We couldn't come any further, there wasn't time. We're all very sorry. Below are a few things we have left for you from the President of the United States. Your old friend Waldo Schmitt.'

Heinz and Rolf went on towards the coast until they discovered a metal container with the crates in. Rolf sniffed around eagerly. 'I think I can smell chocolate!' he cried.

There was clearly a lot more besides chocolate. They broke open the crates, and duly loaded Hannes with the contents. As Heinz had warned Rolf, this was quite enough for the donkey to carry, so Rolf had to walk home, which was a good long walk for a boy of five and a half. But the thought of the chocolate and so many other good things kept him going cheerfully. Heinz told me afterwards he did not whine once. If he occasionally asked: 'Are we nearly home yet, Papa?' that was surely excusable.

They did not get home till late in the evening, when a tired but proud Rolf rushed in to gabble at me all the things he had seen being unpacked. But he was so excited I couldn't take it in. The table nearly broke under the weight of what we emptied on to it: tins of milk, butter and sugar, two bottles of whisky, two bottles of Rhine wine (how very considerate), medicines, cotton wool, gauze, a whole crate full of chocolate (so Rolf had smelt correctly!), and even useful small things like new ribbons for my typewriter. I could only shake my head in wonder and delight. President Roosevelt must have been very familiar with our circumstances, and the sort of things we should want.

As to the cloud of smoke, the Zavalas later explained the answer to that mystery. On seeing the cruiser, they made a big fire from dried branches to show where she could anchor outside Blackbeach. But the bay was far too small to give a good anchorage for the cruiser, so she went first to Post Office Bay.

We were immensely moved by the friendship Waldo Schmitt had shown us, and both Heinz and I wrote him long letters telling him how grateful we were for all the supplies, and asking him to pass on our thanks to the President. The letters, as usual, took some time between their writing and their collection and delivery, but he eventually received them, and in his answer said: 'I deserve very little credit for the gift. We had talked about you and your adventures on board and how much you would appreciate a few things of the sort that he left you. That was some days before we got to Floreana. When we arrived there, I was very pleasantly surprised to have the supply clerk on the ship hand me a list of things that the President suggested and ask me if there was anything else should be added . . .'

Waldo thought we should write a word of thanks to the President himself, and this we at once did. We never in fact had another chance of meeting him, and all our lives we shall regret having missed this chance. Nevertheless, he had called at Floreana specially to see us, had brought us wonderful presents which he had personally selected: the memory of that we shall equally treasure all our lives.

Chapter 13

The visit of the V.I.P. to Floreana certainly enhanced our prestige with the Zavalas, but we soon became involved against our will in a family crisis of theirs. It started only a few days after the *Houston's* departure, when Maruja burst into our house in a state of great agitation. She was followed by her husband, who maintained most of the time the silence of injured dignity.

Did I know the latest news, she demanded hysterically between sobs. I said I did not, and she then poured out in Spanish a torrent of explanation, lamentation and abuse, from which I at last gathered that her daughter Marta had gone off into the bush with Sergio the young fisherman.

In itself there was nothing sensational about this, for according to Maruja herself it was a regular custom on the islands and in the mountains of Ecuador: even in the best families a girl often eloped into the bush with her 'intended,' taking any food either of them could lay hands on. When this ran out, they would hang empty tins on a bush or tree to indicate that additional supplies were urgently needed. If the girl's family still objected to the union, they would ignore the appeal, in which case she generally went home resigned to the loss of her young man. But if they were sympathetic, as more often happened, they would either hang on the same tree or bush the supplies needed, or else just fix a note to it asking the young couple to 'return, all is forgiven' so that the wedding could be celebrated. That shortened the proceedings considerably, and also the period of pre-marital honeymoon.

After hearing this, Heinz was preparing to congratulate her on her future son-in-law, and I asked her why she was so upset if it was often done.

'It may be done in Ecuador and the other islands,' she cried indignantly, 'but not on Floreana, not in my house anyhow. For one thing, who is this Sergio? He's got no possessions at all, no shoes, no socks. I don't believe he has any clothes at all but the ones he's standing up in. What sort of a husband is that for my Marta?'

'But good heavens,' I said, 'is it all so important? They're both young, and can make their own lives, build up something, just as we've done. And after all, Marta herself isn't a great heiress, is she now?'

As I at once realised, this was not the most tactful thing I could have said to the Zavalas, and it was all I could do to mollify them a little by offering some of the excellent whisky President Roosevelt had sent our way.

Even the thought of the President seemed to rub salt in their wounds. 'No!' raged Maruja. 'This wretched pauper shall never have my Marta. Anything that happens here always gets into the American papers, and what will the Americans say, what will His Excellency President Roosevelt say, when he hears that all the tins of food he presented have been taken off into the bush by this whippersnapper, not leaving us any at all? It's absolutely scandalous.'

I gradually realised that they might be more aggrieved over the loss of the tins than over the possible loss of a daughter. 'But there's sure to be a boat in some time bringing you more supplies,' I ventured. 'And if you asked them to come home, they might still have some of the tins left. Anyhow, isn't it really the main thing that they love one another?'

It was no good. 'I don't care a rap about that,' declared Zavala, speaking for the first time. 'I shall never give my consent to this marriage. Never.'

There was clearly nothing more we could say, and afterwards the Zavalas went off to the Conways, hoping perhaps to find a more sympathetic audience. But the Conways felt the same as we did, and believed like us that the angry parents would soon relent.

Two days later the young couple hung out their empty tins on a tree, to which Zavala replied by fixing the traditional note asking them to return home. All unsuspecting, they accepted this invitation, and walked hand in hand to the Zavala house rejoicing that their love had won the day. But before they even reached the house, Zavala and Maruja pounced on them. She snatched her daughter away from Sergio before he could say a word; then she and Zavala began belabouring him with sticks.

Sergio fled to the Conways and spent the night in their house, asking if they would go down to Blackbeach with him the next morning and intercede for him with Marta's parents. The Conways agreed, but they were met at the door by Maruja with a flood of denunciation. Once when she paused for breath, Sergio himself remarked quietly: 'It's the done thing in our country, you know.'

'Not on our island, it isn't!' she screamed. 'Millionaires and Counts and even Presidents come to visit Floreana. What will people like that think if they hear that Don Ezequiel tolerates such *barbarismo*?'

Don Ezequiel showed no signs of tolerating it. He came to the door himself and threw Sergio's few possessions at the boy's feet, crying: 'Never let me see you come to this house again.'

The Conways had no room in their small house to put Sergio up till a ship came, so we let him move into our pirates' cave and former 'residence.' He paid for his keep by working in the garden.

When Maruja heard this, she was furious with us. 'You are supposed to be friends of ours, yet you take in our enemies! It's simply not done.'

'What did you expect Sergio to do if we hadn't taken him in?' I asked mildly. 'We don't get a ship calling every day, you know. Was he to stand on the beach for weeks or months waiting for one to come?'

Perhaps we had spoilt our 'friendship,' for Maruja flounced off, and Sergio stayed with us till a ship came which could take him to Chatham.

As to Marta, she ran off with a soldier two years later, when there was a ship from Chatham in the Bay. Zavala was drinking hard that evening with the ship's crew, and when he woke next morning his daughter had gone. Strangely enough, he merely shrugged his shoulders at this elopement. Marta was equally unlucky, however, with her second young man, who deserted her after six weeks to marry another girl quite officially. She had further 'early honeymoons,' which took her to the mainland; and thereafter her parents lost touch with her completely.

In an island like Floreana, where there were not a dozen inhabitants, the occurrence of some small tragedy or family quarrel inevitably took on an importance out of proportion to its merits, even for us who stood largely outside it. It rarely occurred to us that our own lives were lacking in 'drama.' We were always glad, of course, of the distraction offered by a ship's calling, especially when old friends were on board. But we did not pine to have the humdrum rhythm of our daily lives disturbed. We welcomed that rhythm because it gave us peace and serenity—even though it also meant unremitting hard work with no holidays or long week-ends!

By the time I got up, at half past five, Harry would have put on the water for coffee, and he and Heinz would be in the bush to load their backs with firewood, take it home and chop it up. Then we all had coffee before starting on the daily round.

My first job was to see to the chickens. Although from January to May was the best time for rearing pullets, they needed a lot of attention then, for the hens were always pecking at each other's chicks, and would kill them off if you didn't stop them. The cocks fought among themselves too, of course, and their combs were generally covered with blood.

After that I went to the pigsty, where I was greeted with great squealing, as soon as the pigs heard the clatter of their bucket. Their food was usually green bananas, yucca or otoi tubers which had been boiled with some bones and a little salt the afternoon before in a big old petrol can on a special stone hearth.

Heinz was meanwhile making a morning round of the 'estate' with the dogs, seeing if the wild cattle, which still troubled us as much as ever, had broken in the fence overnight and done any damage to the plantation, in which case repairs must be done during the day.

Then it was time for a proper breakfast. Our bread was 'home-baked,' the flour being made from either wheat flour or corn-meal. Wheat grew on the island, but the sparrows usually picked off most of it, despite the efforts of Puchito Ladrón, before we had started gathering it in; so our wheat had to be bought from ships coming from the mainland. When there wasn't a ship for months and we ran out of flour, I sometimes fried green bananas instead of baking bread. You cut them in slices, fried them in fat until brown, and sprinkled salt over them as soon as they were done; they were very nourishing and tasted excellent. Other days there was hot corn bread, fried in the pan like small pancakes. For spreading on our bread we had pork dripping (when there was no gift butter), jam (which I made from guavas or papaws with bananas and pineapple), also sausage and cold beef.

It had taken a great deal of work before cow, calf or pig meat was ready for the table. Heinz had to go into the bush on a hunting expedition, and he couldn't afford a day off every week for that. When he had shot his animal, it had to be skinned, gutted, taken home and cut up. Then most of it had to be put in salt and afterwards smoked, all in twenty-four hours at most; for in our climate (without a refrigerator) meat would not keep longer than that.

Again, to preserve the meat needed a terrific amount of salt, and getting that was also a considerable operation. Our predecessors on Floreana, the Norwegians who had come in 1927, intended to start a fishing and canning business. They soon gave up, but we inherited from them the salt holes which had been made in a big salt lake about five hours away from us. These holes had to be cleaned out after the rainy season, and the saline in them dried up during the next months under the blazing sun, to form a crust of salt. This was 'ready for harvest' at the end of November or beginning of December, but you couldn't take more than fifty pounds on your back at a time, so Heinz and Harry had to make the ten-hour trek, on a miserable stony track, several times over—five hours there, and five hours back, loaded with salt. Still, when that was done, we had our store of salt for the next months, both for cooking and for salting the meat.

We grew our own coffee, of course, but we drank it much faster than we grew it. It was five years after the little trees were planted before the first coffee beans could be harvested; and here again we had to do most of the work by hand. When the fruit turned scarlet, we knew they were ripe for picking, after which we dried them in the sun, turning them over several times a day. Then we pressed them through rollers to break the dried pulp of the fruit so that the actual beans came out. Then the whole mixture was exposed to the wind so that the pulp got blown away. After this the beans could at last be roasted.

Sugar-cane was one of our best crops, the plants themselves grew very quickly. Every four weeks the leaves had to be pruned when they began to turn brown, so that the sugar ripened faster. When it was ripe, the canes had to be cut close to the ground with a *machete* and taken to our home-made sugar-press. The juicy canes were very heavy, and you couldn't carry more than ten or fifteen at a time.

When it came to the pressing, we used our donkeys as substitute for a motor. They were tied to the press, and had to turn round and round like horses for grandfather's threshing machine. The juice extracted was caught and then boiled in a large container, till the liquid sugar had turned to a thick syrup. The whole process meant a heap of work, and also took an enormous amount of firewood. Harry would push the cane in, Rolf was already trained to drive the donkey, and I stood at the big boiler watching that the sugar should not boil over, or worse still, burn. This happened if you left it boiling a second too long, when all your work was completely wasted. At just the right moment you had to tear the burning log out of the fire hole, then pour the stiff syrup into another big, cold copper and keep on beating it with a wooden shovel till the whole mass became firm sugar. While still hot, it was turned out into wooden moulds, rinsed beforehand with cold water. Then when the sugar was cold, you wrapped the hard brown sugar 'bricks,' each weighing about three pounds, in dry banana leaves, protecting them from damp so that they would keep a long time.

Meat, coffee, sugar, salt, everything that went on to the table, was obtained and prepared only by our own labours. I sometimes reflected how much everything is taken for granted in civilisation, how little people think about the mass of work and worry and effort, of mistakes and setbacks, that go into the food they buy in shops and put on the breakfast table.

After breakfast, between about eight and nine, the 'menfolk' —usually including Rolf—would go off to work, often clearing new land, chopping trees and bushes, digging up the roots and trunks, and working over the cleared ground. It was a laborious business, with hands often replacing tools, and they were all nice and hungry at midday when they returned for dinner after a bathe in the cool spring water. During the morning I had been doing my housework and cooking, like any ordinary housewife, except that I had fewer 'gadgets' to lighten my work.

After the meal the children rested—Harry also needed a rest, although he was very much better—and then there was more work in the plantation, trimming maize, potatoes, sugar-cane and pineapple, and struggling to keep down the weeds, which grew with a profusion and speed far exceeding the worst experiences of suburban gardeners. I worked most of the afternoon in my vegetable garden and with the poultry, which never left me unemployed either!

The sun goes down quickly near the Equator, and it was already dark about six when we were having supper. After supper there would still be beans, peas and maize to shell, and some sewing and darning for me—because clothes were always getting torn in the bush. Rolf would have a story read to him before he went to bed, and then Heinz would go on reading out loud to Harry and me, either from one of our books or from some periodical we had been sent—perhaps months or even years old. Outside there was silence except for the occasional bray of a donkey or the lowing of cattle. The Asilo de la Paz was wrapped in a deep evening peace. The day was over, so much like the day of a family of small farmers anywhere in the world, and yet different because of its long weeks of complete isolation when no ship came. We did not mind this isolation and solitude. It was the life we had chosen ourselves, and on the whole we were well content.

Chapter 14

Rolf's sixth birthday, January 2nd, 1939, had a very exciting finish to it. In the early evening he came bursting into the house, flushed with excitement and so breathless he could scarcely speak. 'Mutti, Mutti,' he cried. 'Harry's caught such a great big calf. He wants Papa to come at once with more rope.'

Heinz equipped himself with the rope and ran off into the bush, Rolf panting after him. There indeed was the calf. The cow had abandoned her, Harry told them, on seeing the dogs. He had quickly put a rope round her neck, and the two dogs were helping guard her till Heinz came.

Quite soon they had brought her home. She was a sturdy well-built calf with a red hide and a white blaze, very wild at present, but we were determined to tame her. We christened her Barbara, and every day I cooked plenty of sweet potatoes and cornmeal for the new member of our family.

The first day only Heinz could hold the bucket while feeding her. But after a few days she was already quite tame, and soon she would let us all touch and stroke her. As soon as she heard the bucket clattering along, Barbara would come hurrying towards it to fetch her food, just like the pigs when I went with their swill.

Three months later Heinz and Harry caught a pitch-black bull-calf. With this pair we had started our cattle-breeding, and in our imagination we were already swimming in milk and butter —although Barbara was still very young, and it would be three years before we could expect any butter from her.

One long-term problem, incidentally, had shown signs of solving itself: that of Rolf's schooling—just as my confident husband had so light-heartedly predicted in the first year of the boy's life. Heinz varied his evening stories with tales of the past and of the big world outside Floreana; in other words, he was giving Rolf a first grounding in history and geography, which he was intending to develop as the boy got older. I managed to supply some elementary lessons in reading and writing, and as for arithmetic Harry was a marvellous teacher for his young brother: when he and Rolf were out in the bush together, he would make Rolf count and do little sums in his head. It was a strange makeshift kindergarten, which yet covered 'the three Rs' and a great deal of practical knowledge besides. But better still, there was now a school on Chatham, and we hoped in due course to send Rolf to that.

The school had been built by Señor Alvear, the enlightened governor of the Galapagos Islands who had succeeded Puente. His wife's parents were German, and though born in Ecuador she had been brought up in Europe. The Alvears were a fine cultured pair, I was amazed at the amount they had read; when they came to see us we had long talks about European music and literature, which was understandably outside the intellectual range of most people in Ecuador. We couldn't have wished for a better governor. He had built the first hospital on the islands as well as the school, and was always anxious to improve conditions of life for the islanders. He showed no less concern for the well-being of foreigners like ourselves, and came to Floreana every two or three months to see how we were getting on. He was full of admiration for our thriving farm, which was naturally pleasant for us to hear, and once he said: 'You have everything you need to make a really happy life, and I can see you *are* happy. I congratulate you.'

The only thing which disturbed us a little was that on one visit he told us that Floreana was going to become a military station with an officer and nine men; this was to be established in July. July passed, however, without any signs of it, and though we knew from irregular newspapers and letters that there was bad trouble in Europe, though we still remembered the warnings of that Polish doctor from the *Dar Pomorza* about rumblings under the surface, it was all too far away for us to take it quite seriously.

On 2nd September I was just getting supper when Rolf charged into the kitchen. 'We've been up on Olympus,' he said excitedly, 'and there we saw a whole lot of men coming up from Blackbeach.'

'Men?' I asked. 'What sort of men?'

'I don't know,' he answered, 'but there were lots of them.'

I heard the dogs barking uneasily. 'Go into the garden and let Papa know,' I told him.

They dashed off, and half an hour later our visitors had arrived, accompanied by Heinz, who had met them on the way. They were the crew of the American fishing boat *Paramount*. 'We really want some fresh meat,' her skipper said. 'Only we can't stay long, because we're having fine catches and ought to get on with our fishing as soon as possible.'

'I'll go out hunting tomorrow morning,' Heinz promised. We were always glad to earn a little in cash or kind by selling something to a ship's crew. Besides meat, when Heinz had a successful day's hunt, we could offer bananas and fresh fruit and vegetables, even a few chickens. Sometimes instead of getting paid we would barter against things we urgently needed.

Being unprepared for guests, I could only give them a modest supper, but the ten men were ready to take pot luck, and after the meal we sat for a long time by the fire. We needed a fire because the weather was distinctly cold; the beginning of September was generally the coldest time on Floreana.

When we had people in the house after weeks of solitude, we were used to cheerful conversation flowing without any difficulty. This evening it dragged badly, there were long silences, and the men seemed depressed. 'Is there anything the matter?' I asked eventually.

'Not for us.' The skipper drew thoughtfully once or twice at his pipe. 'But I'm afraid things look bad for you at home. War may break out any time.'

He told us a little about the international situation, enough to make us very worried, but not enough—he may have been sparing us deliberately—for us to believe the worst could happen. The head of our country's government, whatever disgraceful things he might have done, was surely not mad enough to plunge the world into war: no, it was incredible. With such reflections Heinz and I tried to comfort ourselves, as we tried in vain to get to sleep that night; but the next morning there was so much to do that we were able to forget our fears. Heinz went hunting with some of the crew, and they had a successful day, coming back with a big bull. Anything that our donkey couldn't carry, the sturdy fishermen took down to the shore on their backs. The skipper paid for vegetables and chickens in dollars, for fruit and meat in kind: we got things we badly needed, soap, milk, and working trousers for Heinz and Harry. Finally, I bartered four working shirts for two Alsatian puppies.

The crew of the *Paramount* departed, with the grim word 'war' left hanging in the air. I was only a girl during the terrible conflagration which started in 1914, but I had vivid memories of broken families with menfolk dead, wounded or missing, and I had adult experience of the aftermath of poverty and misery in my defeated country. According to the little we had read, another world war would be far more terrible, whole cities would be razed to the ground; and this time even my loyalties were divided. My father and stepmother with her three daughters were still in Cologne, and there were many friends there for whose safety Heinz and I feared if war came. But my sister was in England, a sworn enemy of all the Nazi party stood for, one of those who believed that there could never be real peace while that party was ruling Germany. So much I had read between the lines in her letters, but should I be getting those letters any more, should I now be completely cut off from her? What would our own position be? Heinz had been a regular officer in the last war, what would the German government demand of him? Heaven only knew the answer to these questions. For the moment we could only wait and see, hoping the lunacy of another war might somehow be averted.

We had a long moment to wait, for it was nearly three months before the next ship called with news of the outside world. By that time we had finished picking the potatoes—eighty sacks, a very satisfactory crop—and were looking forward to Christmas; Heinz and I had big plans for presents for the children. The Zavalas had long 'forgiven' us for having harboured Sergio, but they and we went our separate ways, and we saw little of them. It was therefore rather a surprise, one Sunday afternoon at the end of November, to see Maruja and Marta approaching the house. As they came nearer, they began making agitated gestures, so that I thought we were in for some new family drama.

Maruja was almost in tears, which made it even more difficult than usual to follow her rapid flow of Spanish, but I kept hearing the one word: *Guerra. Guerra.*

Guerra? Often as we had thought and talked of war in the last weeks, it still seemed remote and unreal. Now I felt as if the catastrophe had already come to the shores of Floreana.

'*En Europa, Señora Margarita. En Europa.*'

'*En Europa,*' I echoed in a dazed way, and for a minute or two felt completely sick. When I had recovered a little, I asked Maruja for more details, but she was now sobbing uncontrollably, so that it was some time before I could grasp what she was trying to tell me. Apparently the *Calderón* had been there, and besides the grim news and a lot of mail, had brought the Ecuadorian soldiers for the military station, together with builders who were to put up houses for them in Post Office Bay.

Heinz had been working in the garden when Maruja and Marta arrived. He came in and heard Maruja's tearful ramblings. She was too excited to give us the packet of mail she had brought up for us, but Heinz now quietly opened this, and snatched up the newspapers first of all. They dated from the end of September, and we raced through the front page news. The *Blitzkrieg* against Poland was over, we read, and there was now a lull in the fighting everywhere; but there was no sign that the war with England and France was over. When we came to the letters, there was a short one from my sister, saying she might not be in a position to write to me much after this, and that people in England were preparing for a war of attrition, which might go on for years. She sent all her love, and promised to do her best to keep in touch.

Apart from anxieties about what might have happened in Europe since the end of September, our own position seemed alarmingly insecure. I worried a great deal and got bad headaches, while Heinz maintained an outward calm which I felt was somehow forced.

We already began to feel the effects of the war in Europe, for the Galapagos Islands became a favourite port of call for American warships. The United States were preparing for all eventualities, since it seemed only too probable that the war would not be confined to Europe; there were even rumours of American bases being planned on the islands, which after all were only a thousand miles or so from the Panama Canal. Our American visitors had often stressed the importance of the Canal to their country's economic life and also to its strategic defence: the Galapagos, as we could easily see from the map, might be a vital part of that defence on the Pacific side.

The Conways too were thrown into great uncertainty. Elmer Conway, like Heinz, was on the officer reserve, and had to hold himself in readiness for mobilisation. They had cleared an immense amount of land in their two years on Floreana, and it was developing into a fine plantation. Now they stopped all further clearing operations, but of course had plenty of work looking after the land they already had under cultivation.

Heinz decided to do the same, saying this would keep us quite busy enough till we saw what was going to happen. He insisted, however, on going ahead with our Christmas plans, just in case this might be the last we had together. It was the first year that Inge would really appreciate Christmas as such, and after long discussion, way back in October, Heinz and I had decided to give her a doll.

That is not quite accurate. I had said: 'The nicest thing I can think of for Inge would be a doll.' After the traditional 'all right, go and buy one then,' Heinz remarked: 'I think we'd better make one ourselves. We've managed to produce most things we wanted, why shouldn't we succeed with a doll?'

'That's fine,' I said. 'I'm sure we can do it.'

So he searched in the bush for some wood to cut the doll's head from. The wood from the lechoso tree seemed the most suitable. Most of November, when the rest of us were in bed, he stayed up into the small hours, with the hurricane lamp burning low as he carved a wonderful doll's head with nice wavy hair. We painted her eyes blue, and fitted the head to a body I had cut out, sewn together and stuffed with wood shavings. I also sewed some doll's clothes, and Heinz made a little bed, which he coloured with some remnants of pink we scraped from an old paint pot. It was a beautiful doll, and Heinz finished making the bed after we had our news that Germany was at war. I was glad he did, for as I sewed little blankets and pillows for the doll's bed, I found myself forgetting that news for a while and thinking only what a splendid surprise we had for our darling Inge. I began looking forward to Christmas again as if the world were still at peace.

All three children were going to get a pair of the favourite and imperishable sealskin *Lederhosen*. Heinz had been down to Post Office Bay and gone over the causeway to the tiny 'seal island' of Loveria, half a mile away, where he shot a few sea-lion cubs. He returned that evening extremely tired, carrying the skins, which we cleaned up and put into the tannin solution we had ready. The bark of the guava tree was the best substitute we could find for alum. We shaved it off the trunks, dried it, and ground it up as best we could, then boiled it in hot water and left it standing for several days. The skins stayed in this home-made tannin for several weeks, by which time they were thoroughly tanned and had become proper leather. The leather was well rinsed in fresh water, dried in the shade, and drawn over a log till it got supple. It became so beautifully soft that after Heinz had cut it into trouser lengths I could sew them by hand without too much trouble. True, the needle sometimes broke, which was quite a minor tragedy for us, but the *Lederhosen* were ready in time.

This was going to be a really special Christmas. Perhaps we said that every year, but this year, alas, it had the 'special-ness' of our uncertain future. We picked heaps of flowers, and spread them in vases all over the house, where their scent mingled with the delicious aroma of Christmas baking. The summery weather still didn't fit into European conceptions of Christmas, but these were anyhow completely unfamiliar to Rolf and Inge. I once tried to tell Inge what snow meant, but at the end of my explanations, both in words and with elaborate gestures of hands and feet, she was clearly baffled still. You can't make a child of the tropics understand snow.

For Christmas Eve we had our traditional roast pork, and sat over the meal till sundown. When it was completely dark, we all went up on 'Olympus' to light the brushwood bonfire Rolf and Inge had made. It blazed high and strong, and we all sang *Stille Nacht*.

It was truly a still and holy night, a peaceful night far from the world of war. In front of us blazed the fire. At our feet lay our farm, the work of our own hands and heads and endurance. Away to the left shone the vast and endless sea. Above, in the dark sky, the stars twinkled brightly.

Slowly we went back to the house.

The children were long asleep when Heinz and I began decorating the Christmas tree Heinz had brought over from Germany. It had dug roots in our garden, we used it every year and planted it back—a piece of our native land which was now at war.

Heinz laid the children's presents under the tree. Very early in the morning I took some sweets and chocolate I had saved up, and put those too beneath the tree. I lighted the candles, and when all was ready, I rang a little bell. The children were awake and up, now they dashed out to the tree. I was longing to see Inge's face when she first caught sight of the doll, longing to hear her shouts of delight. Nothing happened, in fact she looked anything but delighted.

'Don't you like your lovely doll?' I asked, very disappointed. She shook her head, equally disappointed. 'Why can't Father Christmas bring me a *machete*?' she demanded. 'Or a hoe or a rake. I want to work in Rolf's garden. I can't do work with a doll.'

We were a little hurt that the doll which had been made with so much loving care and effort meant nothing to Inge, but that was one of the things parents had to accept. The doll disappeared into a cupboard, and has remained there ever since—one of our failures or forgotten masterpieces, according to which way you look at it. I told Frances Conway about it in the afternoon when she and Elmer paid a Christmas visit, but she only laughed. She did try to draw Inge out, however. 'I think it's a lovely doll, Inge, you ought to be very fond of her.'

Inge did not answer, except to give Aunt Frances an expressive sidelong look. Then she vanished, to return a few minutes later holding a little raffia basket with some cheeping chickens in it straight out of the egg. 'Ve,' she said, gazing tenderly at the little yellow chicks, '*éste es lindo*' (this here is lovely). Why she said this in Spanish we never knew.

'She's a real island child, and always will be,' Frances comforted us. 'She'll never learn to play with dolls, because they're not living creatures. Those are what *she* likes.'

Frances was right too. Puppies, kittens, piglets, chickens, donkey foals, were always Inge's favourite playmates. Rolf too was a proper island boy, and he had a disappointment at Christmas too: he didn't get the real gun he had set his heart on. 'We *have* got a gun for him someone gave us,' I remarked to the

Conways when he wasn't there, 'but he's a bit too young at seven, don't you think?'

'Might be if he lived in a town,' Elmer answered. 'But it's not dangerous for a boy like Rolf. Sooner he learns to handle a gun, the less dangerous it will be.'

As a matter of fact Heinz agreed with Elmer, and Rolf never needed to give up hope if he failed to get something he wanted at Christmas: his birthday was only a week later. I baked a birthday cake and decorated it with seven home-made candles. They had turned out a little crooked, I'm afraid, but it still looked very gay. That was the first thing which met Rolf's eye when he came in for breakfast. Then he saw a long package lying on the table across his place. He pounced on this, tore off the wrappings, and found a fine small-bore gun, with which he was thrilled beyond measure: he had a wonderful afternoon with his father being given first lessons in shooting. Every time he fired, Inge came rushing into the house with shining eyes to tell me that Rolf had again made 'Bang-Bang!'

He had shooting practice every Sunday after that, and when he could hit a target more or less adequately, his father one day said to him: 'Now you can shoot a bit, you can take over some of my duties. Every morning when you get up, I'd like you to make a round of the farm and see if and where a bull has broken through the fence. Would you like to do that for me?'

Would he like to! Rolf's face widened in one vast grin. He sure would.

So every morning at six o'clock he set out on his rounds, gun over his shoulder, accompanied by Lump. When he came back, he always had plenty to talk about, and Inge kept begging him to let her come too the next morning, 'I could help you such a terrific lot.' But Rolf wouldn't take a sister with him who wasn't even three yet. She would only get in the way, and it might be risky for her too.

Some weeks later, about ten minutes after he had left, I heard the dogs barking fiercely. Heinz, who was out in the plantation with Harry, also heard them, and went to see what they were making such a noise for. The only thing he saw was Rolf racing towards the house as fast as his legs would carry him.

The boy panted in, white as a sheet, and it was not till I had quickly given him a cup of coffee that he could get out what happened. When he heard the angry dogs, he knew it must be a bull at the boundary fence, and crept very quietly towards the place where the barking came from. Yes, it was a huge black bull. He levelled his gun, took aim, fired. The next time he looked, the bull had vanished, it simply wasn't there any more. After which he ran home.

While the boy was talking, Heinz had come in. He took his own gun, and went back with Rolf to the place where the dogs had 'given tongue.' Lo and behold, there was the bull, stretched out dead over about six feet of ground, the bullet from Rolf's gun had got him straight through the brain.

We had a feast of hamburgers that day, and Rolf 'the white hunter' was rewarded by having two fried eggs with them. Inge eyed these covetously, demanding in a petulant voice: 'Why can't I have two as well?'

Yes, I reflected, we'll soon have to be thinking about a gun for her. 'You shall have two eggs the day you shoot your first bull,' Heinz promised.

'S'pose the hens haven't laid any?'

We laughed, and told her we would see they did, so she was mollified and reverted to admiring her big brother. I wondered if a boy of seven in Europe could have done as much, and I must admit that I myself was very proud of him: he was indeed his father's son.

However, his father had before this made a difficult decision, which he broke to me at the end of January. 'As soon as there's an opportunity,' he said, 'I'm going over to Chatham, and from there I'll cable the consulate at Guayaquil asking what action I'm to take as a reserve officer.'

He had made up his mind on his own without telling me any of his reflections. He said he hadn't wanted to worry me until he was quite certain this was the best thing to do.

I looked stunned. We had seen nothing of the war till now, it had almost seemed to be passing us by. And now my husband was going off to join up . . .

'Just like millions of other men,' he said. 'I expect their wives feel much as you do now. And after all, it isn't certain I'll be needed, they may well not want men of fifty.'

'And you're sure it's the right thing?' I demanded.

'The trouble is,' he admitted, 'that whatever I do may be wrong. You know I'm no politician, and I hate the sound of these Nazis, but they *are* the government of my country, which is at war. They could call me a traitor if I failed to offer my services, and that wouldn't be too good for any of us. If I do offer them, at least it will show willing. Nobody can then say I've shirked my responsibilities as an old soldier. Cheer up, darling, they may not want me.'

It took me a good while to cheer up. We did not tell the children straight away, and they could not understand why I seemed out of sorts. I packed Heinz's things as for a long absence, and then we waited. I still hoped in those tense weeks that he would change his mind, but if he believed what he was doing was best, that was good enough for me.

His chance to go did not come till April, when Señor Alvear arrived, to inspect the conditions of the soldiers on our little military station. He was very ready to take Heinz back to Chatham with him, so the thing I had dreaded was happening at last: quite suddenly, it seemed to me now, when I had had ten weeks to prepare for it.

'Be very good, and help your mother as much as ever you can,' Heinz told the children as he said good-bye to them. With grave faces they promised they would.

When he had gone, we stayed for a long time on 'Olympus' watching him move out of sight. Later we watched the *Calderón* as she glided out to sea, till she disappeared in the mist. All our dogs had to be tied up, they would have liked to run after their master. We could not stop them whining and howling.

Now I was alone with the children. I tried not to think about the future, but the thoughts came beating in on my brain, and would not leave me in peace. Here I was, on a remote and lonely island with my ailing twenty-year-old stepson, a German national like myself, and two small children who were Ecuadorian nationals. Suppose Ecuador declared war on Germany: how would they treat me? Suppose America declared war on Germany, and decided to establish an air-base on Floreana?

With Heinz gone, I had so much extra work, fortunately, that it left me little time for brooding. But the nights were terrible. I could not sleep for the same continual torment of questions I could not answer. What would happen to Heinz, what would happen to me and the children? Would they one day throw us out of Floreana? I believe this was the thing I feared and fought against most of all, that we should have to leave our island, to leave all we had built up with such patience and hope and love.

Chapter 15

Life went on, better than I had anticipated. We killed a pig, because we needed meat, and also a pig less meant that much less work. Harry and Rolf helped with the sticking, the scalding and the gutting, and everything went like clockwork, just as if Heinz had been there. The children were touching in the way they helped me, just as they had promised their father when he said good-bye to them. They sensed how unhappy I was feeling, though I did not say much about it; and they missed their father too.

All of a sudden Harry stopped work, wiped the sweat off his brow with his arm, and looked at me. I could see he had an idea, and waited with interest: Harry's poor eyesight was often made up for not only by the acuteness of his other senses, but by general alertness and 'bright ideas.'

'I've just thought of something, Mother,' he said. 'How about my riding down to the coast tomorrow morning and asking if the soldiers would like to buy some meat and sausage from us? They won't have any themselves, I imagine, so they should need some. It would earn us a bit of money, and we'll need *that* if we have to leave Floreana.'

I had not even talked much to Harry about our having to leave, but he knew it was in my mind, and it was better to have it in the open. 'Yes,' I said, 'that sounds a very good idea. Quite a brainwave, in fact.'

So Harry went off next morning, while I made liver sausage from the offal and some special German sausage according to our old recipe, nobly assisted by Rolf and even little Inge. The rest of the pig we salted, so that we should have fresh meat for a long time. By the time Harry returned, the work was done. 'The soldiers will come tomorrow,' he announced. 'They're ready to take all the sausages we've got.'

They did take all the sausage, and they could have done with more if we had had it, for the little garrison at Post Office Bay now numbered about twenty people: the married soldiers had brought in their wives and children. Our customers were very pleased with our wares, and we were just as pleased with their money, which we divided equally between the children's savings tins and the family strong-box.

Now there was more work instead of less, but that was really to the good. It kept us from worrying about having to leave or what was happening to Heinz. And the next day it was Rolf's turn to have an idea. 'Why don't we also bake *galletas* for the soldiers? Inge and I can help you a lot in that, so when Papa comes back we'll have lots and lots of money.'

So besides making sausage we baked *galletas* (biscuits), and went on baking them. Luckily I had a good stock of flour from the mainland, and heaven knows how many hundredweights I used; I reckon it must have come to something like five hundred —twenty-five tons of flour.

We could not bake the *galletas* fast enough. Our oven was burning continually, and Harry was hard put to it to get in all the wood that was needed. On average we produced fifteen pounds of *galletas* a day, which we sold for 2.50 sucres a pound, about 15 cents in American money.

We killed a second pig, then a third. All our eggs found a rapid sale. We had a 'business,' and three weeks after Heinz had gone, it had built up very nicely.

One day the children were out near the boundary fence, and I was working in the kitchen, when there was a loud knock at the door. I went to see who it was: probably one of our grocery customers. When I opened the door, I nearly collapsed with the shock of joy. There in the doorway, tall, bronzed and smiling, stood my husband. I flung my arms round his neck.

'Anybody could break in here without your knowing,' he remarked casually. 'Where on earth are the children and the dogs?'

'Out on the plantation,' I told him, 'but what about you? How did you get here? What's going to happen?'

'One thing at a time,' he answered. 'How did I get here? In

163

a fishing boat coming from the United States, which put me down at Blackbeach. What's going to happen? Well, as far as I'm concerned, the German Embassy at Quito let me know that at present there was no possibility of my leaving Ecuador. I'm to wait quietly here till I'm called.'

'Thank God!' I breathed. 'That's wonderful, too good to be true. Just go into our bedroom, will you, I'd like to give the children the same surprise you gave me. They'll be in to dinner soon.'

'All right.' He laughed. 'It doesn't occur to you, woman, that I might be hungry myself?'

'Good heavens, I never thought of that. But do go in there for a few minutes, I'll make sure there's enough for you!'

The children came in. 'Well, we've had another customer in while you've been out,' I said. 'I put him in the bedroom.'

'In the bedroom?' They looked blank. 'Whatever for?' Harry sniffed. 'I can smell American tobacco. Has Mr Conway been here?'

'No. Have another guess.' I opened the door. 'Give it up?' I beckoned to Heinz. 'Come out, stranger.'

'Hullo,' he said, coming out. 'All of you been good?'

'Papa!' They rushed at him, and he had to take Inge in his arms and throw her up and down several times, while she and Rolf started telling him everything that had happened on the island while he had been away. 'And do you know, Papa, we've got a business now?'

'Really, Rolf?'

'Yes, we're all in it,' Inge put in, 'Mutti as well, of course.'

They explained to him both at once, but actually he had met some of our satisfied customers on his way up from the coast, who told him how we had won their hearts with sausage and *galletas*. 'Wonder where on earth you get your business sense from?' he said. 'Must be from Mutti, not me. Still, I think it's a jolly good idea. Well done, everyone.' He turned to me. 'I shan't mind leaving you next time if I ever have to, seems to me you can depend on children like these.'

'Well, don't let's talk about your leaving again,' I said. 'It's too good to have you back. So now you can at last have something to eat.'

That was a wonderful day. In three years Heinz and I had

not been parted a single night; and for all the children's devotion, these last weeks had indeed been long and lonely without him. Now he was back, though we knew we were by no means out of the wood yet. Whether we should be allowed to stay on Floreana probably depended on what happened thousands of miles away in Europe, where the war was now in a new stage, as Heinz had heard on the American boat: Germany had first invaded Scandinavia, then the Low Countries. As the summer went on, we learnt at intervals, chiefly through the Ecuadorian garrison, of the fall of France, the British army's evacuation from Dunkirk. Towards the autumn I learnt with horror of the massive German air raids on London, where I assumed my sister would still be (I hadn't heard from her for months), and even then the war didn't end, but dragged on through a second winter.

But apart from the increased shipping in our waters, Floreana remained untouched by the war. We pursued our ordinary life, as if there were no threat of eviction, and were able to celebrate Harry's 21st birthday, 16th September, 1940, with a very happy party, to which all the Ecuadorian garrison and their families were invited; many a chicken had been killed for the occasion, and I had baked mountains of cakes.

About that time, however, we found ourselves waging an increasingly fierce private war against the bulls, which were particularly bad that autumn, breaking into the plantation almost every night. One dark night at the end of the month these nocturnal intrusions reached a climax.

We had not seen the sun for weeks, it rained incessantly, and most of the ground was a quagmire. It was too wet and cold and dark outside to think of keeping up a guard rota all night, and even indoors, with the fire blazing, it was so cold and damp that the best thing to do in the evenings was to go to bed very early.

About one o'clock that night I was woken abruptly from a deep sleep. 'Can you hear a funny noise behind the house?' I heard Heinz asking.

I 'came to' with a start, and sat up in bed. There was indeed a funny noise: a most ominous noise, that is, as if someone were trying to break down our fine 'bedroom door'—which consisted of some old crate lids nailed together and painted. The battering noises behind it increased.

Heinz was already up, lighting the lamp and loading his gun.

I woke Rolf and Inge, and told Rolf to wake Harry (whose room was furthest away from the noise) and stay with him. I took Inge on my left arm—she was over three now, and quite a weight—and Heinz gave me the lamp to hold so that he should have his hands free. So we crept out of the kitchen door to see what exactly was going on behind the bedroom door!

It was a bull, just preparing for a final charge against the unfortunate door. The bull got a shock from the light of the lamp, which I was holding as high as I could, but it was pitch dark outside, and Heinz couldn't get a good aim because the lamp was shaking so much. 'For heaven's sake keep the thing still,' he shouted, but with Inge on the other arm I was finding my function of lamp-holder a bit of a strain: I *couldn't* keep the thing still.

Then the bull turned on us and headed for the kitchen door, and we retreated inside. Harry came to my rescue, taking Inge, who had meanwhile started crying lustily. Even Rolf was very scared and clung to my nightie. 'Hold the lamp high!' yelled Heinz. 'Higher, higher, so that I can see to shoot. Children into the bedroom!'

Harry raced off with the two children, as Heinz took his first shot through the kitchen window, to which the bull had just transferred his attention. It was a good shot but not mortal. Mad with rage, the bull drew back for his last desperate charge, when the second shot hit him. He plunged forward, then dropped to the ground in front of the kitchen door with a crash that sounded as if the house were falling in.

The whole episode had lasted about an hour, and after we had put the children to bed again we couldn't think of sleep. The fire was relighted, and almost automatically I put on some coffee. 'Think I'll have some brandy with that,' said Heinz.

'Yes,' said Harry, 'you certainly deserve it. We could do with some too, eh, Mother?'

'Just for once I think we could,' I agreed.

The door was badly damaged where the bull fell on it, as we found next morning when we got the body to cut it up. During this operation we discovered the full extent of his fury: he had secreted over four pints of bile. I am glad to say it came in handy for me to dye a piece of dull white material an attractive green.

The bulls' offensive relaxed after this episode, and with the worst rains past we could attend to the potato harvest, which was again a very good one. Part of it formed extra wares for selling to the garrison, with whom we were now on very friendly terms. We entertained some of the soldiers and their families over Christmas, and they too appreciated our Christmas tree and German fashion of celebrating the festival. Rolf was eight, and in April 1941 Inge was four, and still our quiet existence was undisturbed, though the warships we saw from Olympus, replacing the millionaires' elegant white pleasure-yachts of peacetimes, were great steel monsters with menacing-looking guns pointed skyward—so that we felt at any moment they might thunder across the sea in our direction.

That summer we had an American warship actually stationed off Post Office Bay, but her captain and officers came up to see us, just as in happier times, and we were asked to supply the ship with fresh food. We were very glad to do so, of course, for we had no quarrel with the Americans. On the contrary, their behaviour was more than correct; we had found them extremely obliging and helpful, bringing us commodities which may have seemed trifles to them but were immensely useful to us.

We began to feel almost safe on Floreana, till all our forebodings returned on hearing that the Conways would soon be leaving. The fine property they had built up in four years would probably revert to wilderness, while we were losing the first inhabitants of the island we could really call friends. We and they had shared so many minor triumphs and troubles, we knew we should miss them very badly. Frances returned to the United States that October of 1941, and how often in the next weeks I found myself saying 'I must tell Frances about that when I see her.'

Then in December came the shattering news of the Japanese attack on Pearl Harbor, followed by Germany and Italy also declaring war on the United States. Then Ecuador broke off relations with Germany, and we felt it was only a matter of time before we were at best turned off the island, at worst interned. We heard that the Angermeyers, a German family living on Santa Cruz, had been ordered to leave and go to Ecuador. In February, 1942, Elmer Conway, who had stayed on Floreana waiting for orders, was sent direct to Seymour—the great airbase to be.

For Ecuador had leased the Galapagos Islands to the United States. The long-standing rumours of a Galapagos air-base had become fact, and we thanked providence most heartily that it was not Floreana which had been selected but Seymour, the small island just north of Santa Cruz (which was some way north of us). Ships from the United States converged on Seymour, bringing a mass of materials and equipment for the building of the base, which was to be the biggest in South America. Hundreds of workmen poured in, not only from the other Galapagos islands and Ecuador but also from Peru and Colombia, Costa Rica and Panama, from all over the sub-continent.

Soon there were thousands of them at work day and night. A pier was built so that big ships could land right on the island. Countless small wooden houses sprang up almost overnight like mushrooms, to accommodate workmen and American service men, together with a row of larger buildings which included a luxurious stone house for the officers' club. A whole town blossomed, with church, cinema, streets and shops and offices, a power station. An aqueduct was being built on Chatham; fresh water would be piped down from about two thousand feet and brought over on ships to supply Seymour. The island itself was not expected to be a theatre of war, so we gathered, but was chiefly intended as an 'acclimatiser,' to get the crews of ships and planes used to the heat before they sailed for the South Seas or the Far East.

We went on with our old peaceful life, hearing periodical reports of operations on Seymour, but otherwise scarcely disturbed by having quite near us one of the largest projects in the world in the process of being built. Who could have guessed a few years before that the air under the blue Galapagos sky would one day be filled with the roar of planes, that whole convoys of ships would pour through the once quiet waters, that one of these remote islands would be humming with ceaseless activity? We still shuddered to think it might have been Floreana, not Seymour, that bore this invasion of thousands of men drawn from their life as small planters by the lure of the mighty dollar.

American ships kept bringing them over from the mainland, and plainly there were many who came only to earn quick money. For the base had to be built with all possible speed, and

168

the Americans were incredibly generous: money was no object at all. They paid their workmen fabulously high wages. For an eight-hour working day any workman got twenty sucres. Overtime was paid higher, with treble rates for Sundays. The average daily earnings were three or four dollars, which before that must have been beyond their wildest dreams.

They were all accommodated in small but solid wooden houses, each house with running water (an amenity few had more than heard of), radio and refrigerator; there was a free laundry service for them. They could buy working clothes quite cheaply in Seymour's new shops. They did not have to worry about furnishing their houses, for everything had been brought over by the Americans. In fact everything was laid on for them, and their lodging cost them nothing. They also got their food delivered free, not paying a single cent for it. Every week they got a carton of cigarettes and every evening two bottles of iced beer. Every three months they had a fortnight's leave, when American ships would take them to the mainland or their home island and bring them back at the end of it.

With such large pay-envelopes and so much given them free, they could have saved enough to bring them in a modest income for a long time ahead. But perhaps understandably, most of them went mad and parted with their dollars as quickly as they had earned them. As an old acquaintance who came over from Seymour described it to us, 'People who before lived quite happily on the fruits Nature gave them will now only eat food from American tins, nothing else is good enough for them. They can't read what is said on the tins, but then they don't care at all about the contents as long as they've got something American— people who used to be thrilled if they were given an empty tin, would find a hundred uses for it and guard it as a treasure. Once they smoked only the tobacco they'd grown on their own land; now they must have American cigarettes.'

The men who worked on Seymour behaved as if the 'golden rain' would never come to an end. A great deal of good earnings went down the drain called '*puro*,' a spirit made from sugar-cane. Years afterwards I met in Ecuador some people who had worked on the air-base for two years and had almost every cent transferred to a bank in Quito. What did they want money for on Seymour, when life cost practically nothing? At the end of two years when the base was completed, they returned to Ecuador with a very large credit at the Quito bank, with which they bought an attractive estate; and today they are still very well off. But among their fellow-workers on the base they were in a very small minority.

The Americans were far from treating us as enemy aliens, and so far we had no restrictions placed on our liberty. We were told that we were under the authority of the head of the Red Cross on Seymour, who proved a most friendly and sympathetic man. Every few weeks he would come over to Floreana himself or else send a representative to see we were all right, and once a dentist was flown over specially to attend to Inge, who was having very bad toothache; he and his assistant stayed the night as our guests. The Red Cross director also arranged for us to receive newspapers, and it was through the Red Cross that we got our very rare mail. We did not hear from Germany at all, but there was an occasional letter from my sister, thank heavens, who had safely survived the 'Blitz' on London. She was still housekeeper to Lady Duke-Elder, the wife of a well-known Harley Street eye specialist. I could also send out messages to her that we had remained on Floreana, and were keeping well.

Yes, we were all right so far, but how long would it go on? We knew that we had no feelings of hostility to America, and that even if we had wanted to be, we could scarcely be much danger to the Americans' war effort. But they would obviously take no chances, and this miraculous immunity might end at any time. We did our work on the farm listlessly, without any of the usual zest; what was the point when you might soon have to abandon both work and farm? And one day in the late spring of 1942 we thought the dreaded time had come at last.

Captain Brindall, in command of the engineers working on Seymour, was an old friend by now, but that morning he had brought along a stranger, whom he introduced as an official in the American War Department. The stranger carried a bulging brief-case, looked very stern and official, and had evidently come over from Washington. 'This is it,' I thought, but as they must have started out very early, I offered them a belated breakfast. They accepted this and ate heartily; there was no serious talk until they had finished, by which time we were more on tenter-hooks than ever. Then Captain Brindall said: 'Well, now we

170

must get down to business. First I must tell you that it has been decided in Washington . . .'

He stopped to clear his throat, thereby unintentionally causing us a last moment of excruciating suspense. How long should we be given to leave Floreana, would he express regret that unfortunately as enemy aliens we should have to be interned, would our farm be requisitioned . . .?

'Decided in Washington,' he repeated, 'that the Wittmer family may stay on Floreana.'

'May stay . . . may stay . . .' I echoed dazedly. The relief was so intense it was all I could do not to burst into tears of joy.

'We are going to build an auxiliary air-base here,' Brindall continued in the same matter-of-fact way, 'and as the matter is urgent, this gentleman has come by air from Panama to make the necessary arrangements.'

'That is so,' the War Department official took over, 'and for some of our arrangements we need your consent.'

Heinz and I looked at each other in amazement. Our consent! It sounded more like a private business deal than the establishment of a military installation by a country at war with Germany. 'It will only be a small base for reconnaissance planes,' he continued, 'which will be making regular patrol flights over the islands and in the Galapagos area. The Ecuadorian government have leased us the use of the island for this purpose. We propose to clear an air-strip very near to your house, on the Pampa Larga, and we need to pipe fresh water there from your spring, as well as building a road up from Blackbeach Bay. This will go past your boundary fence. For both these things we should therefore like your permission.'

Before Heinz or I could say that of course they had no need to ask even, he was proceeding: 'For such permission we are of course ready to make you a certain payment, either in cash or in kind, as you prefer. You will also have the opportunity to sell the produce of your farm, for the air-base will be manned by five officers and seventy-five men, and will also have its own doctor, dentist and radio station. I am sure you will get along together very well with our personnel . . . I think that's about all you'll be wanting to know. If we have your consent we can go ahead straight away. Think it over.'

There was nothing to think over, but he and Brindall seemed

171

determined to give us time to do this, and Brindall said he'd like to see the children. We called them in, and as usual he had candies for them. So had the War Department official. 'This is for you, Rolf . . . and this is for you, Inge.'

Rolf beamed. 'Thank you very much, sir.' He stuck the box under his arm. But Inge looked wide-eyed at the strange American, and did not say a word. Eventually she turned to Heinz and asked: 'May I take it, Papa?'

He laughed. 'Of course you may.'

She gave a rather timid smile, curtsied, and said a shy 'thank you.'

The frightening representative of officialdom laughed too. 'I like your children, Mr Wittmer,' he said.

For five minutes we talked about children and families, and the war was forgotten. Then Captain Brindall said: 'We want to go to the Pampa Larga now, and we'd like you to take us there, Mr Wittmer, as you know the ground so well.' He turned to me. 'And do you think you could possibly let us have some lunch, Mrs Wittmer? We're expecting two of our engineers, so there'll be four of us.'

The Pampa was a quarter of an hour away, and a little below us—about eight hundred feet above sea level. It was a big flat plain about half a mile long, surrounded by thick bush, its grey clayey soil sparsely covered with a weed a little like our clover and studded with black basalt stones. Once these stones were cleared, it would make a very suitable place for small planes to land and take off; and as we had heard, bigger planes would not be coming here. Small prefabricated houses were to be brought over from America for the officers and men, and erected on sites to be cleared from the bush, so they also would need comparatively little construction work. The road was to be fifteen feet wide, carved out of the bush; but bulldozers would soon deal with that.

When the four Americans arrived for lunch, they were gasping with thirst from the unaccustomed heat, and the juice I had squeezed from a sackful of oranges was only just enough. I was able to give them quite a good meal, we had felt no war shortages in food on Floreana. Afterwards, as we were having coffee, the man from Washington looked at me enquiringly. 'Well, Mrs Wittmer,' he said, 'have you come to a decision?'

'A decision?' I asked blankly.

'Have we your consent to go ahead with these arrangements?'

I had thought it was only a formality, this request for our consent; nor had Heinz and I had a moment to discuss the matter on our own. But they were evidently expecting an answer, so I grinned and said: 'Okay.'

He gave a satisfied nod. 'And you, Mr Wittmer?'

'Naturally,' said Heinz. 'If my family and my house are respected, I of course agree to everything you suggest.'

'Good,' said Brindall. 'Well, we shall be coming back in two days to start work. There'll be two officers besides myself and twenty-two men. We should like to sleep in tents inside your grounds, if that's okay, and do you think we could rely on you as far as fresh food is concerned?'

An extra twenty-five mouths to feed! But after all we had always hoped eventually to market our supplies. We promised we would do our best.

Our visitors were anxious to be off, but as they were leaving, the War Department official, collecting papers in his brief-case, suddenly brought out a white envelope, like a rabbit out of a hat. 'Say, I nearly forgot this,' he remarked, handing it over to Heinz. From the big clear handwriting I had already seen who the writer was, and when Heinz tore it open he found a big sheet of paper with only a short message: 'Don't worry, you will all stay on Floreana. Your loyal friend, W.S.'

That was all, but what splendid news there was for us in those few words! We had Waldo Schmitt to thank for our being left on Floreana—him and his friend President Roosevelt. We could not want higher authority than that, and it was wonderfully reassuring. It was true that our cherished solitude was over, we could expect men and ships and planes arriving from many countries. But all over the world cities were burning, great battles were being fought; and we did not even know the sound of a bomb. We certainly had little to complain of, least of all from our 'enemies,' the Americans. The officers and men on Floreana's air-base behaved, like all their countrymen we had known, with exemplary correctness.

We started getting American officers coming over from Seymour. Floreana was still a haven of peace and quiet after the noise and bustle of the big air-base, and soon they made a regular habit of dropping in on days off 'to your fabulous island,' as they put it, and enjoying our hospitality. There was one air force officer we got to know very well, who offered to signal any visits in advance. 'If I fly over your house three times and dip my wings the third time, you'll know you've got folks coming to see you.'

'Thanks very much,' we said, and this sign was always observed.

The colonel in command of the air-base also paid us several visits, and we got on extremely well with him. These American officers were very considerate of our feelings as Germans, and any newcomer to the Asilo de la Paz was warned beforehand to avoid the topic of war so as to spare us any embarrassment. Although it was known that we also hated the Nazis, victories and defeats were bound to mean different things for us and for our American visitors. They also brought us newspapers and magazines, in which we could read more than we wanted about the war.

One day the colonel asked us whether we could supply tomatoes for Seymour. They got most of their vegetables from Santa Cruz, but strangely enough no tomatoes were grown on that island.

Of course we could. 'We shall have to plant hundreds of them, and you can come and collect them when they're ripe.'

'Sure.'

We soon agreed on the price: five dollars for a hundred pounds of tomatoes. This was a fine transaction for us, and the colonel seemed very satisfied.

We set to work with great zeal, planting tomatoes on every spare patch of ground. They came up very well, and just as the first ones were turning yellow, we had a ship called the *Cisney* over from Seymour with Captain Bill Wymer on board, an officer we knew well. I informed him proudly that in three weeks' time the first tomato crop could be collected.

'Fine, fine,' he said, 'but have you heard the latest? There's been a big change of plan. Orders from Washington, you know. Confidentially, we're quite flabbergasted ourselves, but the auxiliary air-base is not going to be on Floreana after all, but on Hood instead.'

Hood was a barren, rocky island, due east from us. It had not been developed at all, and a road would have to be cut through the rocks—whereas *we* had a good track already, the road was progressing fast, and everything was so much simpler.

'But there's no fresh water on Hood,' I protested.

'Maybe not,' said the officer. 'It's not my idea, as I told you. I should be pleased if I were you.'

So we were, of course, in a way: Floreana could revert to its peace and quiet again. But meanwhile the tomatoes were ripening fast, and no one came to fetch them. First we only had a few buckets full. I used them in all possible forms. Then there were whole wheelbarrows full. I invited all the Ecuadorian soldiers stationed at Blackbeach to come and take as many tomatoes as they liked. The Zavalas came too, and took away several donkey-loads. Our donkeys, our pigs, even Barbara the cow, who had given us the hoped-for calf and also the hoped-for milk—all the animals, no less than the human beings, had to live on a staple diet of tomatoes. They couldn't be wasted, even if we weren't to get any dollars for them.

They went on ripening, there was a real glut. I think we must have grown several tons of tomatoes—and no ship came from Seymour for nine weeks. I told the officer who came to us: 'There aren't any more tomatoes now. We've been waiting ages, and the last ones are just going to rot on the plants.'

'Tomatoes? What tomatoes?' No one knew anything about it. For the colonel had been suddenly transferred to Panama and had forgotten to inform his successor of our agreement. The United States Navy and Air Force had far more important matters on hand: that we quite understood. But it was a long time before we wanted to see a tomato again, let alone start planting the things.

Chapter 16

Now the tide of war had receded, as it were, from the shores of Floreana, we could not only go back to work on the farm in the old tranquil atmosphere, but could also afford a little more time for the children's 'schooling.' Our idea of sending Rolf to school at Chatham or even the mainland had long been discarded in war conditions, but we had continued to improvise a 'private education' as best we could between the three of us, for him and also for Inge.

Lessons were whenever occasion served, such as when I was on a cooking job I didn't need to think about. If I had one or both of the children walking at my side when I was riding somewhere on the donkey, I would test their knowledge or get them to recite some well-known poem they had had to learn like any ordinary schoolchildren. Harry would often play his mouth organ and teach them the words of German folk songs and choruses; Rolf's singing was better than it had been, less painful, but I had long accepted the fact that neither he nor Inge was going to be very musical. Harry was also still the 'arithmetic master,' and sometimes talked English and Spanish with them; for they were already learning both these languages through coming into contact with Americans and Ecuadorians. We spoke German in the house, of course, and I had great struggles to instil the rules of grammar, realising for the first time what a difficult language my mother tongue was.

Rolf and Inge had reading and writing between two and four in the afternoon when there wasn't anything special to be done on the farm (which there usually was), and they had 'homework' in the evenings—again like ordinary schoolchildren, except that the light they did it by was not electric but a hurricane lamp.

Heinz was the history and geography expert, and both children got at least some idea of places and peoples, even though Inge had never been off the island and Rolf only when he was a baby.

Altogether Rolf learnt quickly and eagerly, and without any pushing he picked up a lot of scientific and technical information from books, periodicals and newspapers—and from questioning grown-ups: obviously science was already a 'favourite subject.' On the whole, we felt that at eleven he was not far behind most of his contemporaries in academic instruction, and probably far in advance of them in practical intelligence.

Inge, on the other hand, was not prepared to waste much effort on anything she did not see a practical use for. 'Surely it's good enough,' she would declare, 'if I know how to cook properly and bake bread and all that, and work on the farm.' We insisted on her doing the elementary lessons she was up to at seven, but this was an attitude she stuck to all her girlhood. I cannot say it seems to have done her much harm, and she too must have more than compensated by all-round capability.

Both children were badly shaken when in 1944 dear old Lump —now twelve years old—progenitor of all our dogs, whom Rolf and Inge had known all their lives, got very ill, so that in the end there was nothing we could do for him except give him a merciful bullet one day while he was asleep. He had travelled out to Floreana as a puppy, and had been a faithful friend, 'baby-sitter' and watchdog for so long that it was indeed like losing one of the family.

We did not know what he had been suffering from, and in case it was some disease which the other dogs might catch, we decided that his body had better be burnt. Without much reflection we put it on top of a pile of dry branches in the garden, poured paraffin over the pile and lighted it. A cloud of black smoke shot up, then a beacon of flame, and Heinz and I simultaneously realised what we had done. Suppose they could see the fire from Seymour, or suppose a plane came, they might think we were signalling—signalling to the enemy.

'With any luck,' Heinz muttered, 'if a plane comes at all, the fire will have burnt out by then.'

A plane did come, we could hear its engines; and the fire was still blazing. It was a seaplane. It circled a few times above us and the fire, then dipped its wings, that being still the regular signal: within two hours we should have visitors on Floreana, and what they would say we dared not think. I prepared a meal for them, bread and jam, boiled eggs, beautiful golden yellow bananas, pineapple juice to refresh them after a long hot walk, fresh milk and home-made butter—for Barbara, the cow, had lately been giving us about eight pints of milk a day.

Soon our visitors arrived, four people including the colonel commanding the air-base at Seymour and the director of the Red Cross. They greeted us just as usual, asked after the children. I brought water for them to wash in, then offered them the refreshments I had prepared. They chatted quite normally, till I began to think it was just an ordinary visit with no special purpose. My fears subsided till the colonel asked casually : 'You've had a fire on the island, Mr Wittmer?'

Now we were for it. His voice did not sound quite so friendly, and four pairs of eyes seemed to be watching Heinz as he answered. 'Yes,' he stammered, 'we never intended, I mean we didn't realise . . .'

The colonel drummed on the table impatiently with his fingers. 'We just wondered, Mr Wittmer, if it had any special significance. We didn't quite like the look of it, you know.'

'We didn't mean any harm, really,' I broke in. 'We were so sad at losing good old Lump we never thought of anything else . . .' I was in tears as I explained what had happened, how he might have had an infectious disease, and how we had to burn the body. 'We couldn't have buried him, sir, or the other dogs would have dug the body up.'

The colonel and the other three men listened to my story in silence, and looked at each other as if asking whether it was to be believed. Suppose they didn't believe it, we might be turned off the island even now, after five years of war.

'Okay,' he said at last, and I could not help bursting into hysterical laughter while the tears were still running down my face. The colonel gave a slight smile; I knew that he too was a great dog-lover.

'Of course we'll never be so negligent again,' said Heinz.

'Good,' said the colonel. 'Well, that's the end of that then.'

Now the conversation was easy and relaxed once more. The director of the Red Cross promised to return to Floreana the following week to give us a medical and dental check-up.

The colonel talked to the children and gave them all some chocolate. One of the other officers took Heinz aside, and said : 'Do you realise exactly how dangerous what you did was, what the results might have been?'

'More or less,' said Heinz.

'Well, I'll put you wise now. It might easily have been thought that the smoke and the fire were a prearranged signal for a German submarine. You can't blame us for thinking such things, can you? We've got some pretty inflammable stuff on Seymour. You're a German, the war's going badly for Germany, and you might have been forced into it.'

'Yes,' said Heinz.

'I only want to tell you how it could look, Mr Wittmer. Just suppose a German submarine happens to be sighted near the Panama Canal today or tomorrow or the next day. Do you imagine anyone will believe your story about the dead dog then?'

'Probably not,' Heinz admitted.

'Well, there you are,' said the officer. 'Now let's forget it.'

We parted like old friends, and no enemy submarine was sighted, thank heavens, in the vicinity of the Panama Canal in the next few days; or if one was, we did not hear about it. But I was so upset by the whole business that I felt quite ill, and had to stay in bed for two days. It was a bad shock for my nerves, and every trifle scared me to death. Once when a plane flew over the house at night, I started screaming; it was quite a long while before I was really myself again.

Perhaps I had not recovered even then as completely as I had hoped; for in the autumn of 1944 the day came when I lost my nerve worse than I have ever done before or since.

That morning when we got up, we all had headaches and felt a great heaviness in our arms and legs. It was as if we had been drugged, and my first thought was that we must have eaten something bad the day before. I tried to remember what meals had consisted of, but couldn't concentrate; and all the while my mind was going back to a horrible scene ten years earlier: Dr Ritter's agonising death. Food-poisoning, that was the only explanation.

'Have you seen the dogs?' asked Heinz, coming back into the house.

I shook my head.

'They're creeping about so restlessly. When I came they didn't bark, they only whined.'

I went out with him. The dogs crawled towards us, bodies almost touching the ground. 'I'm afraid we've all got food-poisoning,' I muttered, 'the dogs as well.' I felt so faint I had to hold on to his arm. Neither of us said any more, we went a little way up Olympus in silence. There was a fine grey mist lying over the bush. It had not rained for weeks, though the rainy season was not nearly over.

'Perhaps it's because of this queer weather,' Heinz suggested. 'No rain, and yet this mist.'

There was a queer smell about too, something like sulphur; we had never smelt anything like it on the island before. There was also an oppressive silence, not a sound came to us from the bush, not even the call of a bird; nor were there any birds flying past. When we got back near the house, we saw that the chickens were all huddled under the shrubs, sitting there motionless.

Then we heard a dull but prolonged roll of thunder quite a long way away. Automatically we glanced up at the sky, but it was quite cloudless. Only the mist overhead made it look a little grey. It thundered again, a muffled, distant rumbling. Thunder without rain or lightning? Most eerie and unpleasant.

It was like that all day, and our faintness and heaviness did not let up. But we no longer believed it was due to food-poisoning, and we ate normally without having any ill effects. Sometimes the roll of the thunder grew louder, sometimes it died down. We felt at times as if the sound of it were being registered by not only our ears but our whole bodies, as if the air and the ground shook with every rumble. But we put that down to imagination, the result of strung-up nerves.

Late in the afternoon the silence was suddenly rent by a terrific crash, so violent that we felt a shudder going right through the house. The dogs stopped their uneasy crawling round, and suddenly started barking wildly, running from one corner to another as if they had somebody after them.

Work was nearly impossible. The children were afraid to leave the house, and asked again and again what was happening. There was nothing we could tell them. Perhaps there was a battle at sea raging somewhere near, perhaps some German or

Japanese submarines had fired Seymour's petrol dumps containing millions of gallons of fuel—only that was surely too far away for us to hear anything. No, the battle seemed more likely, and we were hearing the distant thunder of ships' guns.

When the children were in bed, I went out of the house again. I thought I heard soft footsteps, as if someone were coming; but no one came. Then I saw something which took my breath away: a gigantic mass of flame rising into the dark sky to the north-west. Despite the distance it looked thousands of feet high and miles wide.

Suddenly Heinz was standing beside me. He had seen it from the window. 'That's Isabela,' he said, pointing in the direction of the flame. 'A volcano's erupted, perhaps the Sierra Azul. Remember the one we saw erupting our first year? But that was only a tiny one compared to this.'

We stared at the sea of flame. The island of Isabela was about forty miles away from Floreana, we could see it from 'Olympus' in a clear sky, only today the mist had hidden it completely. But now, without binoculars, we could see dark clouds of ashes shooting upwards with the flame.

The whole sky above Isabela was blood-red. Now and then the flame spurted twice as high, accompanied by a shattering crash. There was not much sleep for any of us that night. We comforted Rolf and Inge as best we could, but I could not help worrying about whether the rain of ash would reach us. Heinz tried to reassure me: 'Nonsense, the wind can't possibly blow it forty miles.' But I didn't really believe him, I was still afraid. I think it was the first time in my life I realised there are elemental forces against which man is completely powerless.

The next morning the air was full of sulphur. There was a fine grey dust on the plants and shrubs and trees. So the wind could blow the ashes this far. Then another fear came to me: suppose a volcano broke out on Floreana?

'They've been extinct for ages,' said Heinz. 'There's been no movement in the craters for hundreds of years.'

But I was too distraught and frightened to believe him. In my mind's eye I could already see one of our volcanoes erupting, a column of flame shooting skywards, stone and ashes covering the whole island, a stream of molten lava rolling down on us, till there was no escape from the torrent of fire and ashes.

Perhaps we ought to pack, just the bare necessities, in case . . . in case we had suddenly to escape. I saw at once on what stupid lines I was thinking. Where should we escape if we did have to? To the coast—and then? That would be the end of our escape unless there just happened to be a ship in the bay, and of course there wouldn't be.

I could feel the fear constricting my throat. All the same I had to pack. Just the most important things, the things we couldn't do without. Everything else we should have to abandon: the house, the animals, the farm, all we had so laboriously built up in twelve years. Then we should be destitute, even if we managed to escape with our lives.

But it calmed me down a bit deciding what to take and putting it together. Heinz watched me, but made no comment. He himself was completely calm—or was pretending to be. After dinner I caught him trying to steal out of the house with a book in his hand.

'What's the book?' I asked, as he stuck it under his arm.

'Nothing special,' he answered unconvincingly, and indeed I had already seen what it was from the familiar cover: it was William Beebe's *Galapagos, End of the World*, the book that was in its way responsible for our coming here in the first place, responsible for our choosing Floreana as Harry's 'sanatorium.' We had read it so often in Germany before we came and on the long voyage out, fascinated by the strange world Beebe portrayed. Now I knew why Heinz was referring to the book. It told of a volcano erupting on one of the islands, the stream of lava pouring over the island, the ocean seething. That was my fear now, as more dull thunder rumbled over to us; the smell of sulphur had never seemed as pungent and all-pervading as at that moment.

The pillar of flame was still as high as it had been the evening before; you could see it by day now, blazing fantastically forty miles away. When I looked at it, I could picture exactly, in all its details, the eruption over a hundred years ago as Beebe had described it.

It was in 1825, when a small ship called the *Tartar* was lying off the west coast of Isabela. The sea was calm, the air around dead still. Suddenly there was a tremendous blast like a thousand claps of thunder together, accompanied by a huge blare of light, so that the sky was a beacon of fire. The flames shot up thousands of feet from the island of Fernandina, very close to the west of Isabela. The whole island seemed to be ablaze. A wide stream of red-hot liquid lava rolled down the mountain to the sea, and the ocean raged and roared when the molten mass poured into it; the becalmed ship lay helpless in a bay, close to the fire and unable to move away. The air temperature rose quickly to a hundred and twenty, that of the water to a hundred. Then at last a slight breeze sprang up, and the *Tartar* slowly got under way. She had to sail close in to Fernandina, through the hot breath of the lava: there the air temperature was a hundred and fifty degrees, the water temperature a hundred and fifty-five. The men on board nearly fainted with the heat. They were terrified lest the wind should drop. But they escaped from the inferno, pursued for a long way by the blaze of the mighty fire.

'That was only a hundred and twenty years ago,' I told Heinz in my panic, 'and that could happen any day here on this island. Heinz, we must get away from here. Before it's too late.' I really expected to see one of our old volcanoes breaking out at any moment, bringing its rain of fire and death on to Floreana.

I did not calm down till American planes came over from Seymour, which dropped messages that the volcano on Isabela was being watched all the time, that arrangement had been made to notify the inhabitants in case of imminent danger (they had long left the area of immediate risk), and that a ship was lying in readiness to evacuate them.

Big military planes circled continuously round Isabela, to report at once any change for the worse. One bomber flew too near the blaze and crashed right into the midst of the flames. The blaze lasted four weeks, then gradually abated and went out. At the bottom of the crater there were only fragments of the plane left, molten lumps of metal; and of the eleven-man crew no trace could be found.

We had seen an act of God, and eleven men had been lost. But war, the results of man's folly, had left us unscathed while densely populated cities were being smashed to a mass of rubble. The newspapers and magazines brought periodically from Seymour told us of increasingly heavy air raids on Germany, and we knew Cologne had been among the worst hit places. I heard irregularly now from my sister, about every three months, but there had been no direct contact with Germany for years. At the end of 1943 I had written to the Red Cross at Geneva, asking if my father and stepmother were still alive. It looked as if 1944 would be out and I should still have no answer.

One afternoon in November, when the algerobos were starting to bloom—November for us was the beginning of spring—I was giving the children a lesson when we heard planes. That was nothing unusual, but even so I let them go out and up to Olympus to see what the planes might have come for, and soon they came rushing back, Rolf waving a packet with a little yellow flag which showed it had been dropped by a plane. 'Inge,' I said, 'will you go and tell Papa there's been some post dropped?' (Heinz was busy laying out a new maize field, digging up tree stumps and roots.) At first glance there were only a few letters from friends in the United States, but then my heart missed a beat. 'Look,' I said to Heinz, as he came in, 'here's the answer from the Red Cross.' It was written in French. 'The only thing I can understand is the word *morts* . . .' I swallowed hard. 'They're dead.'

'Now try and be brave,' he said, 'and don't let's take anything for granted. I'll go through it with a dictionary.'

He did so, but it made no difference. My father and his wife, the message said, had been missing since the heavy raid on Cologne in June, 1944, and must therefore unfortunately be presumed dead.

Although I had long feared as much, although millions of families had lost their near and dear, the actual news still hit me hard. Heinz and Harry would have liked to stay in to comfort me, but I sent them back to the maize field, saying I would work in the garden with Rolf and Inge: this was the sure way of taking my mind off things.

When they had gone off, Rolf waited a moment, then said to me: 'You know what Inge and I think, Mutti?'

'No,' I said.

'We think,' he declared with all the weight of his nearly twelve years, 'that Opa and Oma aren't *really* dead, and perhaps they'll be found when the war's over. Don't you think so your-self?'

'Yes,' I said with a sigh. 'Yes, you're quite right. Perhaps they will. Only when's the war going to be over?'

At the time I had given my father up for lost, but as it happened the children were right after all. It was over two years, in January 1947, before we got our first news from Germany, telling us that he and my stepmother had survived (as had many of our friends in Germany), although after being evacuated to Saxony, they had then had to retreat across the country, sleeping in ditches, before the advancing Russian armies. My father was over seventy, but he had somehow come through, and was managing to exist in the chaos and poverty of defeated Germany —they had found somewhere to live just outside Cologne.

We had heard from our friends among the American officers on Seymour that pilots were given small quantities of shark's oil to help them see at night; apparently it had an extremely good effect on the eyesight. We often talked, therefore, about trying to catch a shark, to see if the oil would do anything for Harry's blindness; but we no longer had a boat, and you could hardly sit on the beach for hours or days on end waiting for the shark to swim past.

In the end Heinz and the two boys worked out a way of catching a shark. They would use a pig's shoulder for bait, fixed on a big hook with a wire chain at the other end, and about forty feet of good strong rope attached to the chain. They had to make the hook, of course, and also the chain. For the former, they kept beating out and forging an old piece of iron till it was the right shape and about a foot long. The chain was a yard long: the struggling shark might bite through the rope, but not the chain. After days of hard work the equipment was ready, and the 'shark fishing' was fixed for one week-end: Heinz said he was leaving it to the two boys.

So on Saturday Rolf was up at six to go off with the dogs to collect the 'bait.' He returned an hour later having shot a hog. It was cut up, and the two shoulders were loaded on to the donkey together with the large fishhook, camping equipment, food and drinking water, and he and Harry set off for Post Office Bay. They returned on Sunday at three, looking extremely pleased with themselves. Rolf proudly carried gun and hook back into the house, while Harry unloaded the donkey, and the rest of us saw a five-gallon can containing a huge shark's liver. I quickly got something on the table for them to eat and drink, though we were bursting with impatience to know how they had done it. 'You tell them, Rolf,' said Harry, and between mouthfuls, with occasional interjections from Harry, Rolf gave us his account of the expedition.

'Well, when we got to Post Office Bay, we first found a good site for the tent. Then Harry got a fire going, while I made a reconnaissance of the beach, the water, and a good tree to tie the rope to. The tide was right out. I stuck one of the two shoulders of pork firmly on to the hook, fastening the meat to the hook with wire so that it couldn't be pulled up. Then I tied a marker buoy to it, and with Harry feeding out the rope I swam out with the hook till I thought the water was deep enough for sharks to come by. Then we tied the rope to the tree we had selected.

'Then we both went over the causeway to Loveria, to catch the lobsters we promised you we'd bring home. But we hadn't got far before the sea started foaming round our buoy, and I could see the tail of a big fish beating up and down on the water. As it stayed in the same spot, I assumed it must be well and truly caught; so we went on to get our lobsters before the tide had come in too far for us to find their holes.'

'When we'd got enough lobsters,' Harry put in, 'Rolf fetched his gun, and we went back to our tree. We pulled on the rope, and the shark sure had bitten, hadn't he, Rolf!'

'He sure had. He came quite easily as long as he was still in the water, but it was much harder pulling him as soon as he got on dry land.'

'He was probably dead by then of course, but the body was still twitching. To be on the safe side, Rolf fired four shots into his skull, and then I brought the *machete* down as hard as I could to split his head off.'

'Then we felt we could have a breather,' said Rolf, 'and take a look at our catch. He was a huge tiger shark—must be about sixteen feet long.'

'Well, I certainly congratulate you both, getting him out of the water,' said Heinz. He turned to me. 'Not bad for a boy of twelve, eh, on his first shark-fishing expedition? Now let's have a look at the shark, then we'll see how much oil we get from its liver.' Its snout, when wedged open, was the size of a forty-gallon petrol tank; the oil came to five and a half gallons. Alas, it did not after all improve Harry's eyesight, but the memory of their adventure left him and Rolf very exhilarated.

May is the loveliest month on Floreana too. Everything is still green from the rainy season, but it is cooler. Gaily coloured birds flutter around outside singing their songs of joy from full throats. The hens are clucking as if they would lay three eggs every day. The life of nature seems overflowing, and man is revived after the sultry, parched weeks before. You can feel the year turning, and you start making new plans for the future.

We were busy making such plans in May 1945. And one day we heard the noise of planes above us, much nearer and louder than usual. There were about thirty planes, we had never seen so many before. 'Must be some sort of manœuvre,' said Heinz, 'nothing to do with us, I expect.'

They were flying very low, right over our heads. We could see the pilots waving. One of the planes broke formation and circled above us while the rest started climbing again. We kept our eyes on the lone plane till what I expected happened: something was dropped from it, a sack or a package, with a long tail fluttering from it. You couldn't miss it, as we had once done with Roosevelt's message. The children watched excitedly as it dropped, then rushed to the spot.

I stayed dead still, staring up at the sky. Why should thirty planes come over our house to drop a packet for one German family? I didn't like the look of it.

'You've gone quite pale,' said Heinz at my side. 'What's the matter?'

'I don't like it,' I said stubbornly.

'Let's wait, and see,' said Heinz.

The children came back with the package. It contained a few letters for us, and a slip of paper on which the pilot had written in large letters: 'Germany has surrendered. The war's over.'

Without a word I went into the house with the children. I knew Heinz would want to be alone with his thoughts. When he came in after an hour, he had recovered a bit from the shock.

For five and a half years we had lived in wartime on this island, and thanks to the trust and magnanimity of our American and Ecuadorian friends, we had been spared what millions of people all over the world had gone through. We knew only too well what terrible things had been done in our country's name, and we had long seen the collapse coming. But that country was still ours, and six thousand miles away the hour of Germany's surrender was still a bitter one. If only it could mean that this was the end of all wars!

Four days later the *Cisney* came to Floreana, and her officers came up to us, bringing newspapers that told of the surrender. The officers spared our feelings as Germans, restraining their jubilation, and our old friend Bill Wymer said to us solemnly: 'You're free again. The whole world is free. Free from Nazism and war.'

Chapter 17

El Oro, an Ecuadorian ship which called at Floreana a month
or so later, had old friends of ours on board, whom we were
delighted to see: the Angermeyers. They were the German couple
settled on Santa Cruz who had been turned off it in 1941. They
spent most of the war in Ecuador, under the restrictions and
unpopularity normal for 'enemy aliens'; now they were returning
to Santa Cruz, determined to work up again from scratch. Their
confidence and resilience was rather inspiring. It made us count
our blessings all the more in having been left undisturbed, and
encouraged us in our own plans for the future.

We talked a lot in the evenings about what Rolf was going to
do when he grew up. He was very gifted in things mechanical,
and it was tempting to think of him going in for engineering or
some similar career. But to aspire to a place in any technical
college, he would have to go to boarding school in Ecuador,
where there naturally was a strong anti-German feeling
still. His German parentage might make things difficult for
him, besides which it was obvious that academically he would
have a good deal of leeway to make up. Regretfully we
decided that the engineering career did not look feasible; he
would have to make a living on Floreana, farming for half the
year and fishing the other half. When this was put to him, Rolf
himself thought it was splendid, while we could take comfort
from the prospect of continuity for our farm in the next
generation.

However, if these hopes were to be fulfilled, we needed to
expand, clear more acres of bush so as to get new and better
crops, so as to earn and save more money—so as to buy a fishing
boat (with motor): this was one of the chief targets of our 'five-

189

year-plan.' The coming of peace, the Angermeyers' example, gave us a new impetus, and we set to work with a will.

Of course the war with Japan was still going, but our American friends seemed confident that that too would not last much longer, and the air-base at Seymour gradually lost its importance. Ships from Seymour would often call at Floreana, and American officers with more free time and leaves found plenty of opportunities 'to look in on the Wittmers.' One party, in that September, included someone I had been eagerly waiting for, a Catholic chaplain. The reason I was so pleased to see him was that I wanted to consult him about having Inge christened.

The chaplain's name was Father O'Brien. He was very surprised to hear that a girl of eight had not been christened. 'Why didn't you do it yourselves?' he asked. 'What happened about the boy's christening?'

'Oh, that was done when I went back to Germany in 1935. But you mean *we* could have performed the christening?'

'Certainly, if no priest is within reach. You knew that, didn't you?'

'Yes,' I stammered, 'I suppose I did. I must have forgotten.'

Father O'Brien smiled. 'I expect when you were first told, you never thought you'd be in a position to need that dispensation. Anyhow I'll get in touch with church authorities, and tell you what can be done about it.'

A fortnight after this a plane dropped a letter for us, saying that two days later a ship would be coming from Seymour, that Father O'Brien would be on board and had received permission to christen Inge and confirm both her and Rolf. The donkey should be at Blackbeach at seven in the morning to bring up all the appurtenances, and the ship would have to leave Floreana by six in the evening.

This did not give us much time for preparations. Heinz and Harry built an altar against the outside wall of the storeroom, knocking in stakes and putting a roof over in case it should rain. The wall was lined with white material to hide the rawness of the bricks. I decorated the altar table with my best tablecloths, and with crystal vases, treasures I had brought with me from Germany. A carpet was laid in front of the altar table, and a bench put up for the two children. Heinz had hastily to make a second bench for the guests.

I had the children's clothes to see to. Inge wore shorts all the time, and had only one dress. Although this was light blue, not white as it should have been, it had beautiful white embroidery. A friend had sent it from Chile some time before, and having been worn so little it looked as good as new in honour of the occasion. Rolf had a suitable outfit consisting of black trousers and a white shirt. I had made the trousers from the skirt of a black suit of mine, which I had discarded as out of place on a farm. He also possessed a pair of shoes, whereas Inge only had the sandals Heinz had cobbled for her; she would just have to be christened in sandals, there wasn't anything we could do about it.

I had a heap of cooking to get through, for many of our officer friends had said they would like to attend the ceremony. I catered for twenty-five. 'There can't be more than that,' Heinz said—but naturally there were, as he found when he went down to Blackbeach with Harry and Rolf to meet them. Rolf had had a good breakfast first, though of course you were supposed to fast before Holy Communion. But he had three hours' walk to Blackbeach and back, which was too much for a boy of twelve on an empty stomach. Circumstances altered cases.

Heinz rode down on Hector, our horse—yes, we owned a horse as well. He belonged originally to the officer in command of the little Ecuadorian garrison, but there was not enough food for him on the coast, so we were asked to give him a home. Afterwards they forgot to pay for his fodder, the bill accumulated; for a little extra he came into our possession, and the Ecuadorian army did not seem to miss him. He became the pride of our 'riding stables,' and was used as a mount for V.I.P.s—so the procession returning from Blackbeach was led by the padre riding on Hector.

Father O'Brien had time to put up a sort of confessional so as to prepare Inge for the ceremony. She looked at him wide-eyed and listened attentively to what he told her, but did not say a word herself. Then we stood before our modest improvised altar, which yet looked as beautiful and solemn as in any church. We had a house of God built by nature, a church roof formed by the wide spreading branches of tall trees, which were like the pillars of a Gothic cathedral. With goodwill and a little imagination you could feel you were indeed in church.

Father O'Brien gave a short but moving address. 'These

children born on this island,' he said, 'are growing up in quite different conditions from most other children. They are growing up in God's nature, far from all evil. God Himself will look down with joy on them, though they have come to the Lord's table so little prepared; for they have come to Him with a pure heart.'

Even before he had finished, his words about the different conditions were confirmed by our animals. Mephisto the bull, Barbara the cow and their calf Liesel came trotting out of the bush, took up their stand against the fence, and began lowing in chorus, demanding their food. It was high time for them to be fed, christening or no christening.

Father O'Brien smiled, stole a glance at his watch, and brought his address to an end. Harry went off to feed the animals, while I found a meal for the 'humans,' who were equally in need of sustenance: they had not had a bite since a hasty breakfast at four in the morning. I gave them roast chicken followed by cakes and dessert, and they 'fell to' with an appetite most rewarding for the cook. Of course the food I had prepared for twenty-five did not go quite far enough with so many more guests, but everyone seemed content.

After the meal the Padre made a short speech, saying what a memorable day it was in the history of the Galapagos Islands, and asking the officers to write in our visitors' book. 'Though Fate will soon have scattered you to the four winds,' he concluded, 'may the common experience of this day stay alive in your hearts.'

He signed the visitors' book first, writing: 'Our visit to Floreana has left us with a host of memories: the christening, the confirmation of Rolf and Inge, the Holy Mass here in this solitude, and the feast in your home. May your happy life on Floreana continue, may the Lord God bless you and keep you. Father Patrick O'Brien, Chaplain, U.S. Army.'

We couldn't expand much further near the Asilo de la Paz. The ground was too loamy, there were too many stones, and the bush all round us seemed thicker than ever. We turned our attention to an area a quarter of an hour away, between us and the Conways' former estate, where the soil looked very favourable. We cleared some two hundred and fifty square yards of bush to start with; later, if all went well, we hoped to extend it to ten acres. Having cut down trees and fenced round the plot, we planted bananas and coffee, sowed maize, yucca and beans; and very soon the first green shoots were springing up. We hoped for so much from this new plantation that we decided to call it *Esperanza*. It was to belong to the two boys, and Heinz carved a big sign which went over the entrance, saying: *Esperanza—Proprietarios Harry y Rolf Wittmer*.

Meanwhile the small Ecuadorian military garrison at Blackbeach had been replaced by a detachment of marines—a first lieutenant, two petty officers and five sailors—the married men, as before, having their families with them. We had two new civilian settlers as well from Ecuador. One, a man called Cruz, stayed a long while; but the other was so disappointed by the results of all his hard work that he departed the following year, selling his garden to a fellow-countryman called Ulloa with a wife and three children. The crops still did not grow fast enough for Ulloa and Cruz, so they tried to make a business instead from hides and meat. Having reduced considerably the numbers of cattle and pigs, the Ulloas also left the island. But the game on Floreana had often suffered such losses before, and still survived. The bush was too thick; they could always find protection from man, unless he were a good hunter indeed.

In February 1946, we were involved in a different sort of hunt. I heard the dogs barking very loudly, the bark they always gave when strangers were coming; only I couldn't see anyone walking up the track. I turned round to find an American officer behind me, one I had never met before. He scrutinised me long and hard. 'Morning,' he said at last.

'Good morning.'

'Mrs Wittmer?'

'Yes.'

There was a long tear in his khaki shirt, and one of his hands was bleeding; he looked most alarming. 'Where on earth have you come from?' I asked nervously.

Raising his head, he pointed behind him and upwards with his chin. He had come down from the spring, through the bush, and instead of coming in by the gate must have crept through the fence.

He was not alone. Men were now emerging from the bush on

all sides and making for the house. There were about two dozen of them in all, including some ten officers. All were armed. With them as guide, was First Lieutenant Santos, the officer in charge of Floreana's small naval detachment. 'What's all this from?' I asked, pointing to the torn shirts and bleeding hands which most of them had.

'Barbed wire,' said one laconically, wiping blood away with his sleeve.

'But why did you have to crawl through the barbed wire?' I shook my head, quite baffled. 'Why couldn't you come in through the gate like any normal visitors?'

'We wanted to have a bit of a look round.' I thought I saw some of the soldiers grinning at this.

'Have you got anything to drink?' asked one of the officers. It was the rainy season, and the heat that day was terrible, the sweat was pouring down their cheeks. I offered them cool drinks.

'You didn't send a plane saying you were coming,' I remarked. 'That's what generally happens, you know.'

'Maybe,' said one. Some of the others shrugged their shoulders, some again grinned significantly.

'May we look round your house?' asked a captain who appeared to be in charge of the expedition.

'If you like,' I said. 'I'd love to know what it's all about, though.'

The refreshments had relaxed the atmosphere a good deal, and as no one seemed disposed to answer my questions, I chatted about other things. Soon we were all quite friendly, and when the 'search party' returned, the whole lot took their leave of me, apologising for the intrusion, and disappeared again into the bush. Santos was in the rear, and at the last moment he whispered to me: 'I'll tell you something very funny tomorrow.'

I could hardly wait for the next morning to come. Santos turned up then, as promised. 'I don't know if you've been following the papers lately?' he began.

'When we get our papers,' Heinz answered, 'they aren't usually very up-to-date.'

'Well,' said Santos, 'there was something in a Panama paper about Hitler.' He paused, increasing our suspense. 'Something about, er, Hitler having escaped in a submarine to Floreana and being sheltered by the Wittmers.'

For a moment we were completely flabbergasted. Then we burst into roars of laughter.

'And they believed that?' asked Heinz.

'Perhaps.'

'And that's what they were here for yesterday?'

'Yes.'

'Did they find him?'

'No.'

'Even if he had been there, they mightn't have found him,' said Heinz. 'There's too much bush on this island and too many caves. I think you'd need a whole regiment searching for him for days. However, they can save themselves the trouble, for I may as well tell you frankly: he's not here!'

Santos chuckled. 'I didn't think he was.'

There had long been rumours, of course, about Hitler being alive and having escaped to South America. But we were far from being the sort of Germans who would have offered him a retreat, so that on the whole we were more annoyed than amused at our name being coupled with his. However, there were no repercussions from the bizarre incident, after which we continued in the even tenor of our ways, pleasantly interrupted now and again by visits from globe-trotting private sailors, mostly Americans. It was good to see the Johnsons again at the end of 1947, on the fourth cruise of the schooner *Yankee* round the seven seas. By this time, officially at least, we were not so cut off from the outside world, for Floreana had its own radio station: not always working, but at least there. All ships from Ecuador or other countries visiting the Galapagos Islands had now to call first at Chatham, seat of the *Gobernador Marítimo*; and to keep the other inhabited islands in constant touch with Chatham, they all had radio stations established on them. One of the naval detachment's petty officers was the actual radio operator, with a rating as 'leading signalman.'

To keep the engine going, petrol was needed, but petrol on the Galapagos was a precious fluid. Every gallon had to be brought over from the mainland—on a ship, and you might have to wait anything from five to fifteen weeks for the next ship. Our transmitter had been provided with forty gallons, of which its engine used three quarters of a gallon every working hour. Consequently our station was very often not functioning. There were frequent mechanical breakdowns, which always seemed to occur just when there was plenty of fuel. When there was no breakdown, the fuel had run out. When the engine was all right, and there was enough fuel, the operator was usually on leave or had been transferred to another island.

Nevertheless, we were glad the station was there, telling ourselves optimistically that it would soon be functioning properly and that we might one day need it. This was the case, alas, in March 1949, when Harry, who had been pretty well for a long time, got another attack of rheumatic fever. We recognised it by the symptoms: very high temperatures, racing pulse, extreme weakness and inability to move his arms and legs. We were indeed grateful then to be able to send out a radio appeal for help, though it was five long weeks before a ship could bring us drugs. These at least helped to keep the fever under control, but Harry's condition caused us serious anxiety, and once more he had to stay in bed for many months. Sometimes he would feel better for a few days, then there would be a relapse. We remembered the warnings of the Panama doctor in 1937, and were afraid he was at best going to be a permanent invalid.

The air-base on Seymour had been replaced by a small American naval station, and after this we luckily had periodical visits from its doctor, who kept an eye on Harry's health. He seemed to be slowly recovering, but worry about him, plus the extra work, had taken it out of both Heinz and myself. By the summer of 1949 I was terribly run down, I felt there was something wrong with my inside, and the doctor from Seymour advised me to 'go to hospital' for a thorough overhaul. Hospital, of course, meant the mainland, some six hundred miles away, and perhaps an absence of two or three months if one missed one's ship 'connections,' so I was loath to take the doctor's advice. On the other hand, in my present state I was becoming a burden to the family, and Heinz insisted that he and the boys would manage all right; for after long discussion it was decided that Inge should accompany me. Rolf would have loved to come too, but the two farms certainly could not do without three pairs of hands at once, particularly when Harry still had to stay in bed much of the time. The doctor said he should be spared all unnecessary exertion, then he would be fairly all right.

Floreana seemed rather a sad place just then. Zavala, who had stomach trouble for years, now had to be flown to Panama (by arrangement with the Americans on Seymour) for an emergency abdominal operation. This appeared to have been successful, so that he was sent home; but he died a fortnight later. It was the first death on the island since Ritter's, and was distressing for us, even if we and the Zavalas had not always been very friendly. Maruja was inconsolable, but decided to stay on their farm and manage as best she could. She had a sewing machine, and offered to sew clothes for Inge for the great journey. I gladly accepted, hoping it would help take her mind off her loss.

Soon after the war we had been sent wonderful gifts of clothes and other precious articles, through my sister, from Lady Duke-Elder in London; but Inge, of course, could no more get into the clothes originally destined for her. In any case she still wore shorts all day and every day, having only once worn a dress—on the day of her christening. At twelve and a bit she was a tall girl, looked almost grown-up, and was a good deal above average intelligence for her age. But she knew nothing at first hand of the world outside the Galapagos Islands, and said she didn't want to know anything either. I was afraid the clothes Maruja made for her might have as little appeal as the Christmas doll she had received so disdainfully nine years before. Fortunately she quite enjoyed 'dressing up,' as she put it, tried things on, paraded in them, and was suddenly looking forward to the coming journey. We gradually got her finger-nails into decent shape, and for the first time her fair hair was neatly done up in plaits.

It was I who began to be afraid, as of some terrible ordeal ahead. I was a completely different person from the woman who had come to Floreana seventeen years before. I had been on the island continuously for the last twelve of those years, and felt I shouldn't know how to talk to or get on with people away from my familiar environment. The tables were turned, and Inge had to tell me what fun it would all be 'when you're better, Mutti, and we both make all sorts of new friends.' My daughter was happy enough with the company of her family and the animals, but I could see that she was already a little attracted by the prospect of meeting other children of her own age.

We planned to cross in the *Calderón*, the regular Galapagos boat, and as usual she arrived about August. It was ten o'clock at night when one of the Ecuadorian sailors came up to tell us that the *Calderón* was in the bay, and could not wait for us long. Rolf had to ride down on the donkey with our luggage, and there was such a terrific hurry that none of us had any proper time for good-byes—which may have been a good thing.

'Get better and come back soon,' Rolf called after me, as a rowing boat took us out to the *Calderón*. Then he held his hands in front of his mouth like a funnel, and called again: 'Come back soon.' Whatever he said after that, the words were blown away by the wind. We stood at the rail and waved as long as he was in sight. When we couldn't see him any more, Inge's tears began to flow freely, till the captain, Benjamin Chiraboga, an old friend of ours, put an arm round her shoulder and then showed her over the ship. I went on standing at the rail, watching our island shrink into a narrow strip of low-lying blue-grey land. I felt as if I were saying good-bye to it for ever.

When we reached Guayaquil, we stayed for a few days in this first town Inge had ever set foot in, an important commercial centre and port with four hundred thousand inhabitants; lofty buildings in concrete; splendid churches, wide streets and luxurious shops; cars and buses; the great harbour; and all the colour and bustle of a big city. Inge walked through the streets, showing no more than a mild interest in all the hundreds of things she had never seen before, apparently letting them float right past her consciousness.

But one day I watched her standing at the window with an absorbed expression and gazing down at the street. She wouldn't move away from the window, and when I looked over her shoulder I could not for the life of me find anything special or unusual in the scene. 'What's so interesting?' I asked in the end. She turned and said to me incredulously: 'How on earth can people sit on a bicycle, Mutti, and not fall off?'

This was evidently the most sensational thing she had observed on her first visit to the mainland, and I believe it excited her more than the fourteen-hour train journey through lush meadows, virgin forest, up ten-thousand-foot mountains, to Quito at the foot of snow-capped Mount Chimborazo, which was nearer twenty thousand feet.

Quito itself is between eight and nine thousand feet above sea level and is one of the highest capitals in the world. It is set in gloriously fertile and flowery mountain scenery with the beauty of fairyland; and although almost on the Equator, the air is light and fresh, as if it were spring the whole year round. The beauty of nature all round has inspired artists to magnificent compositions, and few towns in the Spanish-speaking world have so many fine works of art—or so many splendid baroque churches. Its atmosphere is a mixture of modern culture and historic tradition, for it is also a very old town.

Centuries before the Spaniards founded the new Quito, it was the capital of the Indian Quitu kingdom. In the fifteenth century the conquering Incas made it the capital of their northern province, and in the areas round present-day Quito there are still 'thoroughbred' Incas living, short dark-skinned people with lank, pitch-black hair, who still practise the traditional Inca crafts, marketing their products in Quito: colourful tapestries of thick wool, belts, bags, skirts, blouses, vases and pottery, painted in superb colours with old Inca patterns. The buyers are not only Ecuadorians but people from half the world over. The big tapestry in the United Nations Building in New York is the work of these Inca artists, who live retiringly in the mountains dropping away eastwards to the inaccessible areas of the River Amazon.

I went to one of the best hospitals in Quito, and had my thorough medical examination. It turned out that I was suffering from gallstones, and although I responded well to the treatment the doctors ordered, they said I needed a very long convalescence. Probably the change of climate, extra comforts, and the kindness of many friends both old and new, all helped to put me to rights. At any rate I soon felt miles better than I had done the last year on Floreana.

Inge was at first terribly homesick for the island, for sea and bush and animals and plants and the Floreana sky, for her father and brothers. But having the chance for the first time to meet plenty of young people, a girl of Inge's friendly nature could not help brightening up. She also grew taller and broader, so that most of the clothes we had brought for her were already on the small side. In six months' time, when I felt altogether myself again and the doctors allowed me to return to island life, Inge was very sorry to leave all the friends we had made. So was I, but of course our sadness was mixed with joyful anticipation. We were both longing to get home.

Instead of travelling the fourteen hours by train, we flew back to Guayaquil. The flight only lasted an hour, and although it was the first time she had been in a plane, Inge took the whole thing in her stride as if it were an everyday occurrence.

We had no more than a fortnight to wait in Guayaquil, and then our good old *Calderón* put out to sea again, heading for the Galapagos. The little ship was crammed with people, most of whom spent the nights in hammocks on the open deck beneath the dark sky of the Pacific.

Rolf was the last person we had seen when we left; now he was the first when we got back. As we climbed out of the landing-boat, he came rushing up to embrace us both. Inge could not help crying for joy when she saw him again, while Rolf, taking a good look at her, remarked teasingly, no doubt to hide his deep emotion: 'How my baby sister has grown!'

His 'baby sister,' just coming from the great world, had scarcely felt *terra firma* beneath her feet again when she sat down on the black lava boulders on the beach and took off her shoes, discarding with this one gesture all the paraphernalia of the great world outside our island. Then she got up, gripped her case firmly, and ran off bare-footed into the bush as fast as she could.

We had only heard from the men once while we were away, and had been half dreading some bad news; you couldn't guess what sort of minor or major calamities might have occurred in a very few weeks. But this time we couldn't have had a better homecoming, for Harry was up all the time and even able to work a little. He and Heinz greeted us as joyfully as Rolf had, to the accompaniment of delighted barking from all our dogs; and after the first excited questions I was able to give them my special news.

When the American air-base at Seymour was dismantled, a fantastic amount of stuff was left behind, and some of the officers who visited us brought over lots of wonderful 'surplus' especially clothes and shoes which lasted us for years. The Government of Ecuador took over all the more permanent installations of the base, and I had heard in Quito that some of the houses the Americans had put up were to be distributed among the settlers under certain conditions. I applied to the Ecuadorian admiral of the fleet for permission to get one of these houses, and he promised to do what he could. He kept his word too, for quite soon afterwards the government decided that in their distribution the settlers already on the Galapagos should be given priority consideration. I was permitted to look for one of the houses on my return journey and afterwards have it brought over to Floreana. Best of all, this would be a gift; we should have nothing to pay for it at all.

When the ship called at Seymour on the way home, I looked round for a suitable house, and chose immodestly one of the biggest, which had served the Americans as a post office. It had several rooms and represented a great deal of timber. That was the important thing, because the trees on Floreana were all too gnarled to make satisfactory timber for building purposes. That was why we had never managed to build a house at Blackbeach, although we had long seen the advantages of it. For one thing the climate was much more temperate on the coast and better for an invalid, so Harry could live there at least during the hot season. Then there were my chickens—now about five hundred of them —which would be better away from the continual rain up at the Asilo de la Paz and Esperanza; they could be transferred to Blackbeach. Finally, there would be enough wood to build not only our own living accommodation and a big hen-house but also a food store, which we had come to realise was urgently necessary for marketing our produce—instead of having to rush it down to the coast at the last minute for ships with no time to wait.

So when I had selected this former post office, I stuck a big notice, saying, 'WITTMER, FLOREANA,' on the house, which by this small formality came into our possession. Rolf would go over to fetch it from Seymour at the earliest opportunity.

Providence seemed to suggest such an opportunity that June of 1950 when we got a letter from Count von Luckner, with whom we were still in regular correspondence. He promised us a visit the month afterwards from a friend of his, Commander Baverstock, who would also be bringing over one of the latest types of new long-range radio equipment for us. The yacht *Inca* came as announced, and the Commander not only agreed to take Rolf to Seymour, but gave him all the necessary tools for dismantling the house and a whole lot of tinned foods as well. This was invaluable help, for you could not get much food from Seymour itself: there was scarcely anything growing or any wild life on the whole island, which was mostly sheer lava.

Rolf dismantled the house and packed the planks into bundles. Apart from the rest of the building material, there were a hundred and twenty bundles of twenty planks each, and when he returned to Floreana six weeks later, the wind was strong and the sea rough, so unloading the bundles was a real feat. They were thrown down from the ship into the water, and three or four bundles at a time were tied to a skiff and so towed to land.

The crew helped nobly, and Rolf himself kept going to and fro with his skiff, so that we hardly saw anything of him. We were busy lugging the landed bundles further up the beach, stopping now and then to get food and plenty of coffee for the crew. The operation took till long past midnight, and it was a very dark night, though the coast was faintly lit up by the ship's lights out in the bay. Suddenly I heard a yell from the sea's edge : 'Tide's coming in!'

It was Inge, who was alone there at the time and saw the sea flooding in fast, with waves breaking higher and higher, till it threatened all our precious wood. We left everything and dashed down to the rescue, dragging the planks still further up the beach out of range of the incoming tide. By the time we had done this, the night was almost over, we were all soaked to the skin and exhausted. Despite our struggles five of the bundles were carried out to sea. We wrote off two, but managed to salvage the other three in the skiff next day when the sea had calmed down.

When the ship arrived that evening, we had been so happy to have Rolf safely back, bringing the haul of timber, that we completely forgot it was the night the moon changed. So we failed to guard against its inevitable concomitant, the spring tide!

That was the middle of August. On the first of November we were able to move into our new house. A dream was fulfilled, we had a two-storey 'mansion' with plenty of room for all the family and two guest-rooms besides. For a whole fortnight our long-suffering donkeys were transporting bits of furniture and hundreds of other things from the old farmhouse down to Blackbeach. And just at the right moment the Ecuadorian cruiser *El Oro* arrived, so that we were able to have a fine housewarming party with her commander and officers, and Father Castillo from the Franciscan Mission. This allowed us to express our heartfelt gratitude to the government of Ecuador for presenting us so generously with the house from Seymour. We made a vow that it would be kept open at all times for officers and men of the Ecuadorian Navy. That vow has been faithfully kept till this day, and I hope future generations of Wittmers will keep it still.

We had a very happy first Christmas in our new house, but New Year's Eve and Rolf's birthday were even happier, for that week we had very old friends staying in one of the guest-rooms, friends who had known Rolf since he was a very small boy : Irving and Electa Johnson in yet another cruise of the *Yankee*. Irving sat up half the night with my menfolk, discussing Rolf's new project, a fishing boat. 'I made quite a decent desk,' Rolf had remarked to him, 'so with your expert advice I should be able to build some sort of a boat.'

He and Heinz had already worked out a construction plan from the specifications in an American magazine, but Irving Johnson was naturally able to modify the design a good deal in the light of his long experience. The only available wood was the surplus from the house building, and it was very hard: it had to be moistened before you could laboriously bend it into shape, and fit one plank to another. However, after three weeks of strenuous joinery the boat was completed, 14½ feet long by 4 feet wide, and was painted bright red. We decided to call her Inge, and invited the whole naval station and the wireless operator to the launching ceremony. We hadn't any champagne, but felt that plenty of home-brewed brandy would serve just as well. Ingeborg Floreanita Wittmer solemnly pronounced the words : 'I hereby name this boat Inge,' and released the bottle against the bow. But the bottle failed to burst, and we all looked a little embarrassed. Then the girl Inge exclaimed, 'Thank heavens for that!' as if a big weight had been taken off her mind.

'What on earth do you mean?' I asked, shocked by this breach with all naval tradition.

She smiled happily, stroking the intact bottle. 'Thank heavens it didn't break, Mutti. Bottles don't grow on trees here, and I'm sure everyone would much rather drink this stuff than see it wasted.'

'Typical Inge!' I murmured in amusement, and all the naval personnel present heartily agreed with her expression of practical economy, as the bottle was carefully uncorked and its contents shared. The good ship Inge was well and truly launched—in the best of spirits.

It was very pleasant to be living by the sea, and we saw more of the fauna for which the Galapagos Islands are famous. Karl Angermeyer on Santa Cruz took one of our Alsatian puppies in exchange for a piglet, a baby iguana and a baby turtle. We gave the turtle to Irving Johnson, who wanted to see if it would have any young, but kept the lizard, which grew up as part of the family! On calls of 'Ana, ana, ana!' it would slither up for the bread and rice we put down. The dogs didn't touch it, recognising it as a pet. The Angermeyers had a whole house-trained colony of iguanas who would swarm into the dining-room at a whistle from Karl, and wait round the table for the scraps he threw them. There were always plenty of iguanas sunning themselves on the lava shelves round our shores.

Our dogs were also on good terms with the seals, or at least the seals had a fine game to amuse them. Somewhere in shallow waters a seal would pop its head out and bark, at which the dogs would splash out towards the place, only to find the seal had now decamped and would emerge in another spot to repeat its mocking bark. The dogs would chase off there, when the same thing would happen. It seemed a wonderful game for both sides; they would play it for hours on end.

The arrival of a ship would be signalled to us in advance by great flights of frigate birds and pelicans; we often had forty or fifty pelicans fighting on the beach to take the food out of our hands. It was fascinating to watch the mother pelican tearing off the head of a fish to swallow it for softening in her stomach, before bringing it up as predigested food to give to her babies.

There were swarms of fish in the waters round Floreana, particularly the *bacalao*, which is rather like cod, only its flesh is extremely tender and tasty, so that, well cooked, it is a great delicacy for the table. Harry and Rolf went out in the boat soon after the launching, and collected plenty of *bacalao*. Soon even 'Inge' would not be good enough, but if they caught enough in her, they could hope to buy their own motorised fishing boat, the original target of our post-war 'five-year-plan.' They could certainly make a good living by fishing during the season and working on the farm the rest of the year, above all planting coffee. When our coffee plantation grew large enough for us to live on coffee exports, they would be able to give up the comparatively laborious business of fishing, but that was a long-term prospect, and at present fishing was first priority.

To preserve the fish you needed masses of salt, so the boys went to the big salt lake and dug new salt holes by its shores. But a month or two later, when they went to collect the salt, it had gone, and this happened twice more. Since the gift of houses from Seymour, several other families had come to Floreana, living either at Blackbeach or up near our farm, and it was pointless trying to find out who had taken our salt. The main thing was to discover somewhere else for the salt holes which would be less easily accessible, and the boys picked a place in the east of the island on the far side of the lake.

Harry, incidentally, was in better health than he had been for ages. He had been up and working for over a year, was putting on a nice lot of weight (he had been terribly thin before), and on his thirty-second birthday, September 16th, 1951, we had a big party, to which literally 'the whole island' was invited: all the settlers and all the naval station. Inge and a friend of hers, daughter of one of the settlers, sang a nice birthday song; and Harry made a little speech saying how happy he was to be able to go out and fish with Rolf once more.

One Sunday morning nearly six weeks later the two of them rowed off at low tide with our friend Vaca, the new operator of the radio station. They said they would be back in the afternoon, and already at one o'clock we saw *Inge's* small sail appearing above the water. 'I'd never have thought she was so fast,' Inge said to her father.

'A real regatta-type yacht,' he answered, laughing, for the boat was a little ungainly and too heavy for her size. The planks were too thick, but they were all we'd had.

I looked at her through the binoculars. I could see the sail very clearly, but there seemed to be only two people in the boat. 'Perhaps you can see a third,' I said in dismay, handing Heinz the binoculars. He looked through them for a long while, saying nothing. His mouth was tight shut. 'No, I can't,' he muttered at last, the binoculars still glued to his eyes. 'Harry's missing, I can't see Harry.' He tried to reassure us, and himself. 'Perhaps he didn't feel well, and is lying down in the bottom of the boat.'

With one accord the three of us ran down to the beach as fast as we could. The boat was nearly in now. The sea was pretty rough. Rolf quickly took in the sail and began to row very hard to bring the boat in. But although he must have seen us, he neither waved nor called to us.

A wave brought her on to the beach. When the next wave came, we all caught hold of her and dragged her on to dry land. Nobody spoke a word. The faces of the two boys were ashen, their arms and legs bleeding. The next wave broke against the boat, then everything was very still. 'Where's Harry?' I broke the long silence at last.

The boys hunched their shoulders. Their arms hung limply at their sides, their eyes were fixed to the ground. Then Rolf lifted his face for the first time. His voice shook. 'Harry's drowned,' he said.

We stared at Rolf incredulously. I saw Heinz going very pale, and I was afraid he might have another heart attack. 'Drowned?' he whispered from bloodless lips. He reeled. 'Drowned? Harry?' He turned away and sat on the edge of the boat.

Now Rolf began to explain, though he was still not fully in control of his voice. 'We had a good wind which took us to the place we wanted to land at. The sea was fairly calm. Then the wind suddenly got up. I was busy trying to land when a huge wave broke on to the boat. We capsized, but all three of us came up again. Harry too. He was quite close to me.' Rolf leaned against the boat for support.

Vaca went on with the account: 'Then Harry wasn't there any more, I could only see Rolf. We were both fighting for our lives, and managed to swim ashore. Directly he felt land, Rolf dropped into the sand exhausted. I hadn't quite got there, but I just made it with my last strength, and crawled along to Rolf. He was already standing up again shouting, 'Harry, Harry!' We couldn't see or hear anything, we thought Harry must have been thrown up somewhere else by another wave. We rushed up and down, but didn't see anything. Then we had to rest, we were just dead beat. Rolf kept vomiting and retching, then I did too . . . from all the salt water we'd swallowed . . .'

We walked slowly up to the house, first in silence, then they told us more details: how they had run a long way round the beach shouting for Harry, but found no trace of him; how they swam out to the boat, which lay keel upwards jammed between large rocks near the spot where she had turned turtle; how they righted her and then laboriously scooped out the water with an old can they had found on the shore; how she twice threatened to capsize again before they at last reached the open sea and could sail for Blackbeach.

It was two o'clock when we got home. They had not had anything to eat or drink, but they were so exhausted they could only drink in small mouthfuls. Rolf started weeping, while Vaca had such a terrible headache that he could not bear to move. I put them both to bed in the boys' room.

As I was going back to the living-room, I saw Inge coming towards me. Her face was deathly pale, and she was crying. 'Papa,' I heard her say, then she ran past me. I went back into the room we called the study. Heinz was lying slumped across his desk. He had had a heart attack. I did not like waking the two boys, but I had to, to help me get Heinz to bed. When he eventually opened his eyes, I was shocked to see that he looked many years older.

Vaca stumbled off to inform the naval station. The news spread round the island like a forest fire, the marines and some of the other settler families came to see what they could do. But it was four o'clock by then, much too late to get to the scene of the accident with a boat, let alone to reach it on foot—for it would be dark in two hours. They tried to comfort us, but there was no comfort in words just then. I remembered bitterly how Harry had twice lain in bed for months with rheumatic fever, facing death for weeks on end, how we had nursed him back to comparative health, so that he could at last look forward to a happy active life; and now the sea had taken him from us.

Probably what the doctors foretold had happened: his weak heart had not stood up to the sudden shock. Our one consolation was that he must have died instantly without any suffering.

The next morning all the inhabitants of the island set off to search the entire sea-shore, in case Harry's body had been cast up somewhere or was lying in the shallows stuck between rocks. The sun was sinking when they returned, and they had not found him. They did find his jacket, which had been washed ashore, also the hat he was wearing, a pouch containing pipe and tobacco, a rope, and the two buckets I had packed their food in.

The coast was searched continually for a fortnight, but there was no trace of the body. In the end we gave it up. We went with Maruja Zavala to the little mound where she had buried her husband, and there we prayed for Harry's soul. He was only thirty-two, but he had lived nearly twenty years in the peace and freedom of our island, the first boy who had grown to manhood on it. He had been a wonderful son to Heinz and me, a wonderful brother to Rolf and Inge, and he not only left us with many happy memories, I knew he had been happy himself—because that was his nature. In the long blank months and years to come, however much we missed him now, I knew that would in the end console both me and his father.

Chapter 18

It took us a long time to recover from the blow. Rolf had continual headaches, I felt very low myself, and had to force myself to work; while Heinz was seriously ill for weeks. For a long time, too, he was completely apathetic, indifferent, and would scarcely answer when I began looking to the future. One day I even started suggesting schemes for our starting a 'Floreana guest-house' when he was better again. At this he suddenly sat up and began opposing my 'crazy plans,' and even putting forward different ones of his own. Nothing came of them, but I knew then that at least his will to live had been restored; and from then on his physical health improved also.

While we were still half stunned by what had happened, only about a week after the tragedy, we were surprised to see two strangers arriving, from inland. There had been no boat at Blackbeach, and we couldn't understand how they had come. One was a young man in his twenties with a pleasant open face, a Belgian called Raoul Falley; the other was a German and about fifty, his name was Strobel, and he looked rather sulky. Falley explained their circumstances:

'We were on the Dutch yacht *Anna Elisabeth* going to Tahiti, and had paid for the whole voyage. We'd also deposited five hundred dollars each with the captain; you had to have this to be allowed to land on Tahiti. The yacht had no permit to call at the Galapagos, but the captain put in at Post Office Bay so that we could come up to your farmhouse and get our letters stamped with the Galapagos stamp. First of all we lost our way. Then when we eventually found the farm there was nobody there, it was getting very late and we had to stay the night up there, we should never have found our way back to Post Office Bay with darkness falling. But when we got back this morning, there was no sign of the *Anna Elisabeth*. Some of our luggage was lying by the post barrel, but there was no message of any sort. The captain had taken the rest of it, plus our five hundred dollars landing money.'

We were much shocked at this recital. It seemed incredible that in our day and age a captain could leave two people on a strange coast without food or water, without their personal belongings or even their passports. Whether you believed it or not, they were here, and needed a roof over their heads. This being one of the many occasions when our radio station was not working, there was no chance either of finding anything out about the two men or of sending a report on their plight. There might not be another ship for six or eight weeks at least, so for the time being we should have to put them up in our house.

My first impressions of Strobel were unfortunately confirmed. He was a conceited, quarrelsome and morose individual, and we were not sorry to see him depart just before Christmas, on a government ship that called. But Raoul Falley took to our way of life, stayed till February 1952, and was a most attractive personality. He went fishing with Rolf, they caught nearly a ton of fish, sharing the proceeds so that Raoul should be able to buy a ticket back to Belgium. He was actually a journalist, as he soon disclosed, and found many things on Floreana to stimulate his professional interest: the weeks he spent on the island were not wasted time for him. His friendliness and cheerful outlook helped us a great deal to get over our sorrow. Heinz's morale improved daily; he even learnt to laugh again, as he chatted to Raoul in his stumbling English and listened to the replies given in Raoul's awkward German. We all thought of Raoul as a good and kind friend, and blessed the fate which had so literally cast him up on our shores.

After his departure Rolf went out fishing with our neighbour Rodrigo, who had now been settled on the island for a few years. Heinz was well again and able to work, though for a long time he was even quieter than usual. But it was his idea, in which I strongly supported him, that Rolf ought to have a chance of seeing a little of the 'outside world.' Perhaps it only registered with me now that the boy would soon be twenty, yet he had not left the Galapagos Islands since he was a baby, and to all intents and purposes had never seen streets and shops and theatres and cinemas, let alone factories and express trains, except in pictures; not even the humble bicycle, the riding of which had so amazed Inge on *her* first visit to the mainland.

'Are you dying to see the world?' Heinz asked him one evening near Christmas time. We both looked at Rolf eagerly, wondering what his answer would be.

'*Dying* to see it?' Rolf echoed. He reflected a moment. 'Well, not exactly that . . . But I'd be terribly glad just to have a squint at it, you know.'

We laughed. 'Well,' said Heinz, 'your mother and I have decided it's high time you did have a squint at something outside Floreana. It'll be a sort of twentieth birthday present—a trip to the mainland.'

Rolf's face lit up. 'Olé!' he cried exuberantly. 'Boy, what a present!'

'Right,' said Heinz, 'that's settled. You shall go the first opportunity after your birthday.'

But this opportunity came from a most unexpected quarter. At the end of January 1953 a big ship arrived, and a small boat landed with a message for us which said: 'I am on board the *Don Lucho* with two colleagues. We plan to stay some time on Floreana in the hope of excavating Inca remains. Could you possibly put us up? Thor Heyerdahl.'

Could we put up the hero of the Kon-Tiki expedition? We certainly could. We sent Rolf out to the ship to tell Thor Heyerdahl that he and his colleagues would be heartily welcome. Soon they came ashore with Rolf, who introduced us to Heyerdahl himself, then to Arne Skjölsvold and Dr Reed.

Getting their luggage ashore took a great deal longer, for they had brought fifty-five large crates, which rapidly turned our house into a warehouse. 'What on earth have you got in all those?' I asked.

'Oh, all sorts of apparatus,' said Heyerdahl. 'Plus supplies of food. And water too, of course.'

'What?' I cried. 'Food and water? Are you cra . . . I mean, did you think you'd starve to death on Floreana?'

'Oh well, we never can tell,' said Heyerdahl with a laugh. 'Have to guard against all eventualities, you know. Anyhow we've got enough stores here to last us six months.'

'I'm sure you could feed the Wittmers too,' I commented. 'Anyhow I'm glad we've got enough space for your "iron rations" as well as yourselves! I'll show you to your rooms now, if you like.'

'Thanks very much. And then we'd like to get down to work as soon as possible. Your son has kindly said he'll take us round a bit.'

So Rolf gave the party a conducted tour, on foot and by boat, and digging was done in several places. But then it began to pour with rain. It went on teeming down for days. All over the island water streamed from the hills in wide runnels, the bush was a luxuriant green, weeds grew thick and fast, and for weeks digging was impossible. Heyerdahl and his party did not like being idle, and they spent most of the time in the study, rattling away at typewriters and no doubt brushing up on the latest archaeological researches.

Their first evening, when we were all sitting together round the big family table, Heyerdahl and the others kept probing us on Floreana's past. We said nobody knew anything certain, though of course there were a few old stories about the pirates, buried treasure, etc.

'We're thinking of something quite different,' said Skjölsvold. 'Much farther back than the pirates, or even the Spaniards. Haven't you found any traces of human life from the Inca times? Fragments of pottery or anything like that.'

Heinz shook his head. 'Nothing at all.'

'What about a face carved in stone?' asked Heyerdahl. 'Surely there's something of that sort. I remember seeing a photograph of it four or five years ago, and all the archaeologists got very excited about it. Do you know the thing I mean?'

Heinz had sat up with a start. 'Well,' he said thoughtfully, 'there *is* a stone face by the spring near our old farm.' He gave me a slight wink, unnoticed by Heyerdahl and the others. 'Tell us more about it from your end, then I'll tell you the little *I* know.'

'All right,' said Heyerdahl, 'it was quite a sensation at the time. It started with Captain Phillips Lord, who was here in 1948.'

'Yes,' I said, 'he's an old friend of ours. I believe that *was* the year he last came.'

'Well, he gave a lecture in New York about his trip, during

which he showed a photograph of a huge stone face which he claimed to have taken on your farm. I was in New York at the time and attended that lecture myself. I can vividly remember a professor of archaeology jumping up and calling out: "That picture couldn't have come from the Galapagos, it must be from Easter Island." Phillips Lord said he'd never even been to Easter Island, and the professor said nothing of the kind had ever been found on any of the Galapagos Islands. This had the archaeologists wrangling furiously for weeks, and I really don't know why nobody came to check up on the spot. But I've always been pretty convinced there *were* Inca remains on the Galapagos Islands, hence my trip here now. So now let's hear what *you* know about this stone face.'

The whole Wittmer family looked at each other. A wide grin spread over four faces.

'I suppose it's my fault,' Rolf said eventually. 'You tell them, Mutti.'

'It was like this,' I began, rather sheepishly now. 'Captain Lord discovered the stone face and photographed it from all sides. Rolf was with him, and afterwards he asked Rolf various questions.'

'He asked me if the stone was there before we came to the island,' Rolf interjected, 'and I said, yes it was. We've always had plenty of stone, or stones rather. You see my English wasn't so good then.'

'Rolf told us about this question afterwards,' said Heinz, 'and we thought it a bit odd, but of course he had answered quite correctly.'

Heyerdahl turned to Heinz eagerly. 'I can't wait to see that stone face. Let's go and find out how old it may be.'

Heinz shook his head. 'I can tell you that now: about ten years, quite modern . . . I'm afraid I did it myself?'

'You did it yourself?' cried Reed. 'What on earth . . .?'

'I was showing Rolf how to sculpt, and I carved that face in tufa. I suppose it came off better than I expected, and then by the time Lord saw and photographed it, it had crumbled a bit and was all overgrown with moss. I can see how somebody might have thought it had been there for centuries. I meant no deception, of course, and you can't blame Lord for getting excited at having discovered a lost masterpiece of prehistoric sculpture.

We knew nothing about the sensation it caused, only I must say I feel very guilty now . . .' But he could not keep the smile off his face, nor could the rest of us.

Heyerdahl, Skjölsvold and Reed gazed at him for a moment, then with one accord burst into roars of laughter. 'What a masterpiece!' exclaimed Heyerdahl. 'We must certainly celebrate this discovery, eh, Arne?'

'I'll say we must,' said Skjölsvold, 'shall I open up that crate?'

One of the fifty crates was opened, and we drank to the stone face carved by 'Homo Wittmerensis,' together with a hope that the party would find true Inca remains somewhere on the islands.

But the frustrating rain continued, cloudburst after cloudburst. The torrents from the hills tore up the soil and washed it away. Miles of sea turned completely brown. Round my henhouse the water cut deep furrows into the soft ground. And in one of these furrows I discovered what looked like clay shards. I shouted for Heyerdahl and Skjölsvold, who happened to be looking out of the window in my direction, 'Come over here, I've found something.'

'Another stone face?' Skjölsvold called back.

'No. Clay shards.'

They came dashing over to the henhouse, and got down into the furrows regardless of the mud. One fragment after another was carefully dug up and brought to the surface. Skjölsvold stood up flushed with enthusiasm and held out to me a particular treasure: 'An old clay pipe.'

Dr Reed, who had by now joined the other two, took a glance at the pipe. 'Must be at least six hundred years old. Long before the Spaniards came . . . Let the chickens out, will you?'

I did as he asked, and the three explorers set to work feverishly, digging up the whole ground below and around the henhouse. It had been well worth the long wait they had had, this was buried treasure indeed. They took all the shards into the house, packed them fondly in paper and cotton wool; and that evening we had another celebration, this time with Wittmer whisky, which went on till the early hours. Soon afterwards the party left for other Galapagos Islands, where they made further discoveries. In due course we saw pictures of our shards illustrating their finds in the Galapagos from pre-Spanish times, and could feel we had redeemed our unwitting fraud over the stone face: Floreana too had its small place in archaeological progress.

The incessant rain went on long after they had gone. It was one of the fiercest rainy seasons we could remember. All the valleys and slopes in the island had turned into rivers. Work on the farm came to a standstill, and fishing activities were confined to preserving the dried fish from going mouldy. Whenever the sun came out of the clouds for half an hour, the fish had to be given a short sunbath. Easter was approaching, and that was the one time in the year when fish were bought and consumed in terrific quantities. So all Rolf's catch ought to be on the mainland by then. It was his first big chance to earn good money, for Thor Heyerdahl had promised to return from excavating on the other islands by way of Floreana, and to take Rolf with him.

This second time the Heyerdahl party paid only the briefest of calls, being in a hurry to get their discoveries to the mainland and from there back to Europe. As often happened with Wittmer departures, therefore, Rolf left in frantic haste on this promised trip to the 'outside world.' For almost the first time in twenty years I was parted from my son.

By Easter I was also cut off from my husband and daughter. They stayed at the farm with Inge's friend Marianita, while I stayed on the coast to look after the chickens. All the tracks were flooded, and you had to wade wherever you went. I felt a little as if I were in the Ark, with sea and sky forming a monstrous alliance of water.

On 30th April I had a visit from the skipper of an American fishing boat and his wife, who had come from Santa Cruz. 'We're in urgent need of fresh produce,' said the skipper. 'Potatoes, yucca, fruit, vegetables, everything you have. The whole of Santa Cruz is a lake, and there's no contact with the farmers in the mountains. We couldn't get a single cabbage head down. We tried to ride up into the mountains, but the donkeys sank deep in the mud with every step. In fact we haven't got anything to eat at all, and if it goes on like this a few days more, we'll be starving. We've already used up all our stores. There should be a ship from the mainland any day now, in fact it ought to have been here long ago.'

'I'm terribly sorry,' I said, 'but I've got hardly anything here. Perhaps someone will come down from the farm this evening. But I'm afraid it's not very likely, with the tracks in the state they are.'

'I'll come back in three days,' he told me. 'Assuming the ship hasn't arrived by then.'

'All right. I'm sorry I can't help you at the moment, but really we're in much the same plight down here as you are.'

When they had gone, I made an attempt to go up to the farm. But the track was now a river thirty yards wide, nobody could possibly have got down from the farm, let alone with a load— not even Rolf, if he had been there.

The next day it was still raining as hard as ever. I fed the pig, the hens and all the little chicks. Then I went into the study and typed some letters so that they could go with the expected ship from the mainland. About noon there was a tremendous cloudburst, and the wind seemed to reach hurricane force. The blast was so furious that I thought the house might cave in at any moment. But it was solidly built and stood firm. The torrential rain beat against the windows from every side in turn. The storm howled and raged round the house, and water came into the living-room through little cracks in the window-frames. Wide puddles collected on the floor. Outside it suddenly got very dark, then the darkness was rent by blinding flashes of lightning. There were crashes of thunder louder than I had ever heard before. I felt alone and terrified.

I remembered the chicks, and put on a bathing-suit to plunge out towards the hen-house. The chicks were almost floating. The pig looked in danger of drowning. I ran for a crowbar to bore a hole through the floor of the sty so that the water could run away.

I managed it somehow, then I saw my big copper in which I melt down fat, beginning to float away. It had been hanging on the wall of the food store—was the water that high already? I dashed after it. Another twenty yards, and it would have been gone for good, washed out to sea. Shoulder deep in water, stumbling over the rubble, I caught it just in time, stuck between some drifting branches. I held on to a solitary tree trunk with one hand, and with the other gripped the copper. I'd got it!— I was pleased as a child who has recovered a precious toy.

But in this salvage operation I had forgotten about the helpless chicks, which now came floating past me, whirled in the eddies like chips of wood. Eighty were carried out to sea. The hens flew round the water squawking madly, then sought refuge on the trees.

When I waded back, I saw that the workshop and food store were in danger. They were only built of mud, yet they had stood up to the rainy seasons before this. But such a flood was irresistible. I got hold of a spade and heaped a wall of earth in front of the two outhouses to divert the water to one side; but a still bigger vortex breached my dam.

I stood in a lake. I had been working like a black for four hours, and when I took a breather for a moment, I suddenly felt my back hurting. Was it the old illness— 'You oughtn't to do any work for a year,' I heard the Quito doctor telling me. Then all thoughts were drowned in the roar of the storm.

I abandoned my struggle with the elements and staggered back to the house. The water had thrown a wall of earth nearly three feet high against the kitchen door. Being so near the sea the house had been built on cement piles, so the front door was high enough above the ground to be still accessible. The whole house was like an island in a boiling sea. The rivers from the hills raged past, carrying with them branches and complete tree trunks. Indoors everything was deep in water like the bilge of a ship.

The pervading damp had long put out the fire in the stove. I was still in my bathing-suit, and as I stood shivering in the kitchen I registered for the first time that I was freezing cold. I decided to go to bed and sleep through the rest of the flood. The possibility that the house might be carried out to sea, bed and all, didn't quite penetrate to my brain. 'On the coast at Santa Cruz they've nothing more to eat, they'll starve in a day or two if no ship comes . . . *Après moi le déluge* . . .' Those were my last thoughts before I dozed off.

But I cannot have slept long before I was woken by an ear-splitting crash, which made me leap out of bed. Half asleep still, I felt round the walls. They were still standing. I put on my raincoat, crept into Heinz's gumboots, far too large for me, and waded out to see what had caused the crash: the workshop and a wall of the food store had caved in. The noise had been made by the zinc roof of the food store coming down.

I couldn't rebuild the wall. The hens, their wings sodden, were huddled up in the trees. They had survived the flood—and so had I. For it was only drizzling now. The thick cloud which had lain above the island dispersed. I could make out the sea again, it had been dyed an ugly yellow-brown from the soil of our island. It looked as if there could not be any soil left on Floreana. All I could see along the coast was rocks and stones, an endless expanse of them. I felt wretched and forlorn in this chaos, very small and helpless.

There was still a fine mist over the sea, but now that too scattered, and I saw a ship lying in the bay. I climbed back into Heinz's soaking gumboots, not even noticing how wet they were inside, and waded through knee-deep water to the beach. It was the government ship *El Oro*. Someone was waving at me from the rail.

Was it Rolf? I could only see a boat being lowered and heading directly for me. One of the people in it was Commander Northia, a friend of ours. 'What on earth has been happening to you here?' he shouted across the water. 'We thought the island had simply disappeared. We've been searching for it five hours.'

'Do you know anything about Rolf?' I shouted back.

'He's on board. He'll be coming with the next boat.'

The boat landed. Officers climbed out with the commander, took off shoes and stockings and rolled up their trouser legs. 'How about getting us some nice hot coffee, Señora Margarita?' they greeted me.

Rolf was indeed in the next boat, which landed a few minutes later. He couldn't have chosen a better time to return than in this bleak hour when I was wading dismally around in the morass between rocks and bits of branches. He looked round the slime and rubble for a moment, and made a gesture as if he would wipe the lot away. 'I see you've been having a bit of rain here,' he remarked as he kissed me.

'Yes,' I said, suddenly cheerful again. 'Yes, we have. Now let's go into the house and make some coffee for our friends.'

It was two days before the tracks down from the farm were clear. Heinz and Inge arrived, fearing the worst, and were greatly relieved when they saw me safe and sound, and Rolf back into the bargain. They inspected the damage. 'It'll mean weeks of extra work for us, Rolf,' Heinz said.

'Doesn't worry me,' the boy answered. 'I'd far rather be here than on the mainland. I sold my fish well and had quite a good time in Ecuador, but from now on I'm for staying on the island.'

It was fine to have him back, and fine that he should feel like this. There was indeed a heap of work to keep him and all of us going, and in a few months' time we should be celebrating his twenty-first birthday. Our preparations for it were interrupted, though very pleasantly, by two minor invasions in the last days of the year. The *Yankee* was on her sixth cruise round the world, and we gave our usual hearty welcome to the Johnsons and their friends.

Then we had to turn hastily from English to our mother tongue, because only a day later a whole shipload of former Germans arrived. Most of them had lost their homes in Germany, and so had settled in Ecuador to build a new life there. Having heard of the Wittmers, they wanted to spend New Year's Eve with us. The house was nearly bursting, but it was a pleasure to be talking to people who had many common memories with Heinz and myself. We saw 1954 in very happily!

For Rolf's coming of age we were by ourselves again; it was as he wanted it. But luckily there was still some birthday cake left when our next visitors arrived—almost a year after the Heyerdahl party.

A big but slender three-master sailed into the bay, then a motor-boat brought four men and a woman to land. I was standing by the sea, still holding the knife with which I was cleaning fish at the time. The first to jump ashore was a man with a well-groomed black beard. 'Are you Mrs Wittmer?' he asked.

I nodded.

'Good. I'm Hans Hass, and we'd just like to sample your cakes. Our mutual friend Thor Heyerdahl raves about your cakes and the bread you bake.'

I dropped my knife, wiped my hands on my shorts, and shook hands; he did not seem to notice the blood still clinging to my fingers. 'And you've come eight thousand miles for that, have you?' I said.

'Well,' he admitted, 'it hasn't been much of a diversion to call on you anyhow.' He introduced his charming wife Lotte and the three other members of his party. 'We're exploring on our yacht *Xarifa*, and we'd very much like to spend the day with you.'

The famous shark-fisher and under-water photographer had time to sample my baking as desired, and to spend an evening on our island, eating fried bacalao from Floreana and drinking Rhine wine from the slim belly of the *Xarifa*. About midnight they went back to the ship, which soon got under way.

We were sorry the time had been so short, but felt exhilarated, even so, by this brief meeting with new friends.

Chapter 19

'When you're over there, Inge'—Rolf told his sister—'look out for a wife for me, will you? You know my taste pretty well.'

'See what I can do,' she said. It was February 1956, and she was just off to Ecuador, to spend three months in a sort of 'finishing school' run by friends of ours.

This exchange between my two children gave me a slight shock, though a pleasant one. I could hardly believe that my son, born in a cave during our first months on the island, was now twenty-three years old. Of course Heinz and I had looked forward to the prospect of our children one day marrying and having children of their own. But in an island where there were only about fifty inhabitants, opportunities of finding a suitable mate were limited, so the prospect seemed a distant one. It was funny for me to hear Rolf and Inge discussing it so light-heartedly, without any self-consciousness, treating the matter as the normal and natural thing it was. Decidedly they had both grown up before their fond mother had properly realised the fact.

Inge enjoyed her three months away. This time she gained a host of new impressions, together with a smattering of culture. She came to the conclusion, however, that too many people on the mainland were only interested in money. 'I'm jolly glad to be back,' she said that May, on her return home, 'it's island life for me every time!'

She had made a lot of new friends, though, and had even invited one of them to stay. The girl, Paquita Garcia, already had a connection with the island—through our former 'problem child,' the radio station. For about a year this had been functioning perfectly, receiving and transmitting messages from the mainland and the other islands, a real bridge with the outside world. It was wonderful that we now knew in advance when the next ship was coming, instead of endlessly waiting in impatience and uncertainty.

The near-miracle had been achieved by the twenty-one-year-old radio-operator, Mario Garcia, youngest child of a family of ten. He had four brothers and five sisters, the youngest of the sisters being Paquita. All ten children had been born on a small farm at the foot of Mount Chimborazo. Their father was in Government service at Quito, their mother ran the farm. Both Paquita and Mario had grown up in the same tradition of self-supporting small farmers as we had developed on our island.

One day, then, Mario Garcia received a radio message from Ecuador: 'Arriving 12th July Paquita.' This seemed a very good omen, for that was the date of my birthday. Everybody was delighted at the prospect of her coming, and when she came, she quickly acclimatised herself to Floreana life. She understood all our hopes and cares on the farm, and took a keen interest in Rolf's fishing operations, which by now were a flourishing concern. It soon became clear that in Rolf's opinion Inge had made an admirable 'choice' for him, while Inge herself took great pleasure in the company of Paquita's brother. The four of them became nearly inseparable, and all at once we had two courting couples on the island.

Some weeks later, on a fine still Sunday in September, Heinz and I were sitting on the veranda watching the distant play of the waves in the glittering sunshine. As they rippled up and down, they carried millions of sun-specks on their quivering backs, reflected unceasingly in a shimmer of light and shade. Up and down went the small waves, up and down; while Heinz and I sat dreaming, or at least busy with our own thoughts. The young people had gone off somewhere together, as they often did on Sunday afternoons, when work could for once be forgotten.

Then we saw them walking up the thin strip of beach between us and the sea. Rolf and Paquita walked in front, his arm round Paquita's waist. Behind were Mario and Inge, linked in the same way! We watched them silently, smiling to ourselves, till Heinz remarked: 'Well, there you are, dear—the Wittmers' younger generation. It won't be too long now, I fancy, before they'll be able to take over from us. It looks a bit like that, don't you think?'

'Yes,' I said, 'it does look a bit like that.'

After that we relapsed into our private reveries till the four of them reached the house. They all looked flushed with suppressed excitement, and it was no surprise to hear Rolf, who could never beat about the bush, come out bold and clear with a statement of fact: 'Paquita and I want to get married. If you both agree, of course.'

I looked at Rolf, then Heinz and I exchanged glances. He didn't say anything for the moment, and I waited to follow his lead. Meanwhile Inge was fidgeting nervously from one foot to the other. 'Us too,' she said.

'What d'you mean?' asked Heinz in a completely expressionless voice. I realised he was putting on an act, but Inge didn't. 'Well, Papa,' she stuttered in rather touching embarrassment, 'Mario and I . . . we both would like . . . we want to get married too . . . if it's all right with you, that is . . .'

Then Heinz put her out of her embarrassment by telling her that it was very much all right with us, and we wished both couples happiness from the bottom of our hearts. We had a joyful private celebration that evening, but decided to have a proper 'engagement party' a little later on—we couldn't have too many holidays because of work and the animals—to coincide with our silver wedding day. And the Garcia parents came over from Ecuador to complete the new family circle on this day of rejoicing.

That morning I gave Inge my engagement ring, which had been forged from my parents' two rings, and Heinz put his own wedding ring on his future son-in-law's finger. 'My dear Mario,' he said, 'by giving you this ring, I am entrusting you with my daughter's future happiness, even before you are married. She is yours in spirit already, so look after her well, and I am sure she will make you very happy.'

Paquita's father and mother put their daughter in Rolf's arms. Then he and Paquita kneeled before them, as is the national custom, to receive the parental blessing.

They stayed with us for a while afterwards, so that we had a real chance to get to know them, then returned to Ecuador, with all plans for our children thoroughly discussed. It was decided that Mario was rather young to marry, so that he and Inge might have to wait a year or two, while the wedding of Rolf and Paquita should take place the following summer, on 12th July, my birthday. That would give us plenty of time for all the preparations that would need to be made, not only for the festivities, but to start the young couple off on their own.

For one thing it meant a lot of new building work, and it was almost like our first years as settlers all over again—except that we had many more willing hands now than we had then. But Heinz set to work with all his old vigour chopping down trees and rolling great boulders to the site of the new house. It was heavy work for a man in his late sixties, but he seemed to thrive on it as he watched the walls growing a little bit higher every day. I think I can say that the interior of the house, though simple enough, was quite distinguished for the Galapagos—and that was chiefly my province. I ordered large quantities of paint from the mainland, even though it would cost half the occupants of my hen-house to pay for it; and after the men had started me off, I began to slap on paint inside and out on any surface that could possibly be painted. I was very proud of my handiwork, and if I quailed at the thought of the bills for all the paint used, it was worth it to see everything bright and gleaming in gay colours. The men even built two little houses for guests, each containing a bed, a table, a wash-basin and two chairs.

Rolf also built a new workshop, out of eight hundred concrete bricks which he had made himself, and on its solid concrete floor went Floreana's latest amenity, our generator. The day of hurricane lamps and candles made from tallow was reaching its end: Mario, as professional electrician, wired the whole house for electricity.

Amidst all these activities we had to prepare for our second state visit. We had the first in April 1956, when His Excellency Dr Valasco Ibarra, President of Ecuador, came to us. It was one of the greatest days in 'Floreana history' when two destroyers of the Ecuadorian Navy came to anchor outside Blackbeach Bay, and President Ibarra landed in a motor-boat. The island's detachment of marines wore gala uniform, and a triumphal arch of coconut palm leaves was erected on the beach.

After the President had been introduced to the settlers, he and his escort entered our house, and we had the chance of telling him about our wishes and hopes, which we shared with the other settlers. 'I promise you,' he told them in his speech, 'that I will see the island gets better connections with the mainland, a new radio station, and also a solid school building for your children.'

His term of office expired a few months later, but he had already kept his promise, for we got our new radio station, much to Mario's delight, and then the school was built. Through the former we received good notice of a visit of the new President, Dr Camilo Ponce-Enriques, which was to take place on 7th January soon after his inauguration, so that we could make all fitting preparations to receive him and his wife, Ecuador's first lady.

After their arrival, settlers were presented to them by the admiral of the fleet; the President and his wife shook hands with every one of them. Señor Cruz, the senior resident from Ecuador, reminded him of the most pressing problem for the islands and their inhabitants, connection with the mainland by sea. The Ecuadorian government had always shown appreciation of this, but a young and rapidly expanding republic had many more urgent matters to settle, so we had waited patiently till they could give it their attention. But President Ponce-Enriques told us our wishes would soon be fulfilled, and this promise too was kept: not long afterwards we had a regular visit every month from the *Tarqui*, the new island ship.

The President stayed a day on Floreana, and this time we had something special to show him and the other notables: an agricultural display, including all the fruits and crops, tropical, sub-tropical and European, that grew on the island: bananas, pineapples, mangoes, figs, ciruela plums, avocados, coffee, medlars, lemons, oranges, guavas, chirimoyas ('regarded by gourmets as nature's supreme synthesis of strawberry and melon'), sugar-cane, potatoes, peppers, aubergines, maize and various European vegetables; also roses, hibiscus, bougainvillea, dahlias and lilies; and shark fins, filleted fish, dried bacalao, lobsters and crabs, exhibited by Rolf. The President and his suite were clearly impressed, not to say amazed, at the display, with its unique variety of crops: where else in the world would you find pineapple and cauliflower growing on one farm? I could see that even now far too little was known on the mainland of all the island could and did produce.

The next important event was Rolf's wedding. He was the first European to be born on the island, now he would be the first to get married. So it was going to be a very special day not only for us but for the whole of Floreana and all our friends. We made ready for the festivities months before, and in doing so discovered how much we were still at the end of the world. The simplest articles, taken for granted on the mainland, became difficult problems. We needed a new pair of navy blue trousers for Heinz, and shoes for him and Rolf; these we ordered from Guayaquil. My sister bought a wedding dress, veil and white shoes in London for Paquita, also frocks for the little bridesmaids. I knew she had sent them off ages ago, but we grew more and more impatient every day, waiting for them to arrive. In June the long-expected ship came at last bringing the parcels from England, but not, alas, the trousers and shoes from Guayaquil. We were in despair.

Then First Lieutenant Quinones, Floreana's 'mayor,' and his wife came to our rescue magnificently. Señora Quinones lent Paquita a pair of shoes, which after long and loving treatment became white again, and Quinones came out with the joyful, providential news that he had once been a tailor. I gave him a few yards of navy blue cloth, from which he had soon made a fine pair of trousers for Heinz. Rolf borrowed a pair of shoes from Mario, his future brother-in-law, in his relief not bothering that they were a size too small for him.

So the wedding could still take place on my birthday, when we should also celebrate our 25th anniversary as settlers. More or less everything was there which was wanted for the wedding, including the cattle, pigs and thirty-five chickens for roasting. Now we had only to wait for the guests to arrive; but at 10 p.m. on 10th July a radio message came in from Señor Solorzano, governor of the Galapagos, saying the patrol launch could not come, having run out of fuel. The next morning I settled down at the radio station to arrange with Chatham that a boat should be chartered to bring the guests, the governor's delegation and above all the Monsignor who was to perform the ceremony.

Everything was ready to receive the guests, but at midnight, when Heinz came down from the farm, there were still no guests to receive. I was growing extremely agitated, but Heinz only laughed: 'Good heavens, woman, nobody would think you'd been twenty-five years on the Galapagos the way you worry about minor delays! Haven't you learnt anything?'

'Oh yes, *paciencia*,' I repeated obediently. 'But if it's *mañana*, it won't be quite soon enough this time.'

'Don't you worry, dear,' he said, patting my shoulder; and sure enough, a radio message was brought us directly afterwards, saying that a private yacht would be bringing over the Monsignor and the governor's delegation. Four hours later we heard a ship's hoot off Blackbeach. In fact this was the ship bringing our guests; the governor's yacht did not arrive till late in the evening. But at least, and at last, everyone was there, including the priest. Our beds were all occupied, but we were able to put up a few guests in the *Capitania*, residence of the island's officer.

Quinones indeed showed great consideration throughout, seeing that everything should be at its most festive, with Floreana's schoolchildren wearing pale blue or white silk dresses for the great day, and the sailors in gala uniform. The civil ceremony took place in the morning in the *Capitania,* and the governor's representative performed it most impressively. He delivered a short address to the bride and groom before declaring them man and wife. Paquita was so wrought up she could scarcely sign her name afterwards, and I thought I noticed that Rolf's eyes were moist.

Then we went to the 'church,' one of the big algerobo near the house. Candles burning, white and coloured tablecloths, a carpet, a sea of gay flowers, bright clothes and uniforms, the bride and groom in the foreground, Paquita in a lovely wedding dress; all under the broad 'roof' of the tree, with the blue sky above. No wedding could have had a more solemn and beautiful scene.

I was a little worried about Rolf, though. It was natural, perhaps, that he should be much moved by the occasion, but why was he turning paler and paler, so that at one point I was really afraid he might faint? But nothing happened, the priest ended the service with his blessing, and all our friends and the schoolchildren came to congratulate the newly-weds and pelt them with rice. The children sang, the bridal procession set off towards the house. Outside the house Rolf took Paquita in his arms and carried her over the threshold. When he returned a few minutes later, his face had regained its colour, and he seemed quite his old self again.

'What was the matter with you?' I whispered.

'I've just changed my shoes,' he hissed back. 'Mario's shoes were much too tight, I thought I'd never get through the service, they were hurting so much!'

I could not help smiling, but was glad he could enjoy the reception unimpeded by pinching shoes. Our first meal on Floreana had been rice pudding cooked in the open on the beach. Now we stood in our fine house near the beach, holding glasses of champagne, drinking toasts to Rolf and Paquita, to Inge and Mario who would also be married in the not too distant future, remembering Harry who would have so much loved to see this day, and sparing a final toast for the first stroke of the *machete* twenty-five years before.

Presents came from all over the world, and when Paquita looked at them after the wedding breakfast, tears streamed down her cheeks. '*Tanto cariño! Tanto cariño para mí!*' She repeated over and over again. 'So much love for me.' Señor Solorzano had sent a splendid Japanese tea-set, and in the evening telegrams of congratulations poured in at the radio station. Among those who had sent them were Ecuador's admiral of the fleet and several cabinet ministers. During the evening, when there was dancing on the concrete ground where I usually hung up my washing, I had the chance of dancing with my husband again for the first time in twenty-five years.

The party lasted till two o'clock. Then the guests retired to bed, and the house lay in silence. Heinz sat smoking his pipe contentedly on the veranda while I finished clearing up in the kitchen. It couldn't be left till the morning, not on the Galapagos, where cats or even rats and mice might cause irreparable damage like a broken teacup from a set.

When I was at last through, I went out to Heinz. It was a full moon and a bright cloudless night with millions of stars glittering. There was no sound except for the splash of the waves rising and falling. We both sat there deep in our own thoughts, but suddenly Heinz put his arm round my shoulder.

'Come on,' he said, 'let's go and stand where we stood twenty-five years ago on just such a splendid moonlit night—remember?'

'Yes,' I said, 'I remember.'

'Today,' he went on when we had reached the spot, 'was the greatest day of my life. We can both be content and happy with our lives here, don't you think? If I asked you to come out with me to the Galapagos Islands, as I did twenty-five years ago —would you do it?'

I breathed deeply. 'Yes,' I answered. 'Every time.'

Rolf had by now been able to buy a motor-boat for his fishing, and a little while after the wedding he invited me on a cruise round the island. I accepted with alacrity, having had far too little time in all these years for a thorough exploration of Floreana even by land. Even our highest mountain, the 1,800-feet Sierra de Paja, I had only been up once or twice. We sailed north from Blackbeach at a fine speed: Rolf's boat went ten times faster than the little fishing boat with which we first arrived at the island. 'It all looks so different,' I remarked.

Rolf turned round to look at me enquiringly. 'What do you mean, different?'

I did not answer, the picture I saw was so fascinating that I scarcely heard his question. He repeated it. 'It looks different?'

'Different from when we first came,' I said. 'Can we go out to sea a bit, I'd like to have a look at Floreana from the outside. Usually when I've come back after being away, I've been bothering too much about how you've all been getting on, and never really taken in the changes—not till today . . . The bush has spread further and further back, and the bare pampas have disappeared, because there are trees growing on them . . .'

I remembered how the only trees on the island in those days were twenty or thirty guava trees, which didn't need any humus —this was still scarce even today on many parts of the island— because its roots absorbed all the moisture and nourishment they needed from the crevices in the lava stone. Today there were plantations of guavas everywhere, the whole landscape looked fresh and green, instead of the parched grey desolation we first came to. 'I know I've often told you before, Rolf, how I was stupidly expecting a romantic south-sea island where fruit fell into your mouth; and how when we first saw it, I was so utterly disheartened I'd have asked your father to take me straight back to Germany if there'd been the slightest chance.'

'I'm glad there wasn't,' said Rolf, as he brought the boat skilfully into Post Office Bay and she glided on to the sand. 'What about you going to see if there's any mail? I'll stay in the boat for a bit, I'd like to clean the engine while I'm waiting.'

'All right.' I walked off to the famous post-barrel which had served for centuries as mail-box; it had recently been given a coat of white paint. It was the first time for ages I had 'been to the post' here and opened the flap to see if there were any letters in the barrel. There weren't any, of course, no ship had called in the last few days.

Before closing the flap again, I made quite sure by sticking my whole arm through and feeling round the bottom of the barrel. I gave a start: my fingers had touched some sort of letter or package which seemed to have stuck to the barrel. I couldn't pry it loose without using a little stick. Then it came, and I picked it out.

It was a thick envelope, shrivelled and yellow with age. The writing was very indistinct, whether from the salty sea water or the sharp salty air. I weighed the envelope long and thoughtfully in my hand as I walked back to the boat, stopping now and again to try to decipher the letters of the address. Gradually I made them out: I read my own name, and noticed that the stamps were German: old German stamps, long withdrawn from circulation. Goodness, what an age this letter must have been lying stuck to the bottom of the post-barrel!

'So there was some mail after all,' said Rolf, as deep in thought I came slowly up to the boat. I shook my head. 'Not really.'

'But you've got a letter in your hand.' He looked very puzzled.

'That's something else.'

He shrugged his shoulders and helped me into the boat, then pushed off from the sand and jumped in himself. He seemed to have let the matter drop.

'Cruise round a bit, and then let's go back home,' I said.

'All right,' replied Rolf, refraining most admirably from asking why I should suddenly want to go home when we had been going to tour the island.

I had put the letter down next to me on the bench, and Rolf could see it. There was no reason why I should hide it from him, but I wanted to think, to be alone with my thoughts. For I knew now who had written it. I could pretty well guess what the letter said without even opening it. I wasn't sure I wanted to open it.

Rolf swung the boat out to sea in a wide arc. I could see he was intrigued by the letter, which was obviously the cause of my abrupt desire to go back. But he maintained his discretion, knowing I would tell him in my own good time, and merely said : 'You seem to be in one of your silent moods.'

'Yes, my dear Rolf, women have their moods, as you'll find out with Paquita, if you haven't already. But we sometimes can't help feeling a bit shaken—for instance when we suddenly get a letter that was sent off twenty-two years ago. Like this one . . .' I handed him the envelope, tapping with my forefinger on the address. He let the boat drift and pored over the letters, spelling them laboriously out because the ink was so faded: 'Frau Margret Wittmer, Isla Floreana, Galapagos, Ecuador, Postlagernd.'

'Postlagernd,' murmured Rolf, 'Poste restante Floreana, eh?' He laughed quietly to himself. 'It's been *restante* quite a while, hasn't it!' Then he said no more, but began watching the sealions which lay on a tiny island of lava rocks—two cubs, the mother and the bull. They barked cheerfully at us as usual, and would have liked us to play with them. But this time we sailed past them. We cruised around for an hour or so more without another word being said between us: my thoughts were far away in time and place, back in October 1935, in Germany, at the end of my first 'home leave.'

I remembered the strange man who had come to see me just as I was preparing for the voyage back to South America. He greatly admired our enterprise, but insisted with vehemence that we had already proved what we could do. There was no point in sticking it out indefinitely on our tiny island at the end of the world, we should only come to a bad end if we did. So he very much wanted us to return to Germany and manage his farm for him; he would even pay our passages home. And when my ship reached Antwerp—how it all came back to me—there was that telegram from him saying something like: 'Hope to see you back here very soon with all your family. Will shortly be sending cheque to Floreana.'

I had stowed the telegram somewhere, and later thrown it

away. Very occasionally, when life on our island got on top of me, seemed particularly difficult or discouraging, when badly needed doctors didn't turn up, when some everyday article was not there, when we thought the war would drive us out of our new home—on such occasions, but they were very rare, I had a fleeting memory of our well-wisher's offer, and half wondered whether we ought to have accepted it. But I never heard from him again—till now!

I came back to the present. Yes, the face of the island had changed indeed, so green and cultivated it looked, so rich in trees and shrubs, plantations and farms. And my face must have changed too in these twenty-five years, though it still had few wrinkles—the air on Floreana was extremely healthy. My life had been too full and happy for me to register properly that I was that much older. But now I was reminded of it by this envelope lying beside me with its long obsolete stamps on and its faded address, Postlagernd Floreana: poste restante our barrel mail-box.

Heinz was at home when we got back. I held out the thick envelope. 'Mail,' I said. 'It's certainly been some time reaching me, hasn't it?' I handed it to him for inspection.

He looked at the faded address and shook his head in a puzzled way. 'Oh well, the most important things often take longest.'

'It's not so important as all that.' I smiled and took it back from him, then slowly opened the envelope. I knew exactly what the man would have written, I could hear him talking to me as we sat there in my father's flat in Cologne: it might have been last week. But when I saw several sheets close written, the ink smudged with damp and the lines running into each other, I realised it would be a terrific job to read the letter. But there was something attached to the letter which made me gasp when I saw it. I kept it out, but refolded the sheets of writing paper and put them back in the envelope.

'Aren't you going to read your letter,' Heinz asked, 'now it's reached you after all this time?'

'It's almost unreadable,' I answered, 'but anyhow I don't need to read it now, I know just what it says. Look at this, though. The ink hasn't faded so badly here, you can make the words out quite easily. And the figures.' I handed him a cheque for a thousand dollars.

Heinz stared at it, completely flabbergasted. 'A thousand dollars . . . but that's . . . that's quite a lot of money . . . it's incredible.'

'Shall we try paying it in?' I said jokingly, feeling extremely happy all of a sudden. Sometimes I laughed without knowing why, but this time I knew why I felt like laughing out loud. It was because I was so exhilarated that that man in Germany had kept his word after all, had actually sent not only a letter but the cheque he promised; and even more exhilarating was the fact that he had been altogether wrong. His dismal prophecies had not been fulfilled, we had not surrendered to isolation and loneliness. We felt at home on Floreana and by God's grace we should live out our lives there. Still, I must try to write and thank him sometime if he could still be traced . . .

When I got back to the island twenty-two years before, I had not told Heinz much about the man who was so anxious to rescue us from our crazy adventure. He only smiled at the time. Now he burst out laughing himself when I explained about the letter which had taken over twenty years to come into our hands.

'Suppose we'd found it then?' I remarked. 'After all, it's a lot of money, as you say.'

'I wouldn't have sold my freedom for a thousand dollars then either.'

'And what do we do now?'

'Now? I should say that we've got money to burn.' He winked at me. 'Literally, if you see what I mean? How about it?'

'Money to burn,' I repeated. 'Yes, I think that's the best thing to do.' I put the cheque back in the envelope along with the closely written sheets. Then I made a taper from newspaper, lit it from the small fire in the stove, and held it under the envelope. Soon the envelope and its contents were turned to ashes. When the last spark was out, Heinz, usually a stickler for tidiness, simply kicked the ashes to one side and chuckled. 'I'm glad the postal service is a bit slow here,' he said. 'Here's to the whaling crews who were clever enough to invent the post-barrel.'

Epilogue

In a quarter of an hour the island ship would be leaving Floreana. Rolf would take me out to her in his motor-boat. In a few days I should be on the mainland, then I should be flying back to Germany; the flight would only take twenty-two hours. Sometimes in the past weeks when I thought of this journey, I felt as if it were a beautiful dream from which there would some time be a sad awakening. But it was no dream, it was reality. I was leaving today. The one case I was taking was already on the sea-shore.

Twenty-seven years before I had sat here on one of the greyish black lava ledges and looked up at the island, over the bleak, sandy, stony shore and the lifeless dried-up trees, to the luxuriant bush above. I felt dreadfully down-hearted and forlorn in the complete loneliness, as the boat which had brought us disappeared in the mist. I had thought of Floreana as a Paradise, and the reality was infinitely disappointing. I did not know then all the cares and ordeals and even tragedies that lay ahead of us; which was just as well.

But I did not guess either that Floreana would become such a wonderful and well-loved new home; that we should build up so fine an 'estate,' that we should be the first people to spend a whole lifetime on the island. It started with such small beginnings, our primitive cave-man existence, but how glad we were then that the caves existed. I could still hear today the sound of the cattle lowing in the deep bush while I lay alone in the living-cave giving birth to my first child: the child who was now a parent himself.

I got up from my lava rock and walked a little way down the beach to where my case stood. In front of me the dogs were having a scuffle in the warm sand. And here was a little girl who toddled over with her arms stretched out towards me, laughing, and piping happily: 'Oma! Oma!' I picked her up, hugged her, and laughed with her, although I myself was not feeling like laughing: because in ten minutes I should be sailing off in that ship, leaving the island and my family behind.

Rolf and Paquita had been married two years already—amazing!—and Margret-Rose, their daughter, was a bonny one-year-old, the third generation of Wittmers on the island. Floreana and Wittmers: they were inseparably associated. Even though there were now some fifty others on the island, we were the pioneers, and the little hill inland just above our farm was now called Wittmerberg. Our address was simply 'Wittmers, Post-lagernd Floreana,' and the island would always stay 'uncivilised' as it was now, without cars or telephones. It was wonderful to think the world still contained spots like this.

Margret-Rose would not let go of my hands, as if she sensed that her Grannie was leaving her. I went down with her to the boat, where Rolf was waiting. Behind came the others to say good-bye, Heinz, Paquita, then Mario and his wife Ingeborg Floreanita, arm in arm. They had been married a month before, another memorable day, which had included a telegram of congratulations from the President of Ecuador.

Yes, a great deal had changed since we Wittmers came to the island. The pirates and whalers and adventurers of past ages had been followed by a few dozen ordinary men and women, planting coffee, fishing, working hard on the land to make a fair living and bring up their families. It had taken a long while for Floreana to awaken from its centuries of slumber. But everything went slowly here, like the giant tortoises, early inhabitants of these islands, which had given them their name of Galapagos. We too had moved slowly over the ground, step by step, poco a poco—but we had got where we wanted in the end.

1982

My birthday! I can hardly believe that I have lived in Floreana for fifty years! Twenty two years have gone by since I returned from my visit to Germany, feeling truly thankful to be once more in our beloved home. Today my thoughts drift back to our first arrival in this 'enchanted' island, when Heinz and I first saw the dreary grey shore with its black lava rocks, and stood dispirited and forlorn as we watched the fishing boat which had brought us, disappearing into the mist. Fortunately we cannot see the future and in 1932 I could not have imagined that I would still be here fifty years later.

We had succeeded in spending a whole lifetime on Floreana, where so many earlier settlers had failed, had given up and gone away. At first just the three of us, Heinz, my stepson Harry and myself, but now, in spite of all the trials and tribulations that have beset us, the Wittmer household consists of fourteen souls.

My beloved Heinz died in 1963; a faithful, loving heart stopped beating. Then in 1969 we lost my son in law Mario who failed to return from a hunting trip.

There are now almost 6,000 people living in the Galapagos Islands, and on Floreana, where for so long only the Wittmer family lived, we have now about fifty inhabitants.

I still run the Post Office as well as the post barrel in Post Office Bay which is used by passing ships, often carrying tourists to our islands. Tourism has flourished and grows from year to year, since now there is an airfield on Baltra where passengers arrive from all over the world. No longer are our islands inaccessible.

The wildlife of the islands is cared for by the Galapagos National Park and the Charles Darwin Foundation. Fur seals which at the beginning of the century were almost extinct, can now be seen on eleven islands and number around ten thousand. Playful sea lions are everywhere, and there are ten different types of tortoises, giant creatures which are the largest in the world.

The Ecuadorian government has now given me the right of possession of the land on the beach, and 7,315 square metres of Floreana are now our property. Truly an asylum of peace in this much troubled world.

As I look back on my life in Floreana I feel deeply happy that destiny brought me to the Galapagos Islands fifty years ago.

Appendix

The Galapagos Islands are an archipelago in the Pacific, some 600 miles off the coast of South America, scattered over a water area of 23,000 square miles, yet only 2,800 square miles in total land area: ten large islands and a score of smaller ones, all of volcanic origin. Most are uninhabited, some still unexplored; and a few like Narborough (Fernandina) and Isabela have seen recent volcanic activity. On all the islands together there are more volcanoes than people.

The 'Humboldt' current, sweeping up from the Antarctic, washes their shores and tempers the climate, which is only tropical from December to March. Many of them are still bare lava deserts all the year round, with hardly a blade of grass growing; but on the larger islands the inland heights trap passing rainclouds, which condense on the hillside and support lush, jungle-like vegetation; both crops and livestock also thrive on the misty uplands.

Opinions still differ among experts as to how the archipelago came to its present form. For various reasons, e.g., the absence of mammals, it seems unlikely that they were ever connected with the mainland, but some geologists have thought they were once joined to each other, splitting off at a later period. Other geologists, however, believe that all the islands were unconnected with each other, being simply thrown up from the sea as separate volcanic peaks. Isabela's five volcanoes, for instance, were once all separate islands, but the peaks have since been reunited by the rising of the sea-bed, though they are still separated by lava deserts. In any case, if the islands were never joined to the mainland, there is an unsolved riddle as to how the flora and fauna got to them in the first place.

To take plants first, their seeds or spores could have been carried from the mainland by winds or sea currents, but neither is very probable because the plants on the islands bear no close resemblance to those on the nearest mainland. Or they could have been brought by the birds of passage, either clinging to wings and feet or kept in the birds' stomachs, to be eventually deposited on the islands among the droppings. Some are special kinds that can only grow from seeds which have passed through a bird or beast's stomach, so this theory of the birds of passage being the original 'planters' is in some ways probable. But it is only a hypothesis, and the riddle remains.

What of the fauna? The only mammals on the islands are those which have been brought over by man: cattle, donkeys, pigs, dogs and cats (all formerly domestic animals which later turned wild again in the bush), mice and rats. The absence of indigenous mammals is one of the arguments against the archipelago having once joined on to the mainland. The only presumably indigenous fauna are the birds and the reptiles; giant tortoises, turtles and lizards (land and marine iguanas). They certainly were not brought over by men, although both might originally have come to the islands of their own accord from somewhere else.

The mystery here is even more puzzling. In the tertiary period, some sixty million years ago, the giant tortoises had a habitat extending over wide surfaces of the northern hemisphere, where their fossilised shells are still found; whereas today they exist only on the Galapagos Islands. There were once fifteen species or races of tortoise on the islands; it was the differences between both tortoises and finches from one island to the other which so much interested Darwin. On Floreana, as on Sante Fé, they have long been extinct owing to the depredations of the whalers, and even today, though it is illegal, islanders still slaughter them for their oil and tasty meat. Wild dogs, cats and pigs feed ruthlessly upon the young whose shells have not yet hardened. But they are still very common on Santa Cruz and Isabela, where there are five distinct species: these are thought to have evolved originally on Isabela's 'separate islands' mentioned above.

The land iguanas (which cannot swim and have no spines) are

confined now to only a few of the islands, but on Floreana and many of the other Galapagos you can still see hundreds of marine iguanas basking on the lava cliffs. Irving Johnson describes how his wife caught one by the tail and held it at arm's length: 'There it writhed mightily, a fearsome monster with clawing talons, bristling horny spines, and prehistoric aspect—but quite harmless.' They eat only seaweed, and are extremely lazy creatures, sunning themselves all day; they would never attack man, and they have no fear of him.

Nor have the seals and sea-lions, which must originally have swum over to these shores, made themselves at home and multiplied. They are friendly, tame and harmless creatures, with no enemies except the sharks, though they are a nuisance to fishermen because they catch too many fish.

There are immense shoals of fish near the shores of the Galapagos, including the bacalao and beautifully coloured fish like the blue-striped ruff (belonging to the perch family, with prickly scales) and the 'rainbow fish.' There are also millions of lobsters and crabs living in water-holes, where they can easily be caught by hand.

All the birds are amazingly tame. Some look quite European, for instance the famous 'Darwin' finches, grey, brown and black, which are very much like our sparrows and are just as greedy. Others are exotic and very beautiful, like the male frigate bird with his scarlet pouch and the metallic sheen of his plumage: the female has no special adornment except a little white marking on her breast, but it is part of the courting process for him to show off his pouch, which in the green of the bush looks like a huge red blossom.

Isabela still has the strange flightless cormorants (largest of the cormorant species) with their stunted, stubby wings which atrophied because they did not need to fly for food or survival. There are several species of heron, and the little heron which fishes in tidal waters and rock pools is found, like the mocking bird, only on the Galapagos. There are also pigeons, gulls, flamingos, albatrosses, oyster-catchers, even pelicans and penguins: this is the furthest north the penguins reach. Especially on Isabela they are smaller than the penguins of the Antarctic, which is their real home, from which they have swum further and further north, drifting part of the way with the Humboldt current.

Although of such immense scientific interest, the fauna of the islands has been so menaced by settlers, visitors and alien animals, that many species peculiar to the islands are threatened with or on the verge of extinction. Laws passed by the government of Ecuador have been difficult to enforce, but in January 1960, a Charles Darwin Foundation for the Galapagos Islands was launched, with Sir Julian Huxley as first chairman: one of its chief plans was to set up a new international research station on the islands, to collaborate with Ecuador government research workers for the study and protection of what is to biologists 'the most precious assembly of animals on the face of the globe.'

HB 12 V